Learning Spark

Holden Karau, Andy Konwinski, Patrick Wendell, and Matei Zaharia

Beijing · Cambridge · Farnham · Köln · Sebastopol · Tokyo

Learning Spark

by Holden Karau, Andy Konwinski, Patrick Wendell, and Matei Zaharia

Printed in the United States of America.

Published by O'Reilly Media, Inc., 1005 Gravenstein Highway North, Sebastopol, CA 95472.

O'Reilly books may be purchased for educational, business, or sales promotional use. Online editions are also available for most titles (*http://safaribooksonline.com*). For more information, contact our corporate/institutional sales department: 800-998-9938 or *corporate@oreilly.com*.

Editors: Ann Spencer and Marie Beaugureau
Production Editor: Kara Ebrahim
Copyeditor: Rachel Monaghan

Proofreader: Charles Roumeliotis
Indexer: Ellen Troutman
Interior Designer: David Futato
Cover Designer: Ellie Volckhausen
Illustrator: Rebecca Demarest

February 2015:   First Edition

Revision History for the First Edition
2015-01-26:   First Release
2015-03-27:   Second Release
2015-05-08:   Third Release

See *http://oreilly.com/catalog/errata.csp?isbn=9781449358624* for release details.

978-1-449-35862-4

[LSI]

Table of Contents

Foreword

In a very short time, Apache Spark has emerged as the next generation big data processing engine, and is being applied throughout the industry faster than ever. Spark improves over Hadoop MapReduce, which helped ignite the big data revolution, in several key dimensions: it is much faster, much easier to use due to its rich APIs, and it goes far beyond batch applications to support a variety of workloads, including interactive queries, streaming, machine learning, and graph processing.

I have been privileged to be closely involved with the development of Spark all the way from the drawing board to what has become the most active big data open source project today, and one of the most active Apache projects! As such, I'm particularly delighted to see Matei Zaharia, the creator of Spark, teaming up with other longtime Spark developers Patrick Wendell, Andy Konwinski, and Holden Karau to write this book.

With Spark's rapid rise in popularity, a major concern has been lack of good reference material. This book goes a long way to address this concern, with 11 chapters and dozens of detailed examples designed for data scientists, students, and developers looking to learn Spark. It is written to be approachable by readers with no background in big data, making it a great place to start learning about the field in general. I hope that many years from now, you and other readers will fondly remember this as *the* book that introduced you to this exciting new field.

—Ion Stoica, CEO of Databricks and
Co-director, AMPlab, UC Berkeley

Preface

As parallel data analysis has grown common, practitioners in many fields have sought easier tools for this task. Apache Spark has quickly emerged as one of the most popular, extending and generalizing MapReduce. Spark offers three main benefits. First, it is easy to use—you can develop applications on your laptop, using a high-level API that lets you focus on the content of your computation. Second, Spark is fast, enabling interactive use and complex algorithms. And third, Spark is a *general* engine, letting you combine multiple types of computations (e.g., SQL queries, text processing, and machine learning) that might previously have required different engines. These features make Spark an excellent starting point to learn about Big Data in general.

This introductory book is meant to get you up and running with Spark quickly. You'll learn how to download and run Spark on your laptop and use it interactively to learn the API. Once there, we'll cover the details of available operations and distributed execution. Finally, you'll get a tour of the higher-level libraries built into Spark, including libraries for machine learning, stream processing, and SQL. We hope that this book gives you the tools to quickly tackle data analysis problems, whether you do so on one machine or hundreds.

Audience

This book targets data scientists and engineers. We chose these two groups because they have the most to gain from using Spark to expand the scope of problems they can solve. Spark's rich collection of data-focused libraries (like MLlib) makes it easy for data scientists to go beyond problems that fit on a single machine while using their statistical background. Engineers, meanwhile, will learn how to write general-purpose distributed programs in Spark and operate production applications. Engineers and data scientists will both learn different details from this book, but will both be able to apply Spark to solve large distributed problems in their respective fields.

Data scientists focus on answering questions or building models from data. They often have a statistical or math background and some familiarity with tools like Python, R, and SQL. We have made sure to include Python and, where relevant, SQL examples for all our material, as well as an overview of the machine learning and library in Spark. If you are a data scientist, we hope that after reading this book you will be able to use the same mathematical approaches to solve problems, except much faster and on a much larger scale.

The second group this book targets is software engineers who have some experience with Java, Python, or another programming language. If you are an engineer, we hope that this book will show you how to set up a Spark cluster, use the Spark shell, and write Spark applications to solve parallel processing problems. If you are familiar with Hadoop, you have a bit of a head start on figuring out how to interact with HDFS and how to manage a cluster, but either way, we will cover basic distributed execution concepts.

Regardless of whether you are a data scientist or engineer, to get the most out of this book you should have some familiarity with one of Python, Java, Scala, or a similar language. We assume that you already have a storage solution for your data and we cover how to load and save data from many common ones, but not how to set them up. If you don't have experience with one of those languages, don't worry: there are excellent resources available to learn these. We call out some of the books available in "Supporting Books" on page xii.

How This Book Is Organized

The chapters of this book are laid out in such a way that you should be able to go through the material front to back. At the start of each chapter, we will mention which sections we think are most relevant to data scientists and which sections we think are most relevant for engineers. That said, we hope that all the material is accessible to readers of either background.

The first two chapters will get you started with getting a basic Spark installation on your laptop and give you an idea of what you can accomplish with Spark. Once we've got the motivation and setup out of the way, we will dive into the Spark shell, a very useful tool for development and prototyping. Subsequent chapters then cover the Spark programming interface in detail, how applications execute on a cluster, and higher-level libraries available on Spark (such as Spark SQL and MLlib).

Supporting Books

If you are a data scientist and don't have much experience with Python, the books *Learning Python* and *Head First Python* (both O'Reilly) are excellent introductions. If you have some Python experience and want more, *Dive into Python* (*http://*

www.diveintopython.net/) (Apress) is a great book to help you get a deeper understanding of Python.

If you are an engineer and after reading this book you would like to expand your data analysis skills, *Machine Learning for Hackers* and *Doing Data Science* are excellent books (both O'Reilly).

This book is intended to be accessible to beginners. We do intend to release a deep-dive follow-up for those looking to gain a more thorough understanding of Spark's internals.

Conventions Used in This Book

The following typographical conventions are used in this book:

Italic
> Indicates new terms, URLs, email addresses, filenames, and file extensions.

`Constant width`
> Used for program listings, as well as within paragraphs to refer to program elements such as variable or function names, databases, data types, environment variables, statements, and keywords.

`Constant width bold`
> Shows commands or other text that should be typed literally by the user.

`Constant width italic`
> Shows text that should be replaced with user-supplied values or by values determined by context.

> This element signifies a tip or suggestion.

> This element indicates a warning or caution.

Code Examples

All of the code examples found in this book are on GitHub. You can examine them and check them out from *https://github.com/databricks/learning-spark*. Code examples are provided in Java, Scala, and Python.

 Our Java examples are written to work with Java version 6 and higher. Java 8 introduces a new syntax called *lambdas* that makes writing inline functions much easier, which can simplify Spark code. We have chosen not to take advantage of this syntax in most of our examples, as most organizations are not yet using Java 8. If you would like to try Java 8 syntax, you can see the Databricks blog post on this topic (*http://bit.ly/1ywZBs4*). Some of the examples will also be ported to Java 8 and posted to the book's GitHub site.

This book is here to help you get your job done. In general, if example code is offered with this book, you may use it in your programs and documentation. You do not need to contact us for permission unless you're reproducing a significant portion of the code. For example, writing a program that uses several chunks of code from this book does not require permission. Selling or distributing a CD-ROM of examples from O'Reilly books does require permission. Answering a question by citing this book and quoting example code does not require permission. Incorporating a significant amount of example code from this book into your product's documentation does require permission.

We appreciate, but do not require, attribution. An attribution usually includes the title, author, publisher, and ISBN. For example: "*Learning Spark* by Holden Karau, Andy Konwinski, Patrick Wendell, and Matei Zaharia (O'Reilly). Copyright 2015 Databricks, 978-1-449-35862-4."

If you feel your use of code examples falls outside fair use or the permission given above, feel free to contact us at *permissions@oreilly.com*.

Safari® Books Online

Safari Books Online is an on-demand digital library that delivers expert content in both book and video form from the world's leading authors in technology and business.

Technology professionals, software developers, web designers, and business and creative professionals use Safari Books Online as their primary resource for research, problem solving, learning, and certification training.

Safari Books Online offers a range of plans and pricing for enterprise, government, education, and individuals.

Members have access to thousands of books, training videos, and prepublication manuscripts in one fully searchable database from publishers like O'Reilly Media, Prentice Hall Professional, Addison-Wesley Professional, Microsoft Press, Sams, Que, Peachpit Press, Focal Press, Cisco Press, John Wiley & Sons, Syngress, Morgan Kaufmann, IBM Redbooks, Packt, Adobe Press, FT Press, Apress, Manning, New Riders, McGraw-Hill, Jones & Bartlett, Course Technology, and hundreds more. For more information about Safari Books Online, please visit us online.

How to Contact Us

Please address comments and questions concerning this book to the publisher:

O'Reilly Media, Inc.
1005 Gravenstein Highway North
Sebastopol, CA 95472
800-998-9938 (in the United States or Canada)
707-829-0515 (international or local)
707-829-0104 (fax)

We have a web page for this book, where we list errata, examples, and any additional information. You can access this page at *http://bit.ly/learning-spark*.

To comment or ask technical questions about this book, send email to *bookques-tions@oreilly.com*.

For more information about our books, courses, conferences, and news, see our website at *http://www.oreilly.com*.

Find us on Facebook: *http://facebook.com/oreilly*

Follow us on Twitter: *http://twitter.com/oreillymedia*

Watch us on YouTube: *http://www.youtube.com/oreillymedia*

Content Updates

May 8, 2015

Information on the following elements was updated for Spark 1.3:

- SparkSQL
- Spark Streaming

- Spark setup
- Maven coordinates

Acknowledgments

The authors would like to thank the reviewers who offered feedback on this book: Joseph Bradley, Dave Bridgeland, Chaz Chandler, Mick Davies, Sam DeHority, Vida Ha, Andrew Gal, Michael Gregson, Jan Joeppen, Stephan Jou, Jeff Martinez, Josh Mahonin, Andrew Or, Mike Patterson, Josh Rosen, Bruce Szalwinski, Xiangrui Meng, and Reza Zadeh.

The authors would like to extend a special thanks to David Andrzejewski, David Buttler, Juliet Hougland, Marek Kolodziej, Taka Shinagawa, Deborah Siegel, Dr. Normen Müller, Ali Ghodsi, and Sameer Farooqui. They provided detailed feedback on the majority of the chapters and helped point out many significant improvements.

We would also like to thank the subject matter experts who took time to edit and write parts of their own chapters. Tathagata Das worked with us on a very tight schedule to finish Chapter 10. Tathagata went above and beyond with clarifying examples, answering many questions, and improving the flow of the text in addition to his technical contributions. Michael Armbrust helped us check the Spark SQL chapter for correctness. Joseph Bradley provided the introductory example for MLlib in Chapter 11. Reza Zadeh provided text and code examples for dimensionality reduction. Xiangrui Meng, Joseph Bradley, and Reza Zadeh also provided editing and technical feedback for the MLlib chapter.

## CHAPTER 1

Introduction to Data Analysis with Spark

This chapter provides a high-level overview of what Apache Spark is. If you are already familiar with Apache Spark and its components, feel free to jump ahead to Chapter 2.

What Is Apache Spark?

Apache Spark is a cluster computing platform designed to be *fast* and *general-purpose*.

On the speed side, Spark extends the popular MapReduce model to efficiently support more types of computations, including interactive queries and stream processing. Speed is important in processing large datasets, as it means the difference between exploring data interactively and waiting minutes or hours. One of the main features Spark offers for speed is the ability to run computations in memory, but the system is also more efficient than MapReduce for complex applications running on disk.

On the generality side, Spark is designed to cover a wide range of workloads that previously required separate distributed systems, including batch applications, iterative algorithms, interactive queries, and streaming. By supporting these workloads in the same engine, Spark makes it easy and inexpensive to *combine* different processing types, which is often necessary in production data analysis pipelines. In addition, it reduces the management burden of maintaining separate tools.

Spark is designed to be highly accessible, offering simple APIs in Python, Java, Scala, and SQL, and rich built-in libraries. It also integrates closely with other Big Data tools. In particular, Spark can run in Hadoop clusters and access any Hadoop data source, including Cassandra.

A Unified Stack

The Spark project contains multiple closely integrated components. At its core, Spark is a "computational engine" that is responsible for scheduling, distributing, and monitoring applications consisting of many computational tasks across many worker machines, or a *computing cluster*. Because the core engine of Spark is both fast and general-purpose, it powers multiple higher-level components specialized for various workloads, such as SQL or machine learning. These components are designed to interoperate closely, letting you combine them like libraries in a software project.

A philosophy of tight integration has several benefits. First, all libraries and higher-level components in the stack benefit from improvements at the lower layers. For example, when Spark's core engine adds an optimization, SQL and machine learning libraries automatically speed up as well. Second, the costs associated with running the stack are minimized, because instead of running 5–10 independent software systems, an organization needs to run only one. These costs include deployment, maintenance, testing, support, and others. This also means that each time a new component is added to the Spark stack, every organization that uses Spark will immediately be able to try this new component. This changes the cost of trying out a new type of data analysis from downloading, deploying, and learning a new software project to upgrading Spark.

Finally, one of the largest advantages of tight integration is the ability to build applications that seamlessly combine different processing models. For example, in Spark you can write one application that uses machine learning to classify data in real time as it is ingested from streaming sources. Simultaneously, analysts can query the resulting data, also in real time, via SQL (e.g., to join the data with unstructured logfiles). In addition, more sophisticated data engineers and data scientists can access the same data via the Python shell for ad hoc analysis. Others might access the data in standalone batch applications. All the while, the IT team has to maintain only one system.

Here we will briefly introduce each of Spark's components, shown in Figure 1-1.

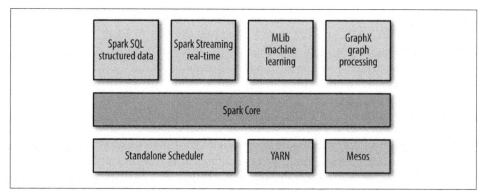

Figure 1-1. The Spark stack

Spark Core

Spark Core contains the basic functionality of Spark, including components for task scheduling, memory management, fault recovery, interacting with storage systems, and more. Spark Core is also home to the API that defines *resilient distributed data-sets* (RDDs), which are Spark's main programming abstraction. RDDs represent a collection of items distributed across many compute nodes that can be manipulated in parallel. Spark Core provides many APIs for building and manipulating these collections.

Spark SQL

Spark SQL is Spark's package for working with structured data. It allows querying data via SQL as well as the Apache Hive variant of SQL—called the Hive Query Language (HQL)—and it supports many sources of data, including Hive tables, Parquet, and JSON. Beyond providing a SQL interface to Spark, Spark SQL allows developers to intermix SQL queries with the programmatic data manipulations supported by RDDs in Python, Java, and Scala, all within a single application, thus combining SQL with complex analytics. This tight integration with the rich computing environment provided by Spark makes Spark SQL unlike any other open source data warehouse tool. Spark SQL was added to Spark in version 1.0.

Shark was an older SQL-on-Spark project out of the University of California, Berkeley, that modified Apache Hive to run on Spark. It has now been replaced by Spark SQL to provide better integration with the Spark engine and language APIs.

Spark Streaming

Spark Streaming is a Spark component that enables processing of live streams of data. Examples of data streams include logfiles generated by production web servers, or queues of messages containing status updates posted by users of a web service. Spark

Streaming provides an API for manipulating data streams that closely matches the Spark Core's RDD API, making it easy for programmers to learn the project and move between applications that manipulate data stored in memory, on disk, or arriving in real time. Underneath its API, Spark Streaming was designed to provide the same degree of fault tolerance, throughput, and scalability as Spark Core.

MLlib

Spark comes with a library containing common machine learning (ML) functionality, called MLlib. MLlib provides multiple types of machine learning algorithms, including classification, regression, clustering, and collaborative filtering, as well as supporting functionality such as model evaluation and data import. It also provides some lower-level ML primitives, including a generic gradient descent optimization algorithm. All of these methods are designed to scale out across a cluster.

GraphX

GraphX is a library for manipulating graphs (e.g., a social network's friend graph) and performing graph-parallel computations. Like Spark Streaming and Spark SQL, GraphX extends the Spark RDD API, allowing us to create a directed graph with arbitrary properties attached to each vertex and edge. GraphX also provides various operators for manipulating graphs (e.g., `subgraph` and `mapVertices`) and a library of common graph algorithms (e.g., PageRank and triangle counting).

Cluster Managers

Under the hood, Spark is designed to efficiently scale up from one to many thousands of compute nodes. To achieve this while maximizing flexibility, Spark can run over a variety of *cluster managers*, including Hadoop YARN, Apache Mesos, and a simple cluster manager included in Spark itself called the Standalone Scheduler. If you are just installing Spark on an empty set of machines, the Standalone Scheduler provides an easy way to get started; if you already have a Hadoop YARN or Mesos cluster, however, Spark's support for these cluster managers allows your applications to also run on them. Chapter 7 explores the different options and how to choose the correct cluster manager.

Who Uses Spark, and for What?

Because Spark is a general-purpose framework for cluster computing, it is used for a diverse range of applications. In the Preface we outlined two groups of readers that this book targets: data scientists and engineers. Let's take a closer look at each group and how it uses Spark. Unsurprisingly, the typical use cases differ between the two, but we can roughly classify them into two categories, *data science* and *data applications.*

Of course, these are imprecise disciplines and usage patterns, and many folks have skills from both, sometimes playing the role of the investigating data scientist, and then "changing hats" and writing a hardened data processing application. Nonetheless, it can be illuminating to consider the two groups and their respective use cases separately.

Data Science Tasks

Data science, a discipline that has been emerging over the past few years, centers on analyzing data. While there is no standard definition, for our purposes a *data scientist* is somebody whose main task is to analyze and model data. Data scientists may have experience with SQL, statistics, predictive modeling (machine learning), and programming, usually in Python, Matlab, or R. Data scientists also have experience with techniques necessary to transform data into formats that can be analyzed for insights (sometimes referred to as *data wrangling*).

Data scientists use their skills to analyze data with the goal of answering a question or discovering insights. Oftentimes, their workflow involves ad hoc analysis, so they use interactive shells (versus building complex applications) that let them see results of queries and snippets of code in the least amount of time. Spark's speed and simple APIs shine for this purpose, and its built-in libraries mean that many algorithms are available out of the box.

Spark supports the different tasks of data science with a number of components. The Spark shell makes it easy to do interactive data analysis using Python or Scala. Spark SQL also has a separate SQL shell that can be used to do data exploration using SQL, or Spark SQL can be used as part of a regular Spark program or in the Spark shell. Machine learning and data analysis is supported through the MLLib libraries. In addition, there is support for calling out to external programs in Matlab or R. Spark enables data scientists to tackle problems with larger data sizes than they could before with tools like R or Pandas.

Sometimes, after the initial exploration phase, the work of a data scientist will be "productized," or extended, hardened (i.e., made fault-tolerant), and tuned to become a production data processing application, which itself is a component of a business application. For example, the initial investigation of a data scientist might lead to the creation of a production recommender system that is integrated into a web application and used to generate product suggestions to users. Often it is a different person or team that leads the process of productizing the work of the data scientists, and that person is often an engineer.

Data Processing Applications

The other main use case of Spark can be described in the context of the engineer persona. For our purposes here, we think of engineers as a large class of software developers who use Spark to build production data processing applications. These developers usually have an understanding of the principles of software engineering, such as encapsulation, interface design, and object-oriented programming. They frequently have a degree in computer science. They use their engineering skills to design and build software systems that implement a business use case.

For engineers, Spark provides a simple way to parallelize these applications across clusters, and hides the complexity of distributed systems programming, network communication, and fault tolerance. The system gives them enough control to monitor, inspect, and tune applications while allowing them to implement common tasks quickly. The modular nature of the API (based on passing distributed collections of objects) makes it easy to factor work into reusable libraries and test it locally.

Spark's users choose to use it for their data processing applications because it provides a wide variety of functionality, is easy to learn and use, and is mature and reliable.

A Brief History of Spark

Spark is an open source project that has been built and is maintained by a thriving and diverse community of developers. If you or your organization are trying Spark for the first time, you might be interested in the history of the project. Spark started in 2009 as a research project in the UC Berkeley RAD Lab, later to become the AMPLab. The researchers in the lab had previously been working on Hadoop MapReduce, and observed that MapReduce was inefficient for iterative and interactive computing jobs. Thus, from the beginning, Spark was designed to be fast for interactive queries and iterative algorithms, bringing in ideas like support for in-memory storage and efficient fault recovery.

Research papers were published about Spark at academic conferences and soon after its creation in 2009, it was already 10–20× faster than MapReduce for certain jobs.

Some of Spark's first users were other groups inside UC Berkeley, including machine learning researchers such as the Mobile Millennium project, which used Spark to monitor and predict traffic congestion in the San Francisco Bay Area. In a very short time, however, many external organizations began using Spark, and today, over 50 organizations list themselves on the Spark PoweredBy page (*http://bit.ly/1yx195p*), and dozens speak about their use cases at Spark community events such as Spark Meetups (*http://www.meetup.com/spark-users/*) and the Spark Summit (*http://spark-summit.org*). In addition to UC Berkeley, major contributors to Spark include Databricks, Yahoo!, and Intel.

In 2011, the AMPLab started to develop higher-level components on Spark, such as Shark (Hive on Spark)[1] and Spark Streaming. These and other components are sometimes referred to as the Berkeley Data Analytics Stack (BDAS) (*https://amplab.cs.berkeley.edu/software/*).

Spark was first open sourced in March 2010, and was transferred to the Apache Software Foundation in June 2013, where it is now a top-level project.

Spark Versions and Releases

Since its creation, Spark has been a very active project and community, with the number of contributors growing with each release. Spark 1.0 had over 100 individual contributors. Though the level of activity has rapidly grown, the community continues to release updated versions of Spark on a regular schedule. Spark 1.0 was released in May 2014. This book focuses primarily on Spark 1.1.0 and beyond, with updates for Spark 1.3, though most of the concepts and examples also work in earlier versions.

Storage Layers for Spark

Spark can create distributed datasets from any file stored in the Hadoop distributed filesystem (HDFS) or other storage systems supported by the Hadoop APIs (including your local filesystem, Amazon S3, Cassandra, Hive, HBase, etc.). It's important to remember that Spark does not require Hadoop; it simply has support for storage systems implementing the Hadoop APIs. Spark supports text files, SequenceFiles, Avro, Parquet, and any other Hadoop InputFormat. We will look at interacting with these data sources in Chapter 5.

---

1 Shark has been replaced by Spark SQL.

## CHAPTER 2

Downloading Spark and Getting Started

In this chapter we will walk through the process of downloading and running Spark in local mode on a single computer. This chapter was written for anybody who is new to Spark, including both data scientists and engineers.

Spark can be used from Python, Java, or Scala. To benefit from this book, you don't need to be an expert programmer, but we do assume that you are comfortable with the basic syntax of at least one of these languages. We will include examples in all languages wherever possible.

Spark itself is written in Scala, and runs on the Java Virtual Machine (JVM). To run Spark on either your laptop or a cluster, all you need is an installation of Java 6 or newer. If you wish to use the Python API you will also need a Python interpreter (version 2.6 or newer). Spark does not yet work with Python 3.

PATHETIC

Check if this has been fixed.

Downloading Spark

The first step to using Spark is to download and unpack it. Let's start by downloading a recent precompiled released version of Spark. Visit *http://spark.apache.org/downloads.html*, select the package type of "Pre-built for Hadoop 2.4 and later," and click "Direct Download." This will download a compressed TAR file, or *tarball*, called *spark-1.3.0-bin-hadoop2.4.tgz*.

> Windows users may run into issues installing Spark into a directory with a space in the name. Instead, install Spark in a directory with no space (e.g., *C:\spark*).

You don't need to have Hadoop, but if you have an existing Hadoop cluster or HDFS installation, download the matching version. You can do so from *http:// spark.apache.org/downloads.html* by selecting a different package type, but they will have slightly different filenames. Building from source is also possible; you can find the latest source code on GitHub (*http://github.com/apache/spark*) or select the package type of "Source Code" when downloading.

free 7-Zip app. to unpack tarballs

Most Unix and Linux variants, including Mac OS X, come with a command-line tool called tar that can be used to unpack TAR files. If your operating system does not have the tar command installed, try searching the Internet for a free TAR extractor—for example, on Windows, you may wish to try 7-Zip.

Now that we have downloaded Spark, let's unpack it and take a look at what comes with the default Spark distribution. To do that, open a terminal, change to the directory where you downloaded Spark, and untar the file. This will create a new directory with the same name but without the final *.tgz* suffix. Change into that directory and see what's inside. You can use the following commands to accomplish all of that:

```
cd ~
tar -xf spark-1.3.0-bin-hadoop2.4.tgz
cd spark-1.3.0-bin-hadoop2.4
ls
```

In the line containing the tar command, the x flag tells tar we are extracting files, and the f flag specifies the name of the tarball. The ls command lists the contents of the Spark directory. Let's briefly consider the names and purposes of some of the more important files and directories you see here that come with Spark:

README.md
Contains short instructions for getting started with Spark.

bin
Contains executable files that can be used to interact with Spark in various ways (e.g., the Spark shell, which we will cover later in this chapter).

core, streaming, python, ...
Contains the source code of major components of the Spark project.

examples
Contains some helpful Spark standalone jobs that you can look at and run to learn about the Spark API.

Don't worry about the large number of directories and files the Spark project comes with; we will cover most of these in the rest of this book. For now, let's dive right in and try out Spark's Python and Scala shells. We will start by running some of the examples that come with Spark. Then we will write, compile, and run a simple Spark job of our own.

All of the work we will do in this chapter will be with Spark running in *local mode*; that is, nondistributed mode, which uses only a single machine. Spark can run in a variety of different modes, or environments. Beyond local mode, Spark can also be run on Mesos, YARN, or the Standalone Scheduler included in the Spark distribution. We will cover the various deployment modes in detail in Chapter 7.

Introduction to Spark's Python and Scala Shells

Spark comes with interactive shells that enable ad hoc data analysis. Spark's shells will feel familiar if you have used other shells such as those in R, Python, and Scala, or operating system shells like Bash or the Windows command prompt.

Unlike most other shells, however, which let you manipulate data using the disk and memory on a single machine, Spark's shells allow you to interact with data that is distributed on disk or in memory across many machines, and Spark takes care of automatically distributing this processing.

Because Spark can load data into memory on the worker nodes, many distributed computations, even ones that process terabytes of data across dozens of machines, can run in a few seconds. This makes the sort of iterative, ad hoc, and exploratory analysis commonly done in shells a good fit for Spark. Spark provides both Python and Scala shells that have been augmented to support connecting to a cluster.

Most of this book includes code in all of Spark's languages, but interactive shells are available only in Python and Scala. Because a shell is very useful for learning the API, we recommend using one of these languages for these examples even if you are a Java developer. The API is similar in every language.

The easiest way to demonstrate the power of Spark's shells is to start using one of them for some simple data analysis. Let's walk through the example from the Quick Start Guide (*http://spark.apache.org/docs/latest/quick-start.html*) in the official Spark documentation.

The first step is to open up one of Spark's shells. To open the Python version of the Spark shell, which we also refer to as the PySpark Shell, go into your Spark directory and type:

```
bin/pyspark
```

Starting PySpark shell

(Or `bin\pyspark` in Windows.) To open the Scala version of the shell, type:

```
bin/spark-shell
```

The shell prompt should appear within a few seconds. When the shell starts, you will notice a lot of log messages. You may need to press Enter once to clear the log output and get to a shell prompt. Figure 2-1 shows what the PySpark shell looks like when you open it.

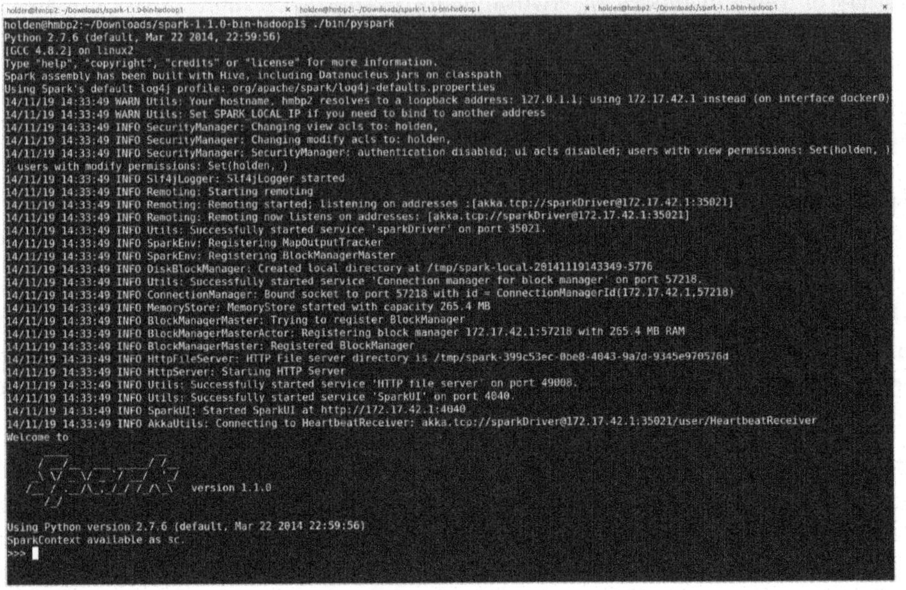

Figure 2-1. The PySpark shell with default logging output

You may find the logging statements that get printed in the shell distracting. You can control the verbosity of the logging. To do this, you can create a file in the *conf* directory called *log4j.properties*. The Spark developers already include a template for this file called *log4j.properties.template*. To make the logging less verbose, make a copy of *conf/log4j.properties.template* called *conf/log4j.properties* and find the following line:

```
log4j.rootCategory=INFO, console
```

Then lower the log level so that we show only the WARN messages, and above by changing it to the following:

```
log4j.rootCategory=WARN, console
```

When you reopen the shell, you should see less output (Figure 2-2).

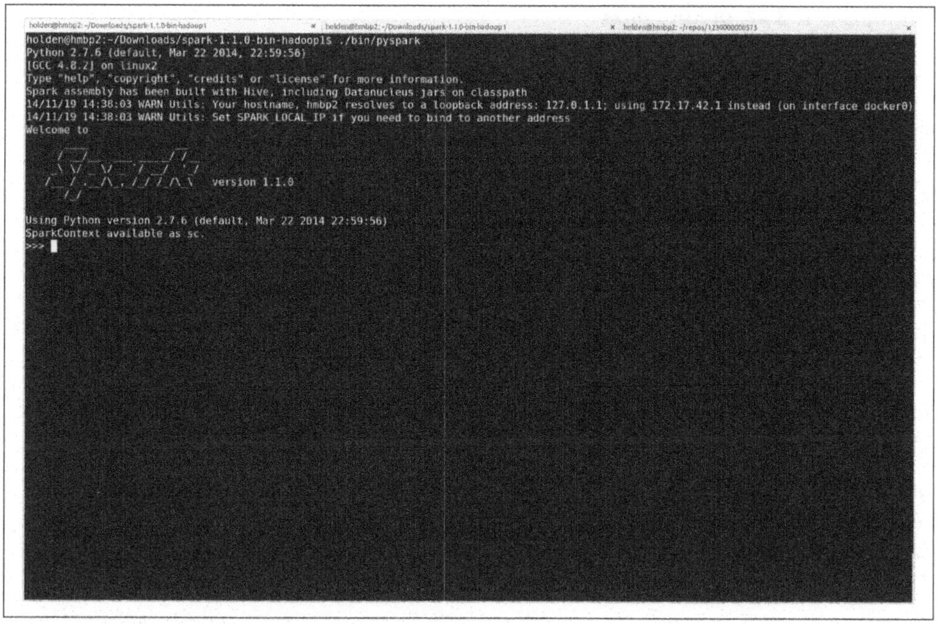

Figure 2-2. The PySpark shell with less logging output

Using IPython

IPython is an enhanced Python shell that many Python users prefer, offering features such as tab completion. You can find instructions for installing it at *http://ipython.org*. You can use IPython with Spark by setting the `IPYTHON` environment variable to 1:

```
IPYTHON=1 ./bin/pyspark
```

To use the IPython Notebook, which is a web-browser-based version of IPython, use:

```
IPYTHON_OPTS="notebook" ./bin/pyspark
```

On Windows, set the variable and run the shell as follows:

```
set IPYTHON=1
bin\pyspark
```

IPython enhanced Python shell

In Spark, we express our computation through operations on distributed collections that are automatically parallelized across the cluster. These collections are called *resilient distributed datasets*, or RDDs. RDDs are Spark's fundamental abstraction for distributed data and computation.

Before we say more about RDDs, let's create one in the shell from a local text file and do some very simple ad hoc analysis by following Example 2-1 for Python or Example 2-2 for Scala.

Example 2-1. Python line count

```
>>> lines = sc.textFile("README.md") # Create an RDD called lines

>>> lines.count() # Count the number of items in this RDD
127
>>> lines.first() # First item in this RDD, i.e. first line of README.md
u'# Apache Spark'
```

Example 2-2. Scala line count

```
scala> val lines = sc.textFile("README.md") // Create an RDD called lines
lines: spark.RDD[String] = MappedRDD[...]

scala> lines.count() // Count the number of items in this RDD
res0: Long = 127

scala> lines.first() // First item in this RDD, i.e. first line of README.md
res1: String = # Apache Spark
```

To exit either shell, press Ctrl-D.

 We will discuss it more in Chapter 7, but one of the messages you may have noticed is INFO SparkUI: Started SparkUI at http://[ipaddress]:4040. You can access the Spark UI there and see all sorts of information about your tasks and cluster.

In Examples 2-1 and 2-2, the variable called lines is an RDD, created here from a text file on our local machine. We can run various parallel operations on the RDD, such as counting the number of elements in the dataset (here, lines of text in the file) or printing the first one. We will discuss RDDs in great depth in later chapters, but before we go any further, let's take a moment now to introduce basic Spark concepts.

Introduction to Core Spark Concepts

Now that you have run your first Spark code using the shell, it's time to learn about programming in it in more detail.

At a high level, every Spark application consists of a *driver program* that launches various parallel operations on a cluster. The driver program contains your application's main function and defines distributed datasets on the cluster, then applies operations to them. In the preceding examples, the driver program was the Spark shell itself, and you could just type in the operations you wanted to run.

Driver programs access Spark through a SparkContext object, which represents a connection to a computing cluster. In the shell, a SparkContext is automatically created for you as the variable called sc. Try printing out sc to see its type, as shown in Example 2-3.

Example 2-3. Examining the sc variable

```
>>> sc
<pyspark.context.SparkContext object at 0x1025b8f90>
```

Once you have a SparkContext, you can use it to build RDDs. In Examples 2-1 and 2-2, we called sc.textFile() to create an RDD representing the lines of text in a file. We can then run various operations on these lines, such as count().

To run these operations, driver programs typically manage a number of nodes called *executors*. For example, if we were running the count() operation on a cluster, different machines might count lines in different ranges of the file. Because we just ran the Spark shell locally, it executed all its work on a single machine—but you can connect the same shell to a cluster to analyze data in parallel. Figure 2-3 shows how Spark executes on a cluster.

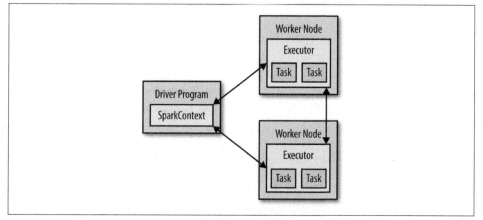

Figure 2-3. Components for distributed execution in Spark

Finally, a lot of Spark's API revolves around passing functions to its operators to run them on the cluster. For example, we could extend our README example by *filtering* the lines in the file that contain a word, such as *Python*, as shown in Example 2-4 (for Python) and Example 2-5 (for Scala).

Example 2-4. Python filtering example

```
>>> lines = sc.textFile("README.md")

>>> pythonLines = lines.filter(lambda line: "Python" in line)
```

```
>>> pythonLines.first()
u'## Interactive Python Shell'
```

Example 2-5. Scala filtering example

```scala
scala> val lines = sc.textFile("README.md") // Create an RDD called lines
lines: spark.RDD[String] = MappedRDD[...]

scala> val pythonLines = lines.filter(line => line.contains("Python"))
pythonLines: spark.RDD[String] = FilteredRDD[...]

scala> pythonLines.first()
res0: String = ## Interactive Python Shell
```

Passing Functions to Spark

If you are unfamiliar with the `lambda` or `=>` syntax in Examples 2-4 and 2-5, it is a shorthand way to define functions inline in Python and Scala. When using Spark in these languages, you can also define a function separately and then pass its name to Spark. For example, in Python:

```python
def hasPython(line):
    return "Python" in line

pythonLines = lines.filter(hasPython)
```

Passing functions to Spark is also possible in Java, but in this case they are defined as classes, implementing an interface called `Function`. For example:

```java
JavaRDD<String> pythonLines = lines.filter(
  new Function<String, Boolean>() {
    Boolean call(String line) { return line.contains("Python"); }
  }
);
```

Java 8 introduces shorthand syntax called *lambdas* that looks similar to Python and Scala. Here is how the code would look with this syntax:

```java
JavaRDD<String> pythonLines = lines.filter(line -> line.contains("Python"));
```

We discuss passing functions further in "Passing Functions to Spark" on page 30.

While we will cover the Spark API in more detail later, a lot of its magic is that function-based operations like `filter` *also* parallelize across the cluster. That is, Spark automatically takes your function (e.g., `line.contains("Python")`) and ships it to executor nodes. Thus, you can write code in a single driver program and automatically have parts of it run on multiple nodes. Chapter 3 covers the RDD API in detail.

Standalone Applications

The final piece missing in this quick tour of Spark is how to use it in standalone pro-grams. Apart from running interactively, Spark can be linked into standalone appli-cations in either Java, Scala, or Python. The main difference from using it in the shell is that you need to initialize your own SparkContext. After that, the API is the same.

The process of linking to Spark varies by language. In Java and Scala, you give your application a Maven dependency on the `spark-core` artifact. As of the time of writ-ing, the latest Spark version is 1.3.0, and the Maven coordinates for that are:

```
groupId = org.apache.spark
artifactId = spark-core_2.10
version = 1.3.0
```

Maven is a popular package management tool for Java-based languages that lets you link to libraries in public repositories. You can use Maven itself to build your project, or use other tools that can talk to the Maven repositories, including Scala's sbt tool or Gradle. Popular integrated development environments like Eclipse also allow you to directly add a Maven dependency to a project.

In Python, you simply write applications as Python scripts, but you must run them using the `bin/spark-submit` script included in Spark. The `spark-submit` script includes the Spark dependencies for us in Python. This script sets up the environ-ment for Spark's Python API to function. Simply run your script with the line given in Example 2-6.

Example 2-6. Running a Python script

```
bin/spark-submit my_script.py
```

(Note that you will have to use backslashes instead of forward slashes on Windows.)

[handwritten margin note: Running a Python script using spark-submit]

Initializing a SparkContext

Once you have linked an application to Spark, you need to import the Spark packages in your program and create a SparkContext. You do so by first creating a `SparkConf` object to configure your application, and then building a SparkContext for it. Exam-ples 2-7 through 2-9 demonstrate this in each supported language.

Example 2-7. Initializing Spark in Python

```
from pyspark import SparkConf, SparkContext

conf = SparkConf().setMaster("local").setAppName("My App")
sc = SparkContext(conf = conf)
```

Example 2-8. Initializing Spark in Scala

```scala
import org.apache.spark.SparkConf
import org.apache.spark.SparkContext
import org.apache.spark.SparkContext._

val conf = new SparkConf().setMaster("local").setAppName("My App")
val sc = new SparkContext(conf)
```

Example 2-9. Initializing Spark in Java

```java
import org.apache.spark.SparkConf;
import org.apache.spark.api.java.JavaSparkContext;

SparkConf conf = new SparkConf().setMaster("local").setAppName("My App");
JavaSparkContext sc = new JavaSparkContext(conf);
```

These examples show the minimal way to initialize a SparkContext, where you pass two parameters:

- A *cluster URL*, namely local in these examples, which tells Spark how to connect to a cluster. local is a special value that runs Spark on one thread on the local machine, without connecting to a cluster.

- An *application name*, namely My App in these examples. This will identify your application on the cluster manager's UI if you connect to a cluster.

Additional parameters exist for configuring how your application executes or adding code to be shipped to the cluster, but we will cover these in later chapters of the book.

After you have initialized a SparkContext, you can use all the methods we showed before to create RDDs (e.g., from a text file) and manipulate them.

Finally, to shut down Spark, you can either call the stop() method on your Spark-Context, or simply exit the application (e.g., with System.exit(0) or sys.exit()).

This quick overview should be enough to let you run a standalone Spark application on your laptop. For more advanced configuration, Chapter 7 will cover how to connect your application to a cluster, including packaging your application so that its code is automatically shipped to worker nodes. For now, please refer to the Quick Start Guide (*http://bit.ly/1upkhfx*) in the official Spark documentation.

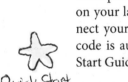
Quick Start

Building Standalone Applications

This wouldn't be a complete introductory chapter of a Big Data book if we didn't have a word count example. On a single machine, implementing word count is simple, but in distributed frameworks it is a common example because it involves reading and combining data from many worker nodes. We will look at building and packaging a simple word count example with both sbt and Maven. All of our examples can be built together, but to illustrate a stripped-down build with minimal dependencies we have a separate smaller project underneath the *learning-spark-examples/mini-complete-example* directory, as you can see in Examples 2-10 (Java) and 2-11 (Scala).

Example 2-10. Word count Java application—don't worry about the details yet

```java
// Create a Java Spark Context
SparkConf conf = new SparkConf().setAppName("wordCount");
JavaSparkContext sc = new JavaSparkContext(conf);
// Load our input data.
JavaRDD<String> input = sc.textFile(inputFile);
// Split up into words.
JavaRDD<String> words = input.flatMap(
  new FlatMapFunction<String, String>() {
    public Iterable<String> call(String x) {
      return Arrays.asList(x.split(" "));
    }});
// Transform into pairs and count.
JavaPairRDD<String, Integer> counts = words.mapToPair(
  new PairFunction<String, String, Integer>(){
    public Tuple2<String, Integer> call(String x){
      return new Tuple2(x, 1);
    }}).reduceByKey(new Function2<Integer, Integer, Integer>(){
        public Integer call(Integer x, Integer y){ return x + y;}});
// Save the word count back out to a text file, causing evaluation.
counts.saveAsTextFile(outputFile);
```

Example 2-11. Word count Scala application—don't worry about the details yet

```scala
// Create a Scala Spark Context.
val conf = new SparkConf().setAppName("wordCount")
val sc = new SparkContext(conf)
// Load our input data.
val input =  sc.textFile(inputFile)
// Split it up into words.
val words = input.flatMap(line => line.split(" "))
// Transform into pairs and count.
val counts = words.map(word => (word, 1)).reduceByKey{case (x, y) => x + y}
// Save the word count back out to a text file, causing evaluation.
counts.saveAsTextFile(outputFile)
```

We can build these applications using very simple build files with both sbt (Example 2-12) and Maven (Example 2-13). We've marked the Spark Core dependency as provided so that, later on, when we use an assembly JAR we don't include the spark-core JAR, which is already on the classpath of the workers.

Example 2-12. sbt build file

```
name := "learning-spark-mini-example"

version := "0.0.1"

scalaVersion := "2.10.4"

// additional libraries
libraryDependencies ++= Seq(
  "org.apache.spark" %% "spark-core" % "1.3.0" % "provided"
)
```

Example 2-13. Maven build file

```
<project>
  <groupId>com.oreilly.learningsparkexamples.mini</groupId>
  <artifactId>learning-spark-mini-example</artifactId>
  <modelVersion>4.0.0</modelVersion>
  <name>example</name>
  <packaging>jar</packaging>
  <version>0.0.1</version>
  <dependencies>
    <dependency> <!-- Spark dependency -->
      <groupId>org.apache.spark</groupId>
      <artifactId>spark-core_2.10</artifactId>
      <version>1.3.0</version>
      <scope>provided</scope>
    </dependency>
  </dependencies>
  <properties>
    <java.version>1.6</java.version>
  </properties>
  <build>
    <pluginManagement>
      <plugins>
        <plugin>    <groupId>org.apache.maven.plugins</groupId>
          <artifactId>maven-compiler-plugin</artifactId>
          <version>3.1</version>
          <configuration>
            <source>${java.version}</source>
            <target>${java.version}</target>
          </configuration> </plugin>
      </plugins>
    </pluginManagement>
  </build>
</project>
```

The spark-core package is marked as provided in case we package our application into an assembly JAR. This is covered in more detail in Chapter 7.

Once we have our build defined, we can easily package and run our application using the bin/spark-submit script. The spark-submit script sets up a number of environment variables used by Spark. From the *mini-complete-example* directory we can build in both Scala (Example 2-14) and Java (Example 2-15).

Example 2-14. Scala build and run

```
sbt clean package
$SPARK_HOME/bin/spark-submit \
  --class com.oreilly.learningsparkexamples.mini.scala.WordCount \
  ./target/...(as above) \
  ./README.md ./wordcounts
```

Example 2-15. Maven build and run

```
mvn clean && mvn compile && mvn package
$SPARK_HOME/bin/spark-submit \
  --class com.oreilly.learningsparkexamples.mini.java.WordCount \
  ./target/learning-spark-mini-example-0.0.1.jar \
  ./README.md ./wordcounts
```

For even more detailed examples of linking applications to Spark, refer to the Quick Start Guide (*http://spark.apache.org/docs/latest/quick-start.html*) in the official Spark documentation. Chapter 7 covers packaging Spark applications in more detail.

Conclusion

In this chapter, we have covered downloading Spark, running it locally on your laptop, and using it either interactively or from a standalone application. We gave a quick overview of the core concepts involved in programming with Spark: a driver program creates a SparkContext and RDDs, and then runs parallel operations on them. In the next chapter, we will dive more deeply into how RDDs operate.

## CHAPTER 3

Programming with RDDs

This chapter introduces Spark's core abstraction for working with data, the resilient distributed dataset (RDD). An RDD is simply a distributed collection of elements. In Spark all work is expressed as either creating new RDDs, transforming existing RDDs, or calling operations on RDDs to compute a result. Under the hood, Spark automatically distributes the data contained in RDDs across your cluster and parallelizes the operations you perform on them.

Both data scientists and engineers should read this chapter, as RDDs are the core concept in Spark. We highly recommend that you try some of these examples in an interactive shell (see "Introduction to Spark's Python and Scala Shells" on page 11). In addition, all code in this chapter is available in the book's GitHub repository (*https://github.com/databricks/learning-spark*).

RDD Basics

An RDD in Spark is simply an immutable distributed collection of objects. Each RDD is split into multiple *partitions*, which may be computed on different nodes of the cluster. RDDs can contain any type of Python, Java, or Scala objects, including user-defined classes.

Users create RDDs in two ways: by loading an external dataset, or by distributing a collection of objects (e.g., a list or set) in their driver program. We have already seen loading a text file as an RDD of strings using SparkContext.textFile(), as shown in Example 3-1.

Example 3-1. Creating an RDD of strings with textFile() in Python

```
>>> lines = sc.textFile("README.md")
```

Once created, RDDs offer two types of operations: *transformations* and *actions*. *Transformations* construct a new RDD from a previous one. For example, one common transformation is filtering data that matches a predicate. In our text file example, we can use this to create a new RDD holding just the strings that contain the word *Python*, as shown in Example 3-2.

Example 3-2. Calling the filter() transformation

```
>>> pythonLines = lines.filter(lambda line: "Python" in line)
```

Actions, on the other hand, compute a result based on an RDD, and either return it to the driver program or save it to an external storage system (e.g., HDFS). One example of an action we called earlier is `first()`, which returns the first element in an RDD and is demonstrated in Example 3-3.

Example 3-3. Calling the first() action

```
>>> pythonLines.first()
u'## Interactive Python Shell'
```

Transformations and actions are different because of the way Spark computes RDDs. Although you can define new RDDs any time, Spark computes them only in a *lazy* fashion—that is, the first time they are used in an action. This approach might seem unusual at first, but makes a lot of sense when you are working with Big Data. For instance, consider Example 3-2 and Example 3-3, where we defined a text file and then filtered the lines that include *Python*. If Spark were to load and store all the lines in the file as soon as we wrote `lines = sc.textFile(...)`, it would waste a lot of storage space, given that we then immediately filter out many lines. Instead, once Spark sees the whole chain of transformations, it can compute just the data needed for its result. In fact, for the `first()` action, Spark scans the file only until it finds the first matching line; it doesn't even read the whole file.

Finally, Spark's RDDs are by default recomputed each time you run an action on them. If you would like to reuse an RDD in multiple actions, you can ask Spark to *persist* it using `RDD.persist()`. We can ask Spark to persist our data in a number of different places, which will be covered in Table 3-6. After computing it the first time, Spark will store the RDD contents in memory (partitioned across the machines in your cluster), and reuse them in future actions. Persisting RDDs on disk instead of memory is also possible. The behavior of not persisting by default may again seem unusual, but it makes a lot of sense for big datasets: if you will not reuse the RDD, there's no reason to waste storage space when Spark could instead stream through the data once and just compute the result.[1]

In practice, you will often use `persist()` to load a subset of your data into memory and query it repeatedly. For example, if we knew that we wanted to compute multiple results about the README lines that contain *Python*, we could write the script shown in Example 3-4.

Example 3-4. Persisting an RDD in memory

```
>>> pythonLines.persist

>>> pythonLines.count()
2

>>> pythonLines.first()
u'## Interactive Python Shell'
```

To summarize, every Spark program and shell session will work as follows:

1. Create some input RDDs from external data.

2. Transform them to define new RDDs using transformations like `filter()`.

3. Ask Spark to `persist()` any intermediate RDDs that will need to be reused.

4. Launch actions such as `count()` and `first()` to kick off a parallel computation, which is then optimized and executed by Spark.

 cache() is the same as calling `persist()` with the default storage level.

In the rest of this chapter, we'll go through each of these steps in detail, and cover some of the most common RDD operations in Spark.

Creating RDDs

Spark provides two ways to create RDDs: loading an external dataset and parallelizing a collection in your driver program.

---

1 The ability to always recompute an RDD is actually why RDDs are called "resilient." When a machine holding RDD data fails, Spark uses this ability to recompute the missing partitions, transparent to the user.

The simplest way to create RDDs is to take an existing collection in your program and pass it to SparkContext's `parallelize()` method, as shown in Examples 3-5 through 3-7. This approach is very useful when you are learning Spark, since you can quickly create your own RDDs in the shell and perform operations on them. Keep in mind, however, that outside of prototyping and testing, this is not widely used since it requires that you have your entire dataset in memory on one machine.

parallelize()

Example 3-5. parallelize() method in Python

```
lines = sc.parallelize(["pandas", "i like pandas"])
```

Example 3-6. parallelize() method in Scala

```
val lines = sc.parallelize(List("pandas", "i like pandas"))
```

Example 3-7. parallelize() method in Java

```
JavaRDD<String> lines = sc.parallelize(Arrays.asList("pandas", "i like pandas"));
```

A more common way to create RDDs is to load data from external storage. Loading external datasets is covered in detail in Chapter 5. However, we already saw one method that loads a text file as an RDD of strings, `SparkContext.textFile()`, which is shown in Examples 3-8 through 3-10.

Example 3-8. textFile() method in Python

```
lines = sc.textFile("/path/to/README.md")
```

Example 3-9. textFile() method in Scala

```
val lines = sc.textFile("/path/to/README.md")
```

Example 3-10. textFile() method in Java

```
JavaRDD<String> lines = sc.textFile("/path/to/README.md");
```

RDD Operations

As we've discussed, RDDs support two types of operations: *transformations* and *actions*. Transformations are operations on RDDs that return a new RDD, such as `map()` and `filter()`. Actions are operations that return a result to the driver program or write it to storage, and kick off a computation, such as `count()` and `first()`. Spark treats transformations and actions very differently, so understanding which type of operation you are performing will be important. If you are ever confused whether a given function is a transformation or an action, you can look at its return type: transformations return RDDs, whereas actions return some other data type.

Transformations

Transformations are operations on RDDs that return a new RDD. As discussed in "Lazy Evaluation" on page 29, transformed RDDs are computed lazily, only when you use them in an action. Many transformations are *element-wise*; that is, they work on one element at a time; but this is not true for all transformations.

As an example, suppose that we have a logfile, *log.txt*, with a number of messages, and we want to select only the error messages. We can use the `filter()` transformation seen before. This time, though, we'll show a filter in all three of Spark's language APIs (Examples 3-11 through 3-13).

Example 3-11. filter() transformation in Python

```
inputRDD = sc.textFile("log.txt")
errorsRDD = inputRDD.filter(lambda x: "error" in x)
```

Example 3-12. filter() transformation in Scala

```
val inputRDD = sc.textFile("log.txt")
val errorsRDD = inputRDD.filter(line => line.contains("error"))
```

Example 3-13. filter() transformation in Java

```
JavaRDD<String> inputRDD = sc.textFile("log.txt");
JavaRDD<String> errorsRDD = inputRDD.filter(
  new Function<String, Boolean>() {
    public Boolean call(String x) { return x.contains("error"); }
  }
});
```

Note that the `filter()` operation does not mutate the existing `inputRDD`. Instead, it returns a pointer to an entirely new RDD. `inputRDD` can still be reused later in the program—for instance, to search for other words. In fact, let's use `inputRDD` again to search for lines with the word *warning* in them. Then, we'll use another transformation, `union()`, to print out the number of lines that contained either *error* or *warning*. We show Python in Example 3-14, but the `union()` function is identical in all three languages.

Example 3-14. union() transformation in Python

```
errorsRDD = inputRDD.filter(lambda x: "error" in x)
warningsRDD = inputRDD.filter(lambda x: "warning" in x)
badLinesRDD = errorsRDD.union(warningsRDD)
```

`union()` is a bit different than `filter()`, in that it operates on two RDDs instead of one. Transformations can actually operate on any number of input RDDs.

> A better way to accomplish the same result as in Example 3-14 would be to simply filter the `inputRDD` once, looking for either *error* or *warning*.

Finally, as you derive new RDDs from each other using transformations, Spark keeps track of the set of dependencies between different RDDs, called the *lineage graph*. It uses this information to compute each RDD on demand and to recover lost data if part of a persistent RDD is lost. Figure 3-1 shows a lineage graph for Example 3-14.

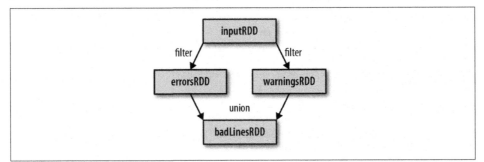

Figure 3-1. RDD lineage graph created during log analysis

Actions

We've seen how to create RDDs from each other with transformations, but at some point, we'll want to actually *do something* with our dataset. Actions are the second type of RDD operation. They are the operations that return a final value to the driver program or write data to an external storage system. Actions force the evaluation of the transformations required for the RDD they were called on, since they need to actually produce output.

Continuing the log example from the previous section, we might want to print out some information about the `badLinesRDD`. To do that, we'll use two actions, `count()`, which returns the count as a number, and `take()`, which collects a number of elements from the RDD, as shown in Examples 3-15 through 3-17.

Example 3-15. Python error count using actions

```python
print "Input had " + badLinesRDD.count() + " concerning lines"
print "Here are 10 examples:"
for line in badLinesRDD.take(10):
    print line
```

Example 3-16. Scala error count using actions

```scala
println("Input had " + badLinesRDD.count() + " concerning lines")
println("Here are 10 examples:")
badLinesRDD.take(10).foreach(println)
```

Example 3-17. Java error count using actions

```java
System.out.println("Input had " + badLinesRDD.count() + " concerning lines")
System.out.println("Here are 10 examples:")
for (String line: badLinesRDD.take(10)) {
  System.out.println(line);
}
```

In this example, we used take() to retrieve a small number of elements in the RDD at the driver program. We then iterate over them locally to print out information at the driver. RDDs also have a collect() function to retrieve the entire RDD. This can be useful if your program filters RDDs down to a very small size and you'd like to deal with it locally. Keep in mind that your entire dataset must fit in memory on a single machine to use collect() on it, so collect() shouldn't be used on large datasets.

In most cases RDDs can't just be collect()ed to the driver because they are too large. In these cases, it's common to write data out to a distributed storage system such as HDFS or Amazon S3. You can save the contents of an RDD using the saveAsTextFile() action, saveAsSequenceFile(), or any of a number of actions for various built-in formats. We will cover the different options for exporting data in Chapter 5.

It is important to note that each time we call a new action, the entire RDD must be computed "from scratch." To avoid this inefficiency, users can *persist* intermediate results, as we will cover in "Persistence (Caching)" on page 44.

Lazy Evaluation

As you read earlier, transformations on RDDs are lazily evaluated, meaning that Spark will not begin to execute until it sees an action. This can be somewhat counter-intuitive for new users, but may be familiar for those who have used functional languages such as Haskell or LINQ-like data processing frameworks.

Lazy evaluation means that when we call a transformation on an RDD (for instance, calling map()), the operation is not immediately performed. Instead, Spark internally records metadata to indicate that this operation has been requested. Rather than thinking of an RDD as containing specific data, it is best to think of each RDD as consisting of instructions on how to compute the data that we build up through transformations. Loading data into an RDD is lazily evaluated in the same way transformations are. So, when we call sc.textFile(), the data is not loaded until it is necessary. As with transformations, the operation (in this case, reading the data) can occur multiple times.

 Although transformations are lazy, you can force Spark to execute them at any time by running an action, such as count(). This is an easy way to test out just part of your program.

Spark uses lazy evaluation to reduce the number of passes it has to take over our data by grouping operations together. In systems like Hadoop MapReduce, developers often have to spend a lot of time considering how to group together operations to minimize the number of MapReduce passes. In Spark, there is no substantial benefit to writing a single complex map instead of chaining together many simple operations. Thus, users are free to organize their program into smaller, more manageable operations.

Passing Functions to Spark

Most of Spark's transformations, and some of its actions, depend on passing in functions that are used by Spark to compute data. Each of the core languages has a slightly different mechanism for passing functions to Spark.

Python

In Python, we have three options for passing functions into Spark. For shorter functions, we can pass in lambda expressions, as we did in Example 3-2, and as Example 3-18 demonstrates. Alternatively, we can pass in top-level functions, or locally defined functions.

Example 3-18. Passing functions in Python

```
word = rdd.filter(lambda s: "error" in s)

def containsError(s):
    return "error" in s
word = rdd.filter(containsError)
```

One issue to watch out for when passing functions is inadvertently serializing the object containing the function. When you pass a function that is the member of an object, or contains references to fields in an object (e.g., self.field), Spark sends the *entire* object to worker nodes, which can be much larger than the bit of information you need (see Example 3-19). Sometimes this can also cause your program to fail, if your class contains objects that Python can't figure out how to pickle.

Example 3-19. Passing a function with field references (don't do this!)

```
class SearchFunctions(object):
  def __init__(self, query):
      self.query = query
  def isMatch(self, s):
      return self.query in s
  def getMatchesFunctionReference(self, rdd):
      # Problem: references all of "self" in "self.isMatch"
      return rdd.filter(self.isMatch)
  def getMatchesMemberReference(self, rdd):
      # Problem: references all of "self" in "self.query"
      return rdd.filter(lambda x: self.query in x)
```

Instead, just extract the fields you need from your object into a local variable and pass that in, like we do in Example 3-20.

Example 3-20. Python function passing without field references

```
class WordFunctions(object):
  ...
  def getMatchesNoReference(self, rdd):
      # Safe: extract only the field we need into a local variable
      query = self.query
      return rdd.filter(lambda x: query in x)
```

Scala

In Scala, we can pass in functions defined inline, references to methods, or static functions as we do for Scala's other functional APIs. Some other considerations come into play, though—namely that the function we pass and the data referenced in it needs to be serializable (implementing Java's Serializable interface). Furthermore, as in Python, passing a method or field of an object includes a reference to that whole object, though this is less obvious because we are not forced to write these references with self. As we did with Python in Example 3-20, we can instead extract the fields we need as local variables and avoid needing to pass the whole object containing them, as shown in Example 3-21.

Example 3-21. Scala function passing

```scala
class SearchFunctions(val query: String) {
  def isMatch(s: String): Boolean = {
    s.contains(query)
  }
  def getMatchesFunctionReference(rdd: RDD[String]): RDD[Boolean] = {
    // Problem: "isMatch" means "this.isMatch", so we pass all of "this"
    rdd.map(isMatch)
  }
  def getMatchesFieldReference(rdd: RDD[String]): RDD[Array[String]] = {
    // Problem: "query" means "this.query", so we pass all of "this"
    rdd.map(x => x.split(query))
  }
  def getMatchesNoReference(rdd: RDD[String]): RDD[Array[String]] = {
    // Safe: extract just the field we need into a local variable
    val query_ = this.query
    rdd.map(x => x.split(query_))
  }
}
```

If NotSerializableException occurs in Scala, a reference to a method or field in a nonserializable class is usually the problem. Note that passing in local serializable variables or functions that are members of a top-level object is always safe.

Java

In Java, functions are specified as objects that implement one of Spark's function interfaces from the org.apache.spark.api.java.function package. There are a number of different interfaces based on the return type of the function. We show the most basic function interfaces in Table 3-1, and cover a number of other function interfaces for when we need to return special types of data, like key/value data, in "Java" on page 43.

Table 3-1. Standard Java function interfaces

Function name	Method to implement	Usage
Function<T, R>	R call(T)	Take in one input and return one output, for use with operations like map() and filter().
Function2<T1, T2, R>	R call(T1, T2)	Take in two inputs and return one output, for use with operations like aggregate() or fold().
FlatMapFunction<T, R>	Iterable<R> call(T)	Take in one input and return zero or more outputs, for use with operations like flatMap().

We can either define our function classes inline as anonymous inner classes (Example 3-22), or create a named class (Example 3-23).

Example 3-22. Java function passing with anonymous inner class

[handwritten: Java Function using an anonymous inner class]

```java
RDD<String> errors = lines.filter(new Function<String, Boolean>() {
  public Boolean call(String x) { return x.contains("error"); }
});
```

Example 3-23. Java function passing with named class

[handwritten: using a named class]

```java
class ContainsError implements Function<String, Boolean>() {
  public Boolean call(String x) { return x.contains("error"); }
}

RDD<String> errors = lines.filter(new ContainsError());
```

The style to choose is a personal preference, but we find that top-level named functions are often cleaner for organizing large programs. One other benefit of top-level functions is that you can give them constructor parameters, as shown in Example 3-24. *[handwritten: agree!]*

Example 3-24. Java function class with parameters

[handwritten: with parameters]

```java
class Contains implements Function<String, Boolean>() {
  private String query;
  public Contains(String query) { this.query = query; }
  public Boolean call(String x) { return x.contains(query); }
}

RDD<String> errors = lines.filter(new Contains("error"));
```

[handwritten: ← what is being queried for passed in with constructor]

In Java 8, you can also use lambda expressions to concisely implement the function interfaces. Since Java 8 is still relatively new as of this writing, our examples use the more verbose syntax for defining classes in previous versions of Java. However, with lambda expressions, our search example would look like Example 3-25.

Example 3-25. Java function passing with lambda expression in Java 8

[handwritten: using a lambda expression]

```java
RDD<String> errors = lines.filter(s -> s.contains("error"));
```

If you are interested in using Java 8's lambda expression, refer to Oracle's documentation (*http://bit.ly/1oHnAAt*) and the Databricks blog post on how to use lambdas with Spark (*http://bit.ly/1ywZBs4*). *[handwritten: ← documents]*

Both anonymous inner classes and lambda expressions can reference any `final` variables in the method enclosing them, so you can pass these variables to Spark just as in Python and Scala.

Common Transformations and Actions

In this chapter, we tour the most common transformations and actions in Spark. Additional operations are available on RDDs containing certain types of data—for example, statistical functions on RDDs of numbers, and key/value operations such as aggregating data by key on RDDs of key/value pairs. We cover converting between RDD types and these special operations in later sections.

Basic RDDs

We will begin by describing what transformations and actions we can perform on all RDDs regardless of the data.

Element-wise transformations

The two most common transformations you will likely be using are `map()` and `fil ter()` (see Figure 3-2). The `map()` transformation takes in a function and applies it to each element in the RDD with the result of the function being the new value of each element in the resulting RDD. The `filter()` transformation takes in a function and returns an RDD that only has elements that pass the `filter()` function.

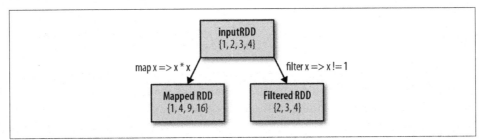

Figure 3-2. Mapped and filtered RDD from an input RDD

We can use `map()` to do any number of things, from fetching the website associated with each URL in our collection to just squaring the numbers. It is useful to note that `map()`'s return type does not have to be the same as its input type, so if we had an RDD `String` and our `map()` function were to parse the strings and return a `Double`, our input RDD type would be `RDD[String]` and the resulting RDD type would be `RDD[Double]`.

Let's look at a basic example of `map()` that squares all of the numbers in an RDD (Examples 3-26 through 3-28).

Example 3-26. Python squaring the values in an RDD

```
nums = sc.parallelize([1, 2, 3, 4])
squared = nums.map(lambda x: x * x).collect()
for num in squared:
    print "%i " % (num)
```

Example 3-27. Scala squaring the values in an RDD

```
val input = sc.parallelize(List(1, 2, 3, 4))
val result = input.map(x => x * x)
println(result.collect().mkString(","))
```

Example 3-28. Java squaring the values in an RDD

```
JavaRDD<Integer> rdd = sc.parallelize(Arrays.asList(1, 2, 3, 4));
JavaRDD<Integer> result = rdd.map(new Function<Integer, Integer>() {
  public Integer call(Integer x) { return x*x; }
});
System.out.println(StringUtils.join(result.collect(), ","));
```

Sometimes we want to produce multiple output elements for each input element. The operation to do this is called `flatMap()`. As with `map()`, the function we provide to `flatMap()` is called individually for each element in our input RDD. Instead of returning a single element, we return an iterator with our return values. Rather than producing an RDD of iterators, we get back an RDD that consists of the elements from all of the iterators. A simple usage of `flatMap()` is splitting up an input string into words, as shown in Examples 3-29 through 3-31.

Example 3-29. flatMap() in Python, splitting lines into words

```
lines = sc.parallelize(["hello world", "hi"])
words = lines.flatMap(lambda line: line.split(" "))
words.first()  # returns "hello"
```

Example 3-30. flatMap() in Scala, splitting lines into multiple words

```
val lines = sc.parallelize(List("hello world", "hi"))
val words = lines.flatMap(line => line.split(" "))
words.first()  // returns "hello"
```

Example 3-31. flatMap() in Java, splitting lines into multiple words

```
JavaRDD<String> lines = sc.parallelize(Arrays.asList("hello world", "hi"));
JavaRDD<String> words = lines.flatMap(new FlatMapFunction<String, String>() {
  public Iterable<String> call(String line) {
    return Arrays.asList(line.split(" "));
  }
});
words.first();  // returns "hello"
```

We illustrate the difference between flatMap() and map() in Figure 3-3. You can think of flatMap() as "flattening" the iterators returned to it, so that instead of ending up with an RDD of lists we have an RDD of the elements in those lists.

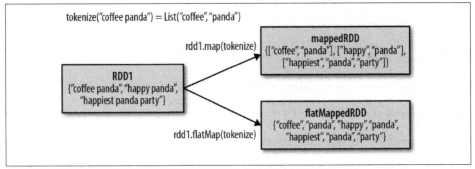

Figure 3-3. Difference between flatMap() and map() on an RDD

Pseudo set operations

RDDs support many of the operations of mathematical sets, such as union and intersection, even when the RDDs themselves are not properly sets. Four operations are shown in Figure 3-4. It's important to note that all of these operations require that the RDDs being operated on are of the same type.

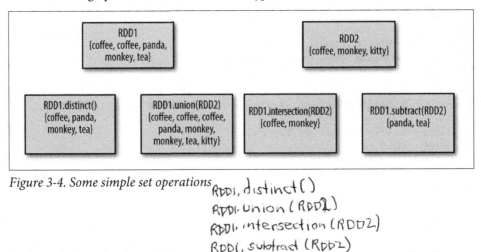

Figure 3-4. Some simple set operations

RDD1. distinct()
RDD1. union (RDD2)
RDD1. intersection (RDD2)
RDD1. subtract (RDD2)

The set property most frequently missing from our RDDs is the uniqueness of elements, as we often have duplicates. If we want only unique elements we can use the RDD.distinct() transformation to produce a new RDD with only distinct items. Note that distinct() is expensive, however, as it requires shuffling all the data over the network to ensure that we receive only one copy of each element. Shuffling, and how to avoid it, is discussed in more detail in Chapter 4.

The simplest set operation is union(other), which gives back an RDD consisting of the data from both sources. This can be useful in a number of use cases, such as processing logfiles from many sources. Unlike the mathematical union(), if there are duplicates in the input RDDs, the result of Spark's union() will contain duplicates (which we can fix if desired with distinct()).

Spark also provides an intersection(other) method, which returns only elements in both RDDs. intersection() also removes all duplicates (including duplicates from a single RDD) while running. While intersection() and union() are two similar concepts, the performance of intersection() is much worse since it requires a shuffle over the network to identify common elements.

Sometimes we need to remove some data from consideration. The subtract(other) function takes in another RDD and returns an RDD that has only values present in the first RDD and not the second RDD. Like intersection(), it performs a shuffle.

We can also compute a Cartesian product between two RDDs, as shown in Figure 3-5. The cartesian(other) transformation returns all possible pairs of (a, b) where a is in the source RDD and b is in the other RDD. The Cartesian product can be useful when we wish to consider the similarity between all possible pairs, such as computing every user's expected interest in each offer. We can also take the Cartesian product of an RDD with itself, which can be useful for tasks like user similarity. Be warned, however, that the Cartesian product is *very expensive* for large RDDs.

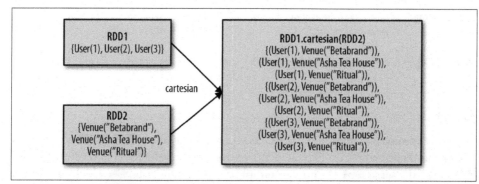

Figure 3-5. Cartesian product between two RDDs

Tables 3-2 and 3-3 summarize these and other common RDD transformations.

Table 3-2. Basic RDD transformations on an RDD containing {1, 2, 3, 3}

Function name	Purpose	Example	Result
map()	Apply a function to each element in the RDD and return an RDD of the result.	rdd.map(x => x + 1)	{2, 3, 4, 4}
flatMap()	Apply a function to each element in the RDD and return an RDD of the contents of the iterators returned. Often used to extract words.	rdd.flatMap(x => x.to(3))	{1, 2, 3, 2, 3, 3, 3}
filter()	Return an RDD consisting of only elements that pass the condition passed to filter().	rdd.filter(x => x != 1)	{2, 3, 3}
distinct()	Remove duplicates.	rdd.distinct()	{1, 2, 3}
sample(withRe placement, frac tion, [seed])	Sample an RDD, with or without replacement.	rdd.sample(false, 0.5)	Nondeterministic

Table 3-3. Two-RDD transformations on RDDs containing {1, 2, 3} and {3, 4, 5}

Function name	Purpose	Example	Result
union()	Produce an RDD containing elements from both RDDs.	rdd.union(other)	{1, 2, 3, 3, 4, 5}
intersec tion()	RDD containing only elements found in both RDDs.	rdd.intersection(other)	{3}
subtract()	Remove the contents of one RDD (e.g., remove training data).	rdd.subtract(other)	{1, 2}
cartesian()	Cartesian product with the other RDD.	rdd.cartesian(other)	{(1, 3), (1, 4), … (3,5)}

Actions

The most common action on basic RDDs you will likely use is reduce(), which takes a function that operates on two elements of the type in your RDD and returns a new element of the same type. A simple example of such a function is +, which we can use to sum our RDD. With reduce(), we can easily sum the elements of our RDD, count the number of elements, and perform other types of aggregations (see Examples 3-32 through 3-34).

reduce()

Example 3-32. reduce() in Python

```
sum = rdd.reduce(lambda x, y: x + y)
```

Example 3-33. reduce() in Scala

```
val sum = rdd.reduce((x, y) => x + y)
```

Example 3-34. reduce() in Java

← HW3 p2

```
Integer sum = rdd.reduce(new Function2<Integer, Integer, Integer>() {
  public Integer call(Integer x, Integer y) { return x + y; }
});
```

fold()

Similar to reduce() is fold(), which also takes a function with the same signature as needed for reduce(), but in addition takes a "zero value" to be used for the initial call on each partition. The zero value you provide should be the identity element for your operation; that is, applying it multiple times with your function should not change the value (e.g., 0 for +, 1 for *, or an empty list for concatenation).

> You can minimize object creation in fold() by modifying and returning the first of the two parameters in place. However, you should not modify the second parameter.

Both fold() and reduce() require that the return type of our result be the same type as that of the elements in the RDD we are operating over. This works well for operations like sum, but sometimes we want to return a different type. For example, when computing a running average, we need to keep track of both the count so far and the number of elements, which requires us to return a pair. We could work around this by first using map() where we transform every element into the element and the number 1, which is the type we want to return, so that the reduce() function can work on pairs.

The aggregate() function frees us from the constraint of having the return be the same type as the RDD we are working on. With aggregate(), like fold(), we supply an initial zero value of the type we want to return. We then supply a function to combine the elements from our RDD with the accumulator. Finally, we need to supply a second function to merge two accumulators, given that each node accumulates its own results locally.

We can use aggregate() to compute the average of an RDD, avoiding a map() before the fold(), as shown in Examples 3-35 through 3-37.

Example 3-35. aggregate() in Python

(handwritten annotations: sum, count with arrows pointing down)

```python
sumCount = nums.aggregate((0, 0),
               (lambda acc, value: (acc[0] + value, acc[1] + 1)),
               (lambda acc1, acc2: (acc1[0] + acc2[0], acc1[1] + acc2[1])))
return sumCount[0] / float(sumCount[1])
```

Example 3-36. aggregate() in Scala

```scala
val result = input.aggregate((0, 0))(
               (acc, value) => (acc._1 + value, acc._2 + 1),
               (acc1, acc2) => (acc1._1 + acc2._1, acc1._2 + acc2._2))
val avg = result._1 / result._2.toDouble
```

Example 3-37. aggregate() in Java

```java
class AvgCount implements Serializable {
  public AvgCount(int total, int num) {
    this.total = total;
    this.num = num;
  }
  public int total;
  public int num;
  public double avg() {
    return total / (double) num;
  }
}
Function2<AvgCount, Integer, AvgCount> addAndCount =
  new Function2<AvgCount, Integer, AvgCount>() {
    public AvgCount call(AvgCount a, Integer x) {
      a.total += x;
      a.num += 1;
      return a;
  }
};
Function2<AvgCount, AvgCount, AvgCount> combine =
  new Function2<AvgCount, AvgCount, AvgCount>() {
    public AvgCount call(AvgCount a, AvgCount b) {
    a.total += b.total;
    a.num += b.num;
    return a;
  }
};
AvgCount initial = new AvgCount(0, 0);
AvgCount result = rdd.aggregate(initial, addAndCount, combine);
System.out.println(result.avg());
```

(handwritten margin note: why 2 Function2's?? No Function1?)

Some actions on RDDs return some or all of the data to our driver program in the form of a regular collection or value.

The simplest and most common operation that returns data to our driver program is collect(), which returns the entire RDD's contents. collect() is commonly used in unit tests where the entire contents of the RDD are expected to fit in memory, as that makes it easy to compare the value of our RDD with our expected result. collect() suffers from the restriction that all of your data must fit on a single machine, as it all needs to be copied to the driver.

take(n) returns n elements from the RDD and attempts to minimize the number of partitions it accesses, so it may represent a biased collection. It's important to note that these operations do not return the elements in the order you might expect.

These operations are useful for unit tests and quick debugging, but may introduce bottlenecks when you're dealing with large amounts of data.

If there is an ordering defined on our data, we can also extract the top elements from an RDD using top(). top() will use the default ordering on the data, but we can supply our own comparison function to extract the top elements.

Sometimes we need a sample of our data in our driver program. The takeSam *takeSample* ple(withReplacement, num, seed) function allows us to take a sample of our data either with or without replacement.

Sometimes it is useful to perform an action on all of the elements in the RDD, but without returning any result to the driver program. A good example of this would be posting JSON to a webserver or inserting records into a database. In either case, the foreach() action lets us perform computations on each element in the RDD without *foreach()* bringing it back locally.

The further standard operations on a basic RDD all behave pretty much exactly as you would imagine from their name. count() returns a count of the elements, and countByValue() returns a map of each unique value to its count. Table 3-4 summarizes these and other actions.

Table 3-4. Basic actions on an RDD containing {1, 2, 3, 3}

Function name	Purpose	Example	Result
collect()	Return all elements from the RDD.	rdd.collect()	{1, 2, 3, 3}
count()	Number of elements in the RDD.	rdd.count()	4
countByValue()	Number of times each element occurs in the RDD.	rdd.countByValue()	{(1, 1), (2, 1), (3, 2)}

Function name	Purpose	Example	Result
take(num)	Return num elements from the RDD.	rdd.take(2)	{1, 2}
top(num)	Return the top num elements the RDD.	rdd.top(2)	{3, 3}
takeOrdered(num)(order ing)	Return num elements based on provided ordering.	rdd.takeOrdered(2) (myOrdering)	{3, 3}
takeSample(withReplace ment, num, [seed])	Return num elements at random.	rdd.takeSample(false, 1)	Nondeterministic
reduce(func)	Combine the elements of the RDD together in parallel (e.g., sum).	rdd.reduce((x, y) => x + y)	9
fold(zero)(func)	Same as reduce() but with the provided zero value.	rdd.fold(0)((x, y) => x + y)	9
aggregate(zeroValue) (seqOp, combOp)	Similar to reduce() but used to return a different type.	rdd.aggregate((0, 0)) ((x, y) => (x._1 + y, x._2 + 1), (x, y) => (x._1 + y._1, x._2 + y._2))	(9, 4)
foreach(func)	Apply the provided function to each element of the RDD.	rdd.foreach(func)	Nothing

Converting Between RDD Types

Some functions are available only on certain types of RDDs, such as mean() and var iance() on numeric RDDs or join() on key/value pair RDDs. We will cover these special functions for numeric data in Chapter 6 and pair RDDs in Chapter 4. In Scala and Java, these methods aren't defined on the standard RDD class, so to access this additional functionality we have to make sure we get the correct specialized class.

Scala

In Scala the conversion to RDDs with special functions (e.g., to expose numeric functions on an RDD[Double]) is handled automatically using implicit conversions. As mentioned in "Initializing a SparkContext" on page 17, we need to add import org.apache.spark.SparkContext._ for these conversions to work. You can see the implicit conversions listed in the SparkContext object's ScalaDoc (*http://bit.ly/1Bc4fNt*). These implicits turn an RDD into various wrapper classes, such as Double RDDFunctions (for RDDs of numeric data) and PairRDDFunctions (for key/value pairs), to expose additional functions such as mean() and variance().

Implicits, while quite powerful, can sometimes be confusing. If you call a function like mean() on an RDD, you might look at the Scaladocs for the RDD class (*http://bit.ly/1KiC7uO*) and notice there is no mean() function. The call manages to succeed because of implicit conversions between RDD[Double] and DoubleRDDFunctions. When searching for functions on your RDD in Scaladoc, make sure to look at functions that are available in these wrapper classes.

Java

In Java the conversion between the specialized types of RDDs is a bit more explicit. In particular, there are special classes called JavaDoubleRDD and JavaPairRDD for RDDs of these types, with extra methods for these types of data. This has the benefit of giving you a greater understanding of what exactly is going on, but can be a bit more cumbersome.

To construct RDDs of these special types, instead of always using the Function class we will need to use specialized versions. If we want to create a DoubleRDD from an RDD of type T, rather than using Function<T, Double> we use DoubleFunction<T>. Table 3-5 shows the specialized functions and their uses.

We also need to call different functions on our RDD (so we can't just create a Double Function and pass it to map()). When we want a DoubleRDD back, instead of calling map(), we need to call mapToDouble() with the same pattern all of the other functions follow.

Table 3-5. Java interfaces for type-specific functions

Function name	Equivalent function*<A, B,...>	Usage
DoubleFlatMapFunction<T>	Function<T, Iterable<Double>>	DoubleRDD from a flatMapToDouble
DoubleFunction<T>	Function<T, double>	DoubleRDD from map ToDouble

Function name	Equivalent function*<A, B,...>	Usage
PairFlatMapFunction<T, K, V>	Function<T, Iterable<Tuple2<K, V>>>	PairRDD<K, V> from a flatMapToPair
PairFunction<T, K, V>	Function<T, Tuple2<K, V>>	PairRDD<K, V> from a mapToPair

We can modify Example 3-28, where we squared an RDD of numbers, to produce a JavaDoubleRDD, as shown in Example 3-38. This gives us access to the additional DoubleRDD specific functions like mean() and variance().

Example 3-38. Creating DoubleRDD in Java

```
JavaDoubleRDD result = rdd.mapToDouble(
  new DoubleFunction<Integer>() {
    public double call(Integer x) {
      return (double) x * x;
    }
});
System.out.println(result.mean());
```

Python

The Python API is structured differently than Java and Scala. In Python all of the functions are implemented on the base RDD class but will fail at runtime if the type of data in the RDD is incorrect.

Persistence (Caching)

As discussed earlier, Spark RDDs are lazily evaluated, and sometimes we may wish to use the same RDD multiple times. If we do this naively, Spark will recompute the RDD and all of its dependencies each time we call an action on the RDD. This can be especially expensive for iterative algorithms, which look at the data many times. Another trivial example would be doing a count and then writing out the same RDD, as shown in Example 3-39.

Example 3-39. Double execution in Scala

```
val result = input.map(x => x*x)
println(result.count())
println(result.collect().mkString(","))
```

To avoid computing an RDD multiple times, we can ask Spark to *persist* the data. When we ask Spark to persist an RDD, the nodes that compute the RDD store their partitions. If a node that has data persisted on it fails, Spark will recompute the lost partitions of the data when needed. We can also replicate our data on multiple nodes if we want to be able to handle node failure without slowdown.

Spark has many levels of persistence to choose from based on what our goals are, as you can see in Table 3-6. In Scala (Example 3-40) and Java, the default `persist()` will store the data in the JVM heap as unserialized objects. In Python, we always serialize the data that persist stores, so the default is instead stored in the JVM heap as pickled objects. When we write data out to disk or off-heap storage, that data is also always serialized.

Table 3-6. Persistence levels from org.apache.spark.storage.StorageLevel and pyspark.StorageLevel; if desired we can replicate the data on two machines by adding _2 to the end of the storage level

Level	Space used	CPU time	In memory	On disk	Comments
MEMORY_ONLY	High	Low	Y	N	
MEMORY_ONLY_SER	Low	High	Y	N	
MEMORY_AND_DISK	High	Medium	Some	Some	Spills to disk if there is too much data to fit in memory.
MEMORY_AND_DISK_SER	Low	High	Some	Some	Spills to disk if there is too much data to fit in memory. Stores serialized representation in memory.
DISK_ONLY	Low	High	N	Y	

 Off-heap caching is experimental and uses Tachyon (*http://Tachyon-project.org/*). If you are interested in off-heap caching with Spark, take a look at the Running Spark on Tachyon guide (*http://Tachyon-project.org/Running-Spark-on-Tachyon.html*).

Example 3-40. persist() in Scala

```
import org.apache.spark.storage.StorageLevel
val result = input.map(x => x * x)
result.persist(StorageLevel.DISK_ONLY)
println(result.count())
println(result.collect().mkString(","))
```

Notice that we called `persist()` on the RDD before the first action. The `persist()` call on its own doesn't force evaluation.

If you attempt to cache too much data to fit in memory, Spark will automatically evict old partitions using a Least Recently Used (LRU) cache policy. For the memory-only storage levels, it will recompute these partitions the next time they are accessed, while for the memory-and-disk ones, it will write them out to disk. In either case, this means that you don't have to worry about your job breaking if you ask Spark to cache too much data. However, caching unnecessary data can lead to eviction of useful data and more recomputation time.

Finally, RDDs come with a method called unpersist() that lets you manually remove them from the cache.

Conclusion

In this chapter, we have covered the RDD execution model and a large number of common operations on RDDs. If you have gotten here, congratulations—you've learned all the core concepts of working in Spark. In the next chapter, we'll cover a special set of operations available on RDDs of key/value pairs, which are the most common way to aggregate or group together data in parallel. After that, we discuss input and output from a variety of data sources, and more advanced topics in working with SparkContext.

## CHAPTER 4

Working with Key/Value Pairs

This chapter covers how to work with RDDs of key/value pairs, which are a common data type required for many operations in Spark. Key/value RDDs are commonly used to perform aggregations, and often we will do some initial ETL (extract, transform, and load) to get our data into a key/value format. Key/value RDDs expose new operations (e.g., counting up reviews for each product, grouping together data with the same key, and grouping together two different RDDs).

We also discuss an advanced feature that lets users control the layout of pair RDDs across nodes: *partitioning*. Using controllable partitioning, applications can sometimes greatly reduce communication costs by ensuring that data will be accessed together and will be on the same node. This can provide significant speedups. We illustrate partitioning using the PageRank algorithm as an example. Choosing the right partitioning for a distributed dataset is similar to choosing the right data structure for a local one—in both cases, data layout can greatly affect performance.

Motivation

Spark provides special operations on RDDs containing key/value pairs. These RDDs are called pair RDDs. Pair RDDs are a useful building block in many programs, as they expose operations that allow you to act on each key in parallel or regroup data across the network. For example, pair RDDs have a `reduceByKey()` method that can aggregate data separately for each key, and a `join()` method that can merge two RDDs together by grouping elements with the same key. It is common to extract fields from an RDD (representing, for instance, an event time, customer ID, or other identifier) and use those fields as keys in pair RDD operations.

Creating Pair RDDs

There are a number of ways to get pair RDDs in Spark. Many formats we explore loading from in Chapter 5 will directly return pair RDDs for their key/value data. In other cases we have a regular RDD that we want to turn into a pair RDD. We can do this by running a map() function that returns key/value pairs. To illustrate, we show code that starts with an RDD of lines of text and keys the data by the first word in each line.

The way to build key-value RDDs differs by language. In Python, for the functions on keyed data to work we need to return an RDD composed of tuples (see Example 4-1).

Example 4-1. Creating a pair RDD using the first word as the key in Python

```
pairs = lines.map(lambda x: (x.split(" ")[0], x))
```

In Scala, for the functions on keyed data to be available, we also need to return tuples (see Example 4-2). An implicit conversion on RDDs of tuples exists to provide the additional key/value functions.

Example 4-2. Creating a pair RDD using the first word as the key in Scala

```
val pairs = lines.map(x => (x.split(" ")(0), x))
```

Java doesn't have a built-in tuple type, so Spark's Java API has users create tuples using the scala.Tuple2 class. This class is very simple: Java users can construct a new tuple by writing new Tuple2(elem1, elem2) and can then access its elements with the ._1() and ._2() methods.

Java users also need to call special versions of Spark's functions when creating pair RDDs. For instance, the mapToPair() function should be used in place of the basic map() function. This is discussed in more detail in "Java" on page 43, but let's look at a simple case in Example 4-3.

Example 4-3. Creating a pair RDD using the first word as the key in Java

```
PairFunction<String, String, String> keyData =
  new PairFunction<String, String, String>() {
  public Tuple2<String, String> call(String x) {
    return new Tuple2(x.split(" ")[0], x);
  }
};
JavaPairRDD<String, String> pairs = lines.mapToPair(keyData);
```

When creating a pair RDD from an in-memory collection in Scala and Python, we only need to call SparkContext.parallelize() on a collection of pairs. To create a pair RDD in Java from an in-memory collection, we instead use `SparkContext.paral lelizePairs()`.

Transformations on Pair RDDs

Pair RDDs are allowed to use all the transformations available to standard RDDs. The same rules apply from "Passing Functions to Spark" on page 30. Since pair RDDs contain tuples, we need to pass functions that operate on tuples rather than on individual elements. Tables 4-1 and 4-2 summarize transformations on pair RDDs, and we will dive into the transformations in detail later in the chapter.

Table 4-1. Transformations on one pair RDD (example: {(1, 2), (3, 4), (3, 6)})

Function name	Purpose	Example	Result
`reduceByKey(func)`	Combine values with the same key.	`rdd.reduceByKey( (x, y) => x + y)`	`{(1, 2), (3, 10)}`
`groupByKey()`	Group values with the same key.	`rdd.groupByKey()`	`{(1, [2]), (3, [4, 6])}`
`combineBy Key(createCombiner, mergeValue, mergeCombiners, partitioner)`	Combine values with the same key using a different result type.	See Examples 4-12 through 4-14.	
`mapValues(func)`	Apply a function to each value of a pair RDD without changing the key.	`rdd.mapValues(x => x+1)`	`{(1, 3), (3, 5), (3, 7)}`
`flatMapValues(func)`	Apply a function that returns an iterator to each value of a pair RDD, and for each element returned, produce a key/value entry with the old key. Often used for tokenization.	`rdd.flatMapValues(x => (x to 5)`	`{(1, 2), (1, 3), (1, 4), (1, 5), (3, 4), (3, 5)}`
`keys()`	Return an RDD of just the keys.	`rdd.keys()`	`{1, 3, 3}`

Function name	Purpose	Example	Result
values()	Return an RDD of just the values.	rdd.values()	{2, 4, 6}
sortByKey()	Return an RDD sorted by the key.	rdd.sortByKey()	{(1, 2), (3, 4), (3, 6)}

Table 4-2. Transformations on two pair RDDs (rdd = {(1, 2), (3, 4), (3, 6)} other = {(3, 9)})

Function name	Purpose	Example	Result
subtractByKey	Remove elements with a key present in the other RDD.	rdd.subtractByKey(other)	{(1, 2)}
join	Perform an inner join between two RDDs.	rdd.join(other)	{(3, (4, 9)), (3, (6, 9))}
rightOuterJoin	Perform a join between two RDDs where the key must be present in the other RDD.	rdd.rightOuterJoin(other)	{(3,(Some(4),9)), (3,(Some(6),9))}
leftOuterJoin	Perform a join between two RDDs where the key must be present in the first RDD.	rdd.leftOuterJoin(other)	{(1,(2,None)), (3, (4,Some(9))), (3, (6,Some(9)))}
cogroup	Group data from both RDDs sharing the same key.	rdd.cogroup(other)	{(1,([2],[])), (3, ([4, 6],[9]))}

We discuss each of these families of pair RDD functions in more detail in the upcoming sections.

Pair RDDs are also still RDDs (of Tuple2 objects in Java/Scala or of Python tuples), and thus support the same functions as RDDs. For instance, we can take our pair RDD from the previous section and filter out lines longer than 20 characters or more, as shown in Examples 4-4 through 4-6 and Figure 4-1.

Example 4-4. Simple filter on second element in Python

```
result = pairs.filter(lambda keyValue: len(keyValue[1]) < 20)
```

Example 4-5. Simple filter on second element in Scala

```
pairs.filter{case (key, value) => value.length < 20}
```

Example 4-6. Simple filter on second element in Java

```
Function<Tuple2<String, String>, Boolean> longWordFilter =
  new Function<Tuple2<String, String>, Boolean>() {
    public Boolean call(Tuple2<String, String> keyValue) {
      return (keyValue._2().length() < 20);
    }
  };
JavaPairRDD<String, String> result = pairs.filter(longWordFilter);
```

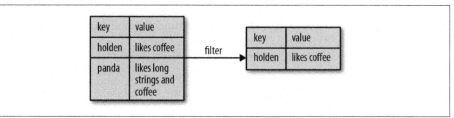

Figure 4-1. Filter on value

Sometimes working with pairs can be awkward if we want to access only the value part of our pair RDD. Since this is a common pattern, Spark provides the mapVal ues(func) function, which is the same as map{case (x, y): (x, func(y))}. We will use this function in many of our examples.

mapValues

We now discuss each of the families of pair RDD functions, starting with aggregations.

Aggregations

When datasets are described in terms of key/value pairs, it is common to want to aggregate statistics across all elements with the same key. We have looked at the fold(), aggregate(), and reduce() actions on basic RDDs, and similar per-key transformations exist on pair RDDs. Spark has a similar set of operations that combines values that have the same key. These operations return RDDs and thus are transformations rather than actions.

reduceByKey() is quite similar to reduce(); both take a function and use it to combine values. reduceByKey() runs several parallel reduce operations, one for each key in the dataset, where each operation combines values that have the same key. Because datasets can have very large numbers of keys, reduceByKey() is not implemented as an action that returns a value to the user program. Instead, it returns a new RDD consisting of each key and the reduced value for that key.

reduceByKey

foldByKey() is quite similar to fold(); both use a zero value of the same type of the data in our RDD and combination function. As with fold(), the provided zero value for foldByKey() should have no impact when added with your combination function to another element.

As Examples 4-7 and 4-8 demonstrate, we can use reduceByKey() along with mapValues() to compute the per-key average in a very similar manner to how fold() and map() can be used to compute the entire RDD average (see Figure 4-2). As with averaging, we can achieve the same result using a more specialized function, which we will cover next.

Example 4-7. Per-key average with reduceByKey() and mapValues() in Python

```
rdd.mapValues(lambda x: (x, 1)).reduceByKey(lambda x, y: (x[0] + y[0], x[1] + y[1]))
```

Example 4-8. Per-key average with reduceByKey() and mapValues() in Scala

```
rdd.mapValues(x => (x, 1)).reduceByKey((x, y) => (x._1 + y._1, x._2 + y._2))
```

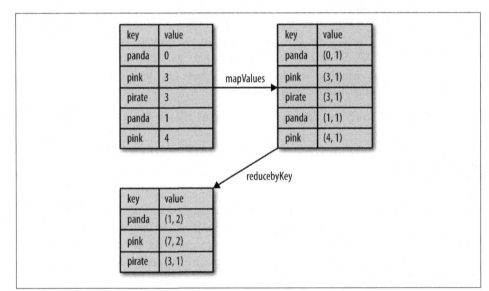

Figure 4-2. Per-key average data flow

 Those familiar with the combiner concept from MapReduce should note that calling reduceByKey() and foldByKey() will automatically perform combining locally on each machine before computing global totals for each key. The user does not need to specify a combiner. The more general combineByKey() interface allows you to customize combining behavior.

We can use a similar approach in Examples 4-9 through 4-11 to also implement the classic distributed word count problem. We will use flatMap() from the previous chapter so that we can produce a pair RDD of words and the number 1 and then sum together all of the words using reduceByKey() as in Examples 4-7 and 4-8.

Example 4-9. Word count in Python

```
rdd = sc.textFile("s3://...")
words = rdd.flatMap(lambda x: x.split(" "))
result = words.map(lambda x: (x, 1)).reduceByKey(lambda x, y: x + y)
```

Example 4-10. Word count in Scala

```
val input = sc.textFile("s3://...")
val words = input.flatMap(x => x.split(" "))
val result = words.map(x => (x, 1)).reduceByKey((x, y) => x + y)
```

Example 4-11. Word count in Java

```
JavaRDD<String> input = sc.textFile("s3://...")
JavaRDD<String> words = input.flatMap(new FlatMapFunction<String, String>() {
  public Iterable<String> call(String x) { return Arrays.asList(x.split(" ")); }
});
JavaPairRDD<String, Integer> result = words.mapToPair(
  new PairFunction<String, String, Integer>() {
    public Tuple2<String, Integer> call(String x) { return new Tuple2(x, 1); }
}).reduceByKey(
  new Function2<Integer, Integer, Integer>() {
    public Integer call(Integer a, Integer b) { return a + b; }
});
```

 We can actually implement word count even faster by using the countByValue() function on the first RDD: input.flatMap(x => x.split(" ")).countByValue().

combineByKey()

combineByKey() is the most general of the per-key aggregation functions. Most of the other per-key combiners are implemented using it. Like aggregate(), combineBy Key() allows the user to return values that are not the same type as our input data.

To understand combineByKey(), it's useful to think of how it handles each element it processes. As combineByKey() goes through the elements in a partition, each element either has a key it hasn't seen before or has the same key as a previous element.

If it's a new element, combineByKey() uses a function we provide, called create Combiner(), to create the initial value for the accumulator on that key. It's important to note that this happens the first time a key is found in each partition, rather than only the first time the key is found in the RDD.

If it is a value we have seen before while processing that partition, it will instead use the provided function, mergeValue(), with the current value for the accumulator for that key and the new value.

Since each partition is processed independently, we can have multiple accumulators for the same key. When we are merging the results from each partition, if two or more partitions have an accumulator for the same key we merge the accumulators using the user-supplied mergeCombiners() function.

 We can disable map-side aggregation in combineByKey() if we know that our data won't benefit from it. For example, groupBy Key() disables map-side aggregation as the aggregation function (appending to a list) does not save any space. If we want to disable map-side combines, we need to specify the partitioner; for now you can just use the partitioner on the source RDD by passing rdd.par titioner.

Since combineByKey() has a lot of different parameters it is a great candidate for an explanatory example. To better illustrate how combineByKey() works, we will look at computing the average value for each key, as shown in Examples 4-12 through 4-14 and illustrated in Figure 4-3.

Example 4-12. Per-key average using combineByKey() in Python

```python
sumCount = nums.combineByKey((lambda x: (x,1)),
                             (lambda x, y: (x[0] + y, x[1] + 1)),
                             (lambda x, y: (x[0] + y[0], x[1] + y[1])))
r = sumCount.map(lambda key, xy: (key, xy[0]/xy[1])).collectAsMap()
print(*r)
```

Example 4-13. Per-key average using combineByKey() in Scala

```scala
val result = input.combineByKey(
  (v) => (v, 1),
  (acc: (Int, Int), v) => (acc._1 + v, acc._2 + 1),
  (acc1: (Int, Int), acc2: (Int, Int)) => (acc1._1 + acc2._1, acc1._2 + acc2._2)
  ).map{ case (key, value) => (key, value._1 / value._2.toFloat) }
  result.collectAsMap().foreach(println(_))
```

Example 4-14. Per-key average using combineByKey() in Java

```java
public static class AvgCount implements Serializable {
  public AvgCount(int total, int num) {   total_ = total;   num_ = num; }
```

```java
  public int total_;
  public int num_;
  public float avg() {   return total_ / (float) num_; }
}

Function<Integer, AvgCount> createAcc = new Function<Integer, AvgCount>() {
  public AvgCount call(Integer x) {
    return new AvgCount(x, 1);
  }
};
Function2<AvgCount, Integer, AvgCount> addAndCount =
  new Function2<AvgCount, Integer, AvgCount>() {
  public AvgCount call(AvgCount a, Integer x) {
    a.total_ += x;
    a.num_ += 1;
    return a;
  }
};
Function2<AvgCount, AvgCount, AvgCount> combine =
  new Function2<AvgCount, AvgCount, AvgCount>() {
  public AvgCount call(AvgCount a, AvgCount b) {
    a.total_ += b.total_;
    a.num_ += b.num_;
    return a;
  }
};
AvgCount initial = new AvgCount(0,0);
JavaPairRDD<String, AvgCount> avgCounts =
  nums.combineByKey(createAcc, addAndCount, combine);
Map<String, AvgCount> countMap = avgCounts.collectAsMap();
for (Entry<String, AvgCount> entry : countMap.entrySet()) {
  System.out.println(entry.getKey() + ":" + entry.getValue().avg());
}
```

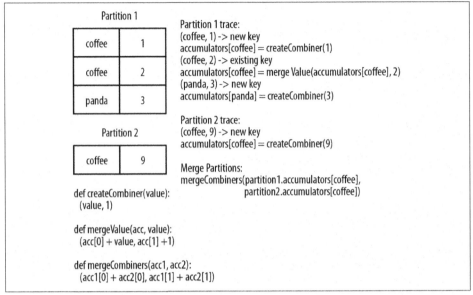

Figure 4-3. combineByKey() sample data flow

There are many options for combining our data by key. Most of them are implemented on top of `combineByKey()` but provide a simpler interface. In any case, using one of the specialized aggregation functions in Spark can be much faster than the naive approach of grouping our data and then reducing it.

Tuning the level of parallelism

So far we have talked about how all of our transformations are distributed, but we have not really looked at how Spark decides how to split up the work. Every RDD has a fixed number of *partitions* that determine the degree of parallelism to use when executing operations on the RDD.

When performing aggregations or grouping operations, we can ask Spark to use a specific number of partitions. Spark will always try to infer a sensible default value based on the size of your cluster, but in some cases you will want to tune the level of parallelism for better performance.

Most of the operators discussed in this chapter accept a second parameter giving the number of partitions to use when creating the grouped or aggregated RDD, as shown in Examples 4-15 and 4-16.

Example 4-15. reduceByKey() with custom parallelism in Python

```python
data = [("a", 3), ("b", 4), ("a", 1)]
sc.parallelize(data).reduceByKey(lambda x, y: x + y)      # Default parallelism
sc.parallelize(data).reduceByKey(lambda x, y: x + y, 10)  # Custom parallelism
```

Example 4-16. reduceByKey() with custom parallelism in Scala

```scala
val data = Seq(("a", 3), ("b", 4), ("a", 1))
sc.parallelize(data).reduceByKey((x, y) => x + y)      // Default parallelism
sc.parallelize(data).reduceByKey((x, y) => x + y, 10)  // Custom parallelism
```

Sometimes, we want to change the partitioning of an RDD outside the context of grouping and aggregation operations. For those cases, Spark provides the `reparti tion()` function, which shuffles the data across the network to create a new set of partitions. Keep in mind that repartitioning your data is a fairly expensive operation. Spark also has an optimized version of `repartition()` called `coalesce()` that allows avoiding data movement, but only if you are decreasing the number of RDD partitions. To know whether you can safely call `coalesce()`, you can check the size of the RDD using `rdd.partitions.size()` in Java/Scala and `rdd.getNumPartitions()` in Python and make sure that you are coalescing it to fewer partitions than it currently has.

Grouping Data

With keyed data a common use case is grouping our data by key—for example, viewing all of a customer's orders together.

If our data is already keyed in the way we want, `groupByKey()` will group our data using the key in our RDD. On an RDD consisting of keys of type `K` and values of type `V`, we get back an RDD of type `[K, Iterable[V]]`.

`groupBy()` works on unpaired data or data where we want to use a different condition besides equality on the current key. It takes a function that it applies to every element in the source RDD and uses the result to determine the key.

groupBy()

> If you find yourself writing code where you `groupByKey()` and then use a `reduce()` or `fold()` on the values, you can probably achieve the same result more efficiently by using one of the per-key aggregation functions. Rather than reducing the RDD to an in-memory value, we reduce the data per key and get back an RDD with the reduced values corresponding to each key. For example, `rdd.reduceByKey(func)` produces the same RDD as `rdd.groupBy Key().mapValues(value => value.reduce(func))` but is more efficient as it avoids the step of creating a list of values for each key.

In addition to grouping data from a single RDD, we can group data sharing the same key from multiple RDDs using a function called cogroup(). cogroup() over two RDDs sharing the same key type, K, with the respective value types V and W gives us back RDD[(K, (Iterable[V], Iterable[W]))]. If one of the RDDs doesn't have elements for a given key that is present in the other RDD, the corresponding Iterable is simply empty. cogroup() gives us the power to group data from multiple RDDs.

cogroup() is used as a building block for the joins we discuss in the next section.

 cogroup() can be used for much more than just implementing joins. We can also use it to implement intersect by key. Additionally, cogroup() can work on three or more RDDs at once.

Joins

Some of the most useful operations we get with keyed data comes from using it together with other keyed data. Joining data together is probably one of the most common operations on a pair RDD, and we have a full range of options including right and left outer joins, cross joins, and inner joins.

The simple join operator is an inner join.[1] Only keys that are present in both pair RDDs are output. When there are multiple values for the same key in one of the inputs, the resulting pair RDD will have an entry for every possible pair of values with that key from the two input RDDs. A simple way to understand this is by looking at Example 4-17.

Example 4-17. Scala shell inner join

```
storeAddress = {
  (Store("Ritual"), "1026 Valencia St"), (Store("Philz"), "748 Van Ness Ave"),
  (Store("Philz"), "3101 24th St"), (Store("Starbucks"), "Seattle")}

storeRating = {
  (Store("Ritual"), 4.9), (Store("Philz"), 4.8))}

storeAddress.join(storeRating) == {
  (Store("Ritual"), ("1026 Valencia St", 4.9)),
  (Store("Philz"), ("748 Van Ness Ave", 4.8)),
  (Store("Philz"), ("3101 24th St", 4.8))}
```

---

1 "Join" (*http://en.wikipedia.org/wiki/Join_(SQL)*) is a database term for combining fields from two tables using common values.

Sometimes we don't need the key to be present in both RDDs to want it in our result. For example, if we were joining customer information with recommendations we might not want to drop customers if there were not any recommendations yet. left OuterJoin(other) and rightOuterJoin(other) both join pair RDDs together by key, where one of the pair RDDs can be missing the key.

With leftOuterJoin() the resulting pair RDD has entries for each key in the source RDD. The value associated with each key in the result is a tuple of the value from the source RDD and an Option (or Optional in Java) for the value from the other pair RDD. In Python, if a value isn't present None is used; and if the value is present the regular value, without any wrapper, is used. As with join(), we can have multiple entries for each key; when this occurs, we get the Cartesian product between the two lists of values.

 Optional is part of Google's Guava library (*https://github.com/ google/guava*) and represents a possibly missing value. We can check isPresent() to see if it's set, and get() will return the contained instance provided data is present.

rightOuterJoin() is almost identical to leftOuterJoin() except the key must be present in the other RDD and the tuple has an option for the source rather than the other RDD.

We can revisit Example 4-17 and do a leftOuterJoin() and a rightOuterJoin() between the two pair RDDs we used to illustrate join() in Example 4-18.

Example 4-18. leftOuterJoin() and rightOuterJoin()

```
storeAddress.leftOuterJoin(storeRating) ==
{(Store("Ritual"),("1026 Valencia St",Some(4.9))),
  (Store("Starbucks"),("Seattle",None)),
  (Store("Philz"),("748 Van Ness Ave",Some(4.8))),
  (Store("Philz"),("3101 24th St",Some(4.8)))}

storeAddress.rightOuterJoin(storeRating) ==
{(Store("Ritual"),(Some("1026 Valencia St"),4.9)),
  (Store("Philz"),(Some("748 Van Ness Ave"),4.8)),
  (Store("Philz"), (Some("3101 24th St"),4.8))}
```

Sorting Data

Having sorted data is quite useful in many cases, especially when you're producing downstream output. We can sort an RDD with key/value pairs provided that there is an ordering defined on the key. Once we have sorted our data, any subsequent call on the sorted data to collect() or save() will result in ordered data.

Since we often want our RDDs in the reverse order, the sortByKey() function takes a parameter called ascending indicating whether we want it in ascending order (it defaults to true). Sometimes we want a different sort order entirely, and to support this we can provide our own comparison function. In Examples 4-19 through 4-21, we will sort our RDD by converting the integers to strings and using the string comparison functions.

Example 4-19. Custom sort order in Python, sorting integers as if strings

```python
rdd.sortByKey(ascending=True, numPartitions=None, keyfunc = lambda x: str(x))
```

Example 4-20. Custom sort order in Scala, sorting integers as if strings

```scala
val input: RDD[(Int, Venue)] = ...
implicit val sortIntegersByString = new Ordering[Int] {
  override def compare(a: Int, b: Int) = a.toString.compare(b.toString)
}
rdd.sortByKey()
```

Example 4-21. Custom sort order in Java, sorting integers as if strings

```java
class IntegerComparator implements Comparator<Integer> {
   public int compare(Integer a, Integer b) {
      return String.valueOf(a).compareTo(String.valueOf(b))
   }
}
rdd.sortByKey(comp)
```

Actions Available on Pair RDDs

As with the transformations, all of the traditional actions available on the base RDD are also available on pair RDDs. Some additional actions are available on pair RDDs to take advantage of the key/value nature of the data; these are listed in Table 4-3.

Table 4-3. Actions on pair RDDs (example ({(1, 2), (3, 4), (3, 6)}))

Function	Description	Example	Result
countByKey()	Count the number of elements for each key.	rdd.countByKey()	{(1, 1), (3, 2)}
collectAsMap()	Collect the result as a map to provide easy lookup.	rdd.collectAsMap()	Map{(1, 2), (3, 4), (3, 6)}
lookup(key)	Return all values associated with the provided key.	rdd.lookup(3)	[4, 6]

There are also multiple other actions on pair RDDs that save the RDD, which we will describe in Chapter 5.

Data Partitioning (Advanced)

The final Spark feature we will discuss in this chapter is how to control datasets' partitioning across nodes. In a distributed program, communication is very expensive, so laying out data to minimize network traffic can greatly improve performance. Much like how a single-node program needs to choose the right data structure for a collection of records, Spark programs can choose to control their RDDs' partitioning to reduce communication. Partitioning will not be helpful in all applications—for example, if a given RDD is scanned only once, there is no point in partitioning it in advance. It is useful only when a dataset is reused *multiple times* in key-oriented operations such as joins. We will give some examples shortly.

Spark's partitioning is available on all RDDs of key/value pairs, and causes the system to group elements based on a function of each key. Although Spark does not give explicit control of which worker node each key goes to (partly because the system is designed to work even if specific nodes fail), it lets the program ensure that a *set* of keys will appear together on *some* node. For example, you might choose to hash-partition an RDD into 100 partitions so that keys that have the same hash value modulo 100 appear on the same node. Or you might range-partition the RDD into sorted ranges of keys so that elements with keys in the same range appear on the same node.

As a simple example, consider an application that keeps a large table of user information in memory—say, an RDD of (UserID, UserInfo) pairs, where UserInfo contains a list of topics the user is subscribed to. The application periodically combines this table with a smaller file representing events that happened in the past five minutes—say, a table of (UserID, LinkInfo) pairs for users who have clicked a link on a website in those five minutes. For example, we may wish to count how many users visited a link that was *not* to one of their subscribed topics. We can perform this combination with Spark's join() operation, which can be used to group the User Info and LinkInfo pairs for each UserID by key. Our application would look like Example 4-22.

Example 4-22. Scala simple application

```
// Initialization code; we load the user info from a Hadoop SequenceFile on HDFS.
// This distributes elements of userData by the HDFS block where they are found,
// and doesn't provide Spark with any way of knowing in which partition a
// particular UserID is located.
val sc = new SparkContext(...)
val userData = sc.sequenceFile[UserID, UserInfo]("hdfs://...").persist()

// Function called periodically to process a logfile of events in the past 5 minutes;
```

```
// we assume that this is a SequenceFile containing (UserID, LinkInfo) pairs.
def processNewLogs(logFileName: String) {
  val events = sc.sequenceFile[UserID, LinkInfo](logFileName)
  val joined = userData.join(events)// RDD of (UserID, (UserInfo, LinkInfo)) pairs
  val offTopicVisits = joined.filter {
    case (userId, (userInfo, linkInfo)) => // Expand the tuple into its components
      !userInfo.topics.contains(linkInfo.topic)
  }.count()
  println("Number of visits to non-subscribed topics: " + offTopicVisits)
}
```

This code will run fine as is, but it will be inefficient. This is because the `join()` operation, called each time `processNewLogs()` is invoked, does not know anything about how the keys are partitioned in the datasets. By default, this operation will hash all the keys of *both* datasets, sending elements with the same key hash across the network to the same machine, and then join together the elements with the same key on that machine (see Figure 4-4). Because we expect the `userData` table to be much larger than the small log of `events` seen every five minutes, this wastes a lot of work: the `userData` table is hashed and shuffled across the network on every call, even though it doesn't change.

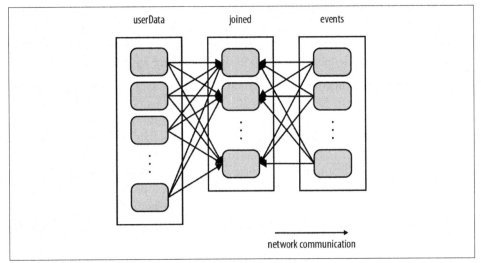

Figure 4-4. Each join of userData and events without using partitionBy()

Fixing this is simple: just use the `partitionBy()` transformation on `userData` to hash-partition it at the start of the program. We do this by passing a `org.apache.spark.HashPartitioner` object to `partitionBy`, as shown in Example 4-23.

Example 4-23. Scala custom partitioner

```
val sc = new SparkContext(...)
val userData = sc.sequenceFile[UserID, UserInfo]("hdfs://...")
                 .partitionBy(new HashPartitioner(100))   // Create 100 partitions
                 .persist()
```

The processNewLogs() method can remain unchanged: the events RDD is local to processNewLogs(), and is used only once within this method, so there is no advantage in specifying a partitioner for events. Because we called partitionBy() when building userData, Spark will now know that it is hash-partitioned, and calls to join() on it will take advantage of this information. In particular, when we call user Data.join(events), Spark will shuffle only the events RDD, sending events with each particular UserID to the machine that contains the corresponding hash partition of userData (see Figure 4-5). The result is that a lot less data is communicated over the network, and the program runs significantly faster.

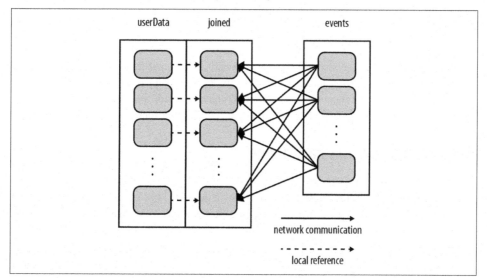

Figure 4-5. Each join of userData and events using partitionBy()

Note that partitionBy() is a transformation, so it always returns a *new* RDD—it does not change the original RDD in place. RDDs can never be modified once created. Therefore it is important to persist and save as userData the result of parti tionBy(), not the original sequenceFile(). Also, the 100 passed to partitionBy() represents the number of partitions, which will control how many parallel tasks perform further operations on the RDD (e.g., joins); in general, make this at least as large as the number of cores in your cluster.

Failure to persist an RDD after it has been transformed with `parti tionBy()` will cause subsequent uses of the RDD to repeat the partitioning of the data. Without persistence, use of the partitioned RDD will cause reevaluation of the RDDs complete lineage. That would negate the advantage of `partitionBy()`, resulting in repeated partitioning and shuffling of data across the network, similar to what occurs without any specified partitioner.

In fact, many other Spark operations automatically result in an RDD with known partitioning information, and many operations other than `join()` will take advantage of this information. For example, `sortByKey()` and `groupByKey()` will result in range-partitioned and hash-partitioned RDDs, respectively. On the other hand, operations like `map()` cause the new RDD to *forget* the parent's partitioning information, because such operations could theoretically modify the key of each record. The next few sections describe how to determine how an RDD is partitioned, and exactly how partitioning affects the various Spark operations.

Partitioning in Java and Python

Spark's Java and Python APIs benefit from partitioning in the same way as the Scala API. However, in Python, you cannot pass a `Hash Partitioner` object to `partitionBy`; instead, you just pass the number of partitions desired (e.g., `rdd.partitionBy(100)`).

Determining an RDD's Partitioner

In Scala and Java, you can determine how an RDD is partitioned using its `parti tioner` property (or `partitioner()` method in Java).[2] This returns a `scala.Option` object, which is a Scala class for a container that may or may not contain one item. You can call `isDefined()` on the `Option` to check whether it has a value, and `get()` to get this value. If present, the value will be a `spark.Partitioner` object. This is essentially a function telling the RDD which partition each key goes into; we'll talk more about this later.

The `partitioner` property is a great way to test in the Spark shell how different Spark operations affect partitioning, and to check that the operations you want to do in your program will yield the right result (see Example 4-24).

---

2 The Python API does not yet offer a way to query partitioners, though it still uses them internally.

Example 4-24. Determining partitioner of an RDD

```
scala> val pairs = sc.parallelize(List((1, 1), (2, 2), (3, 3)))
pairs: spark.RDD[(Int, Int)] = ParallelCollectionRDD[0] at parallelize at <console>:12

scala> pairs.partitioner
res0: Option[spark.Partitioner] = None

scala> import org.apache.spark.HashPartitioner
import org.apache.spark.HashPartitioner

scala> val partitioned = pairs.partitionBy(new HashPartitioner(2))
partitioned: spark.RDD[(Int, Int)] = ShuffledRDD[1] at partitionBy at <console>:14

scala> partitioned.partitioner
res1: Option[spark.Partitioner] = Some(spark.HashPartitioner@5147788d)
```

In this short session, we created an RDD of (Int, Int) pairs, which initially have no partitioning information (an Option with value None). We then created a second RDD by hash-partitioning the first. If we actually wanted to use partitioned in further operations, then we should have appended persist() to the third line of input, in which partitioned is defined. This is for the same reason that we needed persist() for userData in the previous example: without persist(), subsequent RDD actions will evaluate the entire lineage of partitioned, which will cause pairs to be hash-partitioned over and over.

Operations That Benefit from Partitioning

Many of Spark's operations involve shuffling data by key across the network. All of these will benefit from partitioning. As of Spark 1.0, the operations that benefit from partitioning are cogroup(), groupWith(), join(), leftOuterJoin(), rightOuter Join(), groupByKey(), reduceByKey(), combineByKey(), and lookup().

For operations that act on a single RDD, such as reduceByKey(), running on a pre-partitioned RDD will cause all the values for each key to be computed *locally* on a single machine, requiring only the final, locally reduced value to be sent from each worker node back to the master. For binary operations, such as cogroup() and join(), pre-partitioning will cause at least one of the RDDs (the one with the known partitioner) to not be shuffled. If both RDDs have the *same* partitioner, and if they are cached on the same machines (e.g., one was created using mapValues() on the other, which preserves keys and partitioning) or if one of them has not yet been computed, then no shuffling across the network will occur.

Operations That Affect Partitioning

Spark knows internally how each of its operations affects partitioning, and automatically sets the `partitioner` on RDDs created by operations that partition the data. For example, suppose you called `join()` to join two RDDs; because the elements with the same key have been hashed to the same machine, Spark knows that the result is hash-partitioned, and operations like `reduceByKey()` on the join result are going to be significantly faster.

The flipside, however, is that for transformations that *cannot* be guaranteed to produce a known partitioning, the output RDD will not have a `partitioner` set. For example, if you call `map()` on a hash-partitioned RDD of key/value pairs, the function passed to `map()` can in theory change the key of each element, so the result will not have a `partitioner`. Spark does not analyze your functions to check whether they retain the key. Instead, it provides two other operations, `mapValues()` and `flatMap Values()`, which guarantee that each tuple's key remains the same.

All that said, here are all the operations that result in a partitioner being set on the output RDD: `cogroup()`, `groupWith()`, `join()`, `leftOuterJoin()`, `rightOuter Join()`, `groupByKey()`, `reduceByKey()`, `combineByKey()`, `partitionBy()`, `sort()`, `mapValues()` (if the parent RDD has a partitioner), `flatMapValues()` (if parent has a partitioner), and `filter()` (if parent has a partitioner). All *other* operations will produce a result with no partitioner.

Finally, for binary operations, *which* partitioner is set on the output depends on the parent RDDs' partitioners. By default, it is a hash partitioner, with the number of partitions set to the level of parallelism of the operation. However, if one of the parents has a `partitioner` set, it will be that partitioner; and if both parents have a `parti tioner` set, it will be the partitioner of the first parent.

Example: PageRank

As an example of a more involved algorithm that can benefit from RDD partitioning, we consider PageRank. The PageRank algorithm, named after Google's Larry Page, aims to assign a measure of importance (a "rank") to each document in a set based on how many documents have links to it. It can be used to rank web pages, of course, but also scientific articles, or influential users in a social network.

PageRank is an iterative algorithm that performs many joins, so it is a good use case for RDD partitioning. The algorithm maintains two datasets: one of (`pageID`, `link List`) elements containing the list of neighbors of each page, and one of (`pageID`, `rank`) elements containing the current rank for each page. It proceeds as follows:

1. Initialize each page's rank to 1.0.

2. On each iteration, have page p send a contribution of `rank(p)/numNeighbors(p)` to its neighbors (the pages it has links to).

3. Set each page's rank to `0.15 + 0.85 * contributionsReceived`.

The last two steps repeat for several iterations, during which the algorithm will converge to the correct PageRank value for each page. In practice, it's typical to run about 10 iterations.

Example 4-25 gives the code to implement PageRank in Spark.

Example 4-25. Scala PageRank

```
// Assume that our neighbor list was saved as a Spark objectFile
val links = sc.objectFile[(String, Seq[String])]("links")
              .partitionBy(new HashPartitioner(100))
              .persist()

// Initialize each page's rank to 1.0; since we use mapValues, the resulting RDD
// will have the same partitioner as links
var ranks = links.mapValues(v => 1.0)

// Run 10 iterations of PageRank
for (i <- 0 until 10) {
  val contributions = links.join(ranks).flatMap {
    case (pageId, (pageLinks, rank)) =>
      pageLinks.map(dest => (dest, rank / pageLinks.size))
  }
  ranks = contributions.reduceByKey((x, y) => x + y).mapValues(v => 0.15 + 0.85*v)
}

// Write out the final ranks
ranks.saveAsTextFile("ranks")
```

That's it! The algorithm starts with a `ranks` RDD initialized at 1.0 for each element, and keeps updating the `ranks` variable on each iteration. The body of PageRank is pretty simple to express in Spark: it first does a `join()` between the current `ranks` RDD and the static `links` one, in order to obtain the link list and rank for each page ID together, then uses this in a `flatMap` to create "contribution" values to send to each of the page's neighbors. We then add up these values by page ID (i.e., by the page receiving the contribution) and set that page's rank to `0.15 + 0.85 * contributionsReceived`.

Although the code itself is simple, the example does several things to ensure that the RDDs are partitioned in an efficient way, and to minimize communication:

1. Notice that the links RDD is joined against ranks on each iteration. Since links is a static dataset, we partition it at the start with partitionBy(), so that it does not need to be shuffled across the network. In practice, the links RDD is also likely to be much larger in terms of bytes than ranks, since it contains a list of neighbors for each page ID instead of just a Double, so this optimization saves considerable network traffic over a simple implementation of PageRank (e.g., in plain MapReduce).

2. For the same reason, we call persist() on links to keep it in RAM across iterations.

3. When we first create ranks, we use mapValues() instead of map() to preserve the partitioning of the parent RDD (links), so that our first join against it is cheap.

4. In the loop body, we follow our reduceByKey() with mapValues(); because the result of reduceByKey() is already hash-partitioned, this will make it more efficient to join the mapped result against links on the next iteration.

 To maximize the potential for partitioning-related optimizations, you should use mapValues() or flatMapValues() whenever you are not changing an element's key.

Custom Partitioners

While Spark's HashPartitioner and RangePartitioner are well suited to many use cases, Spark also allows you to tune how an RDD is partitioned by providing a custom Partitioner object. This can help you further reduce communication by taking advantage of domain-specific knowledge.

For example, suppose we wanted to run the PageRank algorithm in the previous section on a set of web pages. Here each page's ID (the key in our RDD) will be its URL. Using a simple hash function to do the partitioning, pages with similar URLs (e.g., *http://www.cnn.com/WORLD* and *http://www.cnn.com/US*) might be hashed to completely different nodes. However, we know that web pages within the same domain tend to link to each other a lot. Because PageRank needs to send a message from each page to each of its neighbors on each iteration, it helps to group these pages into the same partition. We can do this with a custom Partitioner that looks at just the domain name instead of the whole URL.

To implement a custom partitioner, you need to subclass the `org.apache.spark.Par titioner` class and implement three methods:

- `numPartitions: Int`, which returns the number of partitions you will create.
- `getPartition(key: Any): Int`, which returns the partition ID (0 to `numPartitions-1`) for a given key.
- `equals()`, the standard Java equality method. This is important to implement because Spark will need to test your `Partitioner` object against other instances of itself when it decides whether two of your RDDs are partitioned the same way!

One gotcha is that if you rely on Java's `hashCode()` method in your algorithm, it can return negative numbers. You need to be careful to ensure that `getPartition()` always returns a nonnegative result.

Example 4-26 shows how we would write the domain-name-based partitioner sketched previously, which hashes only the domain name of each URL.

Example 4-26. Scala custom partitioner

```scala
class DomainNamePartitioner(numParts: Int) extends Partitioner {
  override def numPartitions: Int = numParts
  override def getPartition(key: Any): Int = {
    val domain = new java.net.URL(key.toString).getHost()
    val code = (domain.hashCode % numPartitions)
    if (code < 0) {
      code + numPartitions  // Make it non-negative
    } else {
      code
    }
  }
  // Java equals method to let Spark compare our Partitioner objects
  override def equals(other: Any): Boolean = other match {
    case dnp: DomainNamePartitioner =>
      dnp.numPartitions == numPartitions
    case _ =>
      false
  }
}
```

Note that in the `equals()` method, we used Scala's pattern matching operator (`match`) to test whether `other` is a `DomainNamePartitioner`, and cast it if so; this is the same as using `instanceof()` in Java.

Using a custom `Partitioner` is easy: just pass it to the `partitionBy()` method. Many of the shuffle-based methods in Spark, such as `join()` and `groupByKey()`, can also take an optional `Partitioner` object to control the partitioning of the output.

Creating a custom `Partitioner` in Java is very similar to Scala: just extend the `spark.Partitioner` class and implement the required methods.

In Python, you do not extend a `Partitioner` class, but instead pass a hash function as an additional argument to `RDD.partitionBy()`. Example 4-27 demonstrates.

Example 4-27. Python custom partitioner

```
import urlparse

def hash_domain(url):
    return hash(urlparse.urlparse(url).netloc)

rdd.partitionBy(20, hash_domain)  # Create 20 partitions
```

Note that the hash function you pass will be compared *by identity* to that of other RDDs. If you want to partition multiple RDDs with the same partitioner, pass the same function object (e.g., a global function) instead of creating a new `lambda` for each one!

Conclusion

In this chapter, we have seen how to work with key/value data using the specialized functions available in Spark. The techniques from Chapter 3 also still work on our pair RDDs. In the next chapter, we will look at how to load and save data.

## CHAPTER 5

Loading and Saving Your Data

Both engineers and data scientists will find parts of this chapter useful. Engineers may wish to explore more output formats to see if there is something well suited to their intended downstream consumer. Data scientists can likely focus on the format that their data is already in.

Motivation

We've looked at a number of operations we can perform on our data once we have it distributed in Spark. So far our examples have loaded and saved all of their data from a native collection and regular files, but odds are that your data doesn't fit on a single machine, so it's time to explore our options for loading and saving.

Spark supports a wide range of input and output sources, partly because it builds on the ecosystem available for Hadoop. In particular, Spark can access data through the InputFormat and OutputFormat interfaces used by Hadoop MapReduce, which are available for many common file formats and storage systems (e.g., S3, HDFS, Cassandra, HBase, etc.).[1] The section "Hadoop Input and Output Formats" on page 83 shows how to use these formats directly.

More commonly, though, you will want to use higher-level APIs built on top of these raw interfaces. Luckily, Spark and its ecosystem provide many options here. In this chapter, we will cover three common sets of data sources:

File formats and filesystems
    For data stored in a local or distributed filesystem, such as NFS, HDFS, or Amazon S3, Spark can access a variety of file formats including text, JSON,

---

1 InputFormat and OutputFormat are Java APIs used to connect a data source with MapReduce.

SequenceFiles, and protocol buffers. We will show how to use several common formats, as well as how to point Spark to different filesystems and configure compression.

Structured data sources through Spark SQL

The Spark SQL module, covered in Chapter 9, provides a nicer and often more efficient API for structured data sources, including JSON and Apache Hive. We will briefly sketch how to use Spark SQL, but leave the bulk of the details to Chapter 9.

Databases and key/value stores

We will sketch built-in and third-party libraries for connecting to Cassandra, HBase, Elasticsearch, and JDBC databases.

We chose most of the methods here to be available in all of Spark's languages, but some libraries are still Java and Scala only. We will point out when that is the case.

File Formats

Spark makes it very simple to load and save data in a large number of file formats. Formats range from unstructured, like text, to semistructured, like JSON, to structured, like SequenceFiles (see Table 5-1). Spark wraps a number of input formats through methods like `textFile()`, and as part of the wrapper, automatically handles compression based on file extension.

Table 5-1. Common supported file formats

Format name	Structured	Comments
Text files	No	Plain old text files. Records are assumed to be one per line.
JSON	Semi	Common text-based format, semistructured; most libraries require one record per line.
CSV	Yes	Very common text-based format, often used with spreadsheet applications.
SequenceFiles	Yes	A common Hadoop file format used for key/value data.
Protocol buffers	Yes	A fast, space-efficient multilanguage format.
Object files	Yes	Useful for saving data from a Spark job to be consumed by shared code. Breaks if you change your classes, as it relies on Java Serialization.

In addition to the output mechanisms supported directly in Spark, we can use both Hadoop's new and old file APIs for keyed (or paired) data. We can use these only with key/value data, because the Hadoop interfaces require key/value data, even though some formats ignore the key. In cases where the format ignores the key, it is common to use a dummy key (such as `null`).

Text Files

Text files are very simple to load from and save to with Spark. When we load a single text file as an RDD, each input line becomes an element in the RDD. We can also load multiple whole text files at the same time into a pair RDD, with the key being the name and the value being the contents of each file.

Loading text files

Loading a single text file is as simple as calling the `textFile()` function on our SparkContext with the path to the file, as you can see in Examples 5-1 through 5-3. If we want to control the number of partitions we can also specify `minPartitions`.

Example 5-1. Loading a text file in Python

```
input = sc.textFile("file:///home/holden/repos/spark/README.md")
```

Example 5-2. Loading a text file in Scala

```
val input = sc.textFile("file:///home/holden/repos/spark/README.md")
```

Example 5-3. Loading a text file in Java

```
JavaRDD<String> input = sc.textFile("file:///home/holden/repos/spark/README.md")
```

Multipart inputs in the form of a directory containing all of the parts can be handled in two ways. We can just use the same `textFile` method and pass it a directory and it will load all of the parts into our RDD. Sometimes it's important to know which file each piece of input came from (such as time data with the key in the file) or we need to process an entire file at a time. If our files are small enough, then we can use the [*key is file name*] `SparkContext.wholeTextFiles()` method and get back a pair RDD where the key is the name of the input file.

`wholeTextFiles()` can be very useful when each file represents a certain time [*← suspect this is how DAF works*] period's data. If we had files representing sales data from different periods, we could easily compute the average for each period, as shown in Example 5-4.

Example 5-4. Average value per file in Scala

```
val input = sc.wholeTextFiles("file:///home/holden/salesFiles")
val result = input.mapValues{y =>
  val nums = y.split(" ").map(x => x.toDouble)
```

```
nums.sum / nums.size.toDouble
}
```

 Spark supports reading all the files in a given directory and doing
wildcard expansion on the input (e.g., `part-*.txt`). This is useful
since large datasets are often spread across multiple files, especially
if other files (like success markers) may be in the same directory.

Saving text files

Outputting text files is also quite simple. The method `saveAsTextFile()`, demonstrated in Example 5-5, takes a path and will output the contents of the RDD to that
file. The path is treated as a directory and Spark will output multiple files underneath
that directory. This allows Spark to write the output from multiple nodes. With this
method we don't get to control which files end up with which segments of our data,
but there are other output formats that do allow this.

Example 5-5. Saving as a text file in Python

```
result.saveAsTextFile(outputFile)
```

JSON

JSON is a popular semistructured data format. The simplest way to load JSON data is
by loading the data as a text file and then mapping over the values with a JSON
parser. Likewise, we can use our preferred JSON serialization library to write out the
values to strings, which we can then write out. In Java and Scala we can also work
with JSON data using a custom Hadoop format. "JSON" on page 173 also shows how to
load JSON data with Spark SQL.

Loading JSON

Loading the data as a text file and then parsing the JSON data is an approach that we
can use in all of the supported languages. This works assuming that you have one
JSON record per row; if you have multiline JSON files, you will instead have to load
the whole file and then parse each file. If constructing a JSON parser is expensive in
your language, you can use `mapPartitions()` to reuse the parser; see "Working on a
Per-Partition Basis" on page 107 for details.

There are a wide variety of JSON libraries available for the three languages we are
looking at, but for simplicity's sake we are considering only one library per language.
In Python we will use the built-in library (*http://bit.ly/1upkGOV*) (Example 5-6), and
in Java and Scala we will use Jackson (*http://bit.ly/17k6vli*) (Examples 5-7 and 5-8).
These libraries have been chosen because they perform reasonably well and are also

relatively simple. If you spend a lot of time in the parsing stage, look at other JSON libraries for Scala (*http://bit.ly/1xP8JFK*) or for Java (*http://bit.ly/1upkJu1*).

Example 5-6. Loading unstructured JSON in Python

```python
import json
data = input.map(lambda x: json.loads(x))
```

In Scala and Java, it is common to load records into a class representing their schemas. At this stage, we may also want to skip invalid records. We show an example of loading records as instances of a Person class.

Example 5-7. Loading JSON in Scala

```scala
import com.fasterxml.jackson.module.scala.DefaultScalaModule
import com.fasterxml.jackson.module.scala.experimental.ScalaObjectMapper
import com.fasterxml.jackson.databind.ObjectMapper
import com.fasterxml.jackson.databind.DeserializationFeature
...
case class Person(name: String, lovesPandas: Boolean) // Must be a top-level class
...
// Parse it into a specific case class. We use flatMap to handle errors
// by returning an empty list (None) if we encounter an issue and a
// list with one element if everything is ok (Some(_)).
val result = input.flatMap(record => {
  try {
    Some(mapper.readValue(record, classOf[Person]))
  } catch {
    case e: Exception => None
  }})
```

Example 5-8. Loading JSON in Java

```java
class ParseJson implements FlatMapFunction<Iterator<String>, Person> {
  public Iterable<Person> call(Iterator<String> lines) throws Exception {
    ArrayList<Person> people = new ArrayList<Person>();
    ObjectMapper mapper = new ObjectMapper();
    while (lines.hasNext()) {
      String line = lines.next();
      try {
        people.add(mapper.readValue(line, Person.class));
      } catch (Exception e) {
        // skip records on failure
      }
    }
    return people;
  }
}
JavaRDD<String> input = sc.textFile("file.json");
JavaRDD<Person> result = input.mapPartitions(new ParseJson());
```

Handling incorrectly formatted records can be a big problem, especially with semistructured data like JSON. With small datasets it can be acceptable to stop the world (i.e., fail the program) on malformed input, but often with large datasets malformed input is simply a part of life. If you do choose to skip incorrectly formatted data, you may wish to look at using accumulators to keep track of the number of errors.

Saving JSON

Writing out JSON files is much simpler compared to loading it, because we don't have to worry about incorrectly formatted data and we know the type of the data that we are writing out. We can use the same libraries we used to convert our RDD of strings into parsed JSON data and instead take our RDD of structured data and convert it into an RDD of strings, which we can then write out using Spark's text file API.

Let's say we were running a promotion for people who love pandas. We can take our input from the first step and filter it for the people who love pandas, as shown in Examples 5-9 through 5-11.

Example 5-9. Saving JSON in Python

```python
(data.filter(lambda x: x['lovesPandas']).map(lambda x: json.dumps(x))
  .saveAsTextFile(outputFile))
```

Example 5-10. Saving JSON in Scala

```scala
result.filter(p => P.lovesPandas).map(mapper.writeValueAsString(_))
  .saveAsTextFile(outputFile)
```

Example 5-11. Saving JSON in Java

```java
class WriteJson implements FlatMapFunction<Iterator<Person>, String> {
  public Iterable<String> call(Iterator<Person> people) throws Exception {
    ArrayList<String> text = new ArrayList<String>();
    ObjectMapper mapper = new ObjectMapper();
    while (people.hasNext()) {
      Person person = people.next();
      text.add(mapper.writeValueAsString(person));
    }
    return text;
  }
}

JavaRDD<Person> result = input.mapPartitions(new ParseJson()).filter(
  new LikesPandas());
JavaRDD<String> formatted = result.mapPartitions(new WriteJson());
formatted.saveAsTextFile(outfile);
```

We can thus easily load and save JSON data with Spark by using the existing mechanism for working with text and adding JSON libraries.

Comma-Separated Values and Tab-Separated Values

Comma-separated value (CSV) files are supposed to contain a fixed number of fields per line, and the fields are separated by a comma (or a tab in the case of tab-separated value, or TSV, files). Records are often stored one per line, but this is not always the case as records can sometimes span lines. CSV and TSV files can sometimes be inconsistent, most frequently with respect to handling newlines, escaping, and rendering non-ASCII characters, or noninteger numbers. CSVs cannot handle nested field types natively, so we have to unpack and pack to specific fields manually.

In addition to writing CSV loading code by hand, there is a package on *http://www.spark-packages.org* called spark-csv to load csv data as a Spark SQL data source.

Unlike with JSON fields, each record doesn't have field names associated with it; instead we get back row numbers. It is common practice in single CSV files to make the first row's column values the names of each field.

Loading CSV

Loading CSV/TSV data is similar to loading JSON data in that we can first load it as text and then process it. The lack of standardization of format leads to different versions of the same library sometimes handling input in different ways.

As with JSON, there are many different CSV libraries, but we will use only one for each language. Once again, in Python we use the included csv (*https://docs.python.org/2/library/csv.html*) library. In both Scala and Java we use opencsv (*http://opencsv.sourceforge.net/*).

There is also a Hadoop InputFormat, CSVInputFormat (*http://bit.ly/1FigUkq*), that we can use to load CSV data in Scala and Java, although it does not support records containing newlines.

If your CSV data happens to not contain newlines in any of the fields, you can load your data with textFile() and parse it, as shown in Examples 5-12 through 5-14.

Example 5-12. Loading CSV with textFile() in Python

```python
import csv
import StringIO
...
def loadRecord(line):
    """Parse a CSV line"""
    input = StringIO.StringIO(line)
    reader = csv.DictReader(input, fieldnames=["name", "favouriteAnimal"])
    return reader.next()
input = sc.textFile(inputFile).map(loadRecord)
```

Example 5-13. Loading CSV with textFile() in Scala

```scala
import java.io.StringReader
import au.com.bytecode.opencsv.CSVReader
...
val input = sc.textFile(inputFile)
val result = input.map{ line =>
  val reader = new CSVReader(new StringReader(line));
  reader.readNext();
}
```

Example 5-14. Loading CSV with textFile() in Java

```java
import au.com.bytecode.opencsv.CSVReader;
import java.io.StringReader;
...
public static class ParseLine implements Function<String, String[]> {
  public String[] call(String line) throws Exception {
    CSVReader reader = new CSVReader(new StringReader(line));
    return reader.readNext();
  }
}
JavaRDD<String> csvFile1 = sc.textFile(inputFile);
JavaPairRDD<String[]> csvData = csvFile1.map(new ParseLine());
```

If there are embedded newlines in fields, we will need to load each file in full and parse the entire segment, as shown in Examples 5-15 through 5-17. This is unfortunate because if each file is large it can introduce bottlenecks in loading and parsing. The different text file loading methods are described "Loading text files" on page 73.

Example 5-15. Loading CSV in full in Python

```python
def loadRecords(fileNameContents):
    """Load all the records in a given file"""
    input = StringIO.StringIO(fileNameContents[1])
    reader = csv.DictReader(input, fieldnames=["name", "favoriteAnimal"])
    return reader
fullFileData = sc.wholeTextFiles(inputFile).flatMap(loadRecords)
```

Example 5-16. Loading CSV in full in Scala

```scala
case class Person(name: String, favoriteAnimal: String)

val input = sc.wholeTextFiles(inputFile)
val result = input.flatMap{ case (_, txt) =>
  val reader = new CSVReader(new StringReader(txt));
  reader.readAll().map(x => Person(x(0), x(1)))
}
```

Example 5-17. Loading CSV in full in Java

```java
public static class ParseLine
  implements FlatMapFunction<Tuple2<String, String>, String[]> {
  public Iterable<String[]> call(Tuple2<String, String> file) throws Exception {
    CSVReader reader = new CSVReader(new StringReader(file._2()));
    return reader.readAll();
  }
}
JavaPairRDD<String, String> csvData = sc.wholeTextFiles(inputFile);
JavaRDD<String[]> keyedRDD = csvData.flatMap(new ParseLine());
```

 If there are only a few input files, and you need to use the whole TextFiles() method, you may want to repartition your input to allow Spark to effectively parallelize your future operations.

Saving CSV

As with JSON data, writing out CSV/TSV data is quite simple and we can benefit from reusing the output encoding object. Since in CSV we don't output the field name with each record, to have a consistent output we need to create a mapping. One of the easy ways to do this is to just write a function that converts the fields to given positions in an array. In Python, if we are outputting dictionaries the CSV writer can do this for us based on the order in which we provide the fieldnames when constructing the writer.

The CSV libraries we are using output to files/writers so we can use StringWriter/ StringIO to allow us to put the result in our RDD, as you can see in Examples 5-18 and 5-19.

Example 5-18. Writing CSV in Python

```python
def writeRecords(records):
    """Write out CSV lines"""
    output = StringIO.StringIO()
    writer = csv.DictWriter(output, fieldnames=["name", "favoriteAnimal"])
    for record in records:
```

```
    writer.writerow(record)
  return [output.getvalue()]
```

```
pandaLovers.mapPartitions(writeRecords).saveAsTextFile(outputFile)
```

Example 5-19. Writing CSV in Scala

```
pandaLovers.map(person => List(person.name, person.favoriteAnimal).toArray)
.mapPartitions{people =>
  val stringWriter = new StringWriter();
  val csvWriter = new CSVWriter(stringWriter);
  csvWriter.writeAll(people.toList)
  Iterator(stringWriter.toString)
}.saveAsTextFile(outFile)
```

As you may have noticed, the preceding examples work only provided that we know all of the fields that we will be outputting. However, if some of the field names are determined at runtime from user input, we need to take a different approach. The simplest approach is going over all of our data and extracting the distinct keys and then taking another pass for output.

SequenceFiles

SequenceFiles are a popular Hadoop format composed of flat files with key/value pairs. SequenceFiles have sync markers that allow Spark to seek to a point in the file and then resynchronize with the record boundaries. This allows Spark to efficiently read SequenceFiles in parallel from multiple nodes. SequenceFiles are a common input/output format for Hadoop MapReduce jobs as well, so if you are working with an existing Hadoop system there is a good chance your data will be available as a SequenceFile.

SequenceFiles consist of elements that implement Hadoop's Writable interface, as Hadoop uses a custom serialization framework. Table 5-2 lists some common types and their corresponding Writable class. The standard rule of thumb is to try adding the word *Writable* to the end of your class name and see if it is a known subclass of `org.apache.hadoop.io.Writable` (*http://bit.ly/1FilfEu*). If you can't find a Writable for the data you are trying to write out (for example, a custom case class), you can go ahead and implement your own Writable class by overriding `readFields` and `write` from `org.apache.hadoop.io.Writable`.

 Hadoop's RecordReader reuses the same object for each record, so directly calling `cache` on an RDD you read in like this can fail; instead, add a simple `map()` operation and cache its result. Furthermore, many Hadoop Writable classes do not implement `java.io.Serializable`, so for them to work in RDDs we need to convert them with a `map()` anyway.

Table 5-2. Corresponding Hadoop Writable types

Scala type	Java type	Hadoop Writable
Int	Integer	IntWritable or VIntWritable[a]
Long	Long	LongWritable or VLongWritable[a]
Float	Float	FloatWritable
Double	Double	DoubleWritable
Boolean	Boolean	BooleanWritable
Array[Byte]	byte[]	BytesWritable
String	String	Text
Array[T]	T[]	ArrayWritable<TW>[b]
List[T]	List<T>	ArrayWritable<TW>[b]
Map[A, B]	Map<A, B>	MapWritable<AW, BW>[b]

[a] ints and longs are often stored as a fixed size. Storing the number 12 takes the same amount of space as storing the number 2**30. If you might have a large number of small numbers use the variable sized types, VIntWritable and VLongWritable, which will use fewer bits to store smaller numbers.

[b] The templated type must also be a Writable type.

In Spark 1.0 and earlier, SequenceFiles were available only in Java and Scala, but Spark 1.1 added the ability to load and save them in Python as well. Note that you will need to use Java and Scala to define custom Writable types, however. The Python Spark API knows only how to convert the basic Writables available in Hadoop to Python, and makes a best effort for other classes based on their available getter methods.

Loading SequenceFiles

Spark has a specialized API for reading in SequenceFiles. On the SparkContext we can call sequenceFile(path, keyClass, valueClass, minPartitions). As mentioned earlier, SequenceFiles work with Writable classes, so our keyClass and valueClass will both have to be the correct Writable class. Let's consider loading people and the number of pandas they have seen from a SequenceFile. In this case our keyClass would be Text, and our valueClass would be IntWritable or VIntWritable, but for simplicity we'll work with IntWritable in Examples 5-20 through 5-22.

Example 5-20. Loading a SequenceFile in Python

```python
data = sc.sequenceFile(inFile,
  "org.apache.hadoop.io.Text", "org.apache.hadoop.io.IntWritable")
```

Example 5-21. Loading a SequenceFile in Scala

```scala
val data = sc.sequenceFile(inFile, classOf[Text], classOf[IntWritable]).
  map{case (x, y) => (x.toString, y.get())}
```

Example 5-22. Loading a SequenceFile in Java

```java
public static class ConvertToNativeTypes implements
  PairFunction<Tuple2<Text, IntWritable>, String, Integer> {
  public Tuple2<String, Integer> call(Tuple2<Text, IntWritable> record) {
    return new Tuple2(record._1.toString(), record._2.get());
  }
}

JavaPairRDD<Text, IntWritable> input = sc.sequenceFile(fileName, Text.class,
  IntWritable.class);
JavaPairRDD<String, Integer> result = input.mapToPair(
  new ConvertToNativeTypes());
```

In Scala there is a convenience function that can automatically convert Writables to their corresponding Scala type. Instead of specifying the keyClass and valueClass, we can call sequence File[Key, Value](path, minPartitions) and get back an RDD of native Scala types.

Saving SequenceFiles

Writing the data out to a SequenceFile is fairly similar in Scala. First, because SequenceFiles are key/value pairs, we need a PairRDD with types that our SequenceFile can write out. Implicit conversions between Scala types and Hadoop Writables exist for many native types, so if you are writing out a native type you can just save your PairRDD by calling saveAsSequenceFile(path), and it will write out the data for you. If there isn't an automatic conversion from our key and value to Writable, or we want to use variable-length types (e.g., VIntWritable), we can just map over the data and convert it before saving. Let's consider writing out the data that we loaded in the previous example (people and how many pandas they have seen), as shown in Example 5-23.

Example 5-23. Saving a SequenceFile in Scala

```scala
val data = sc.parallelize(List(("Panda", 3), ("Kay", 6), ("Snail", 2)))
data.saveAsSequenceFile(outputFile)
```

In Java saving a SequenceFile is slightly more involved, due to the lack of a `saveAsSe quenceFile()` method on the `JavaPairRDD`. Instead, we use Spark's ability to save to custom Hadoop formats, and we will show how to save to a SequenceFile in Java in "Hadoop Input and Output Formats" on page 83.

Object Files

Object files are a deceptively simple wrapper around SequenceFiles that allows us to save our RDDs containing just values. Unlike with SequenceFiles, with object files the values are written out using Java Serialization.

 If you change your classes—for example, to add and remove fields —old object files may no longer be readable. Object files use Java Serialization, which has some support for managing compatibility across class versions but requires programmer effort to do so.

Using Java Serialization for object files has a number of implications. Unlike with normal SequenceFiles, the output will be different than Hadoop outputting the same objects. Unlike the other formats, object files are mostly intended to be used for Spark jobs communicating with other Spark jobs. Java Serialization can also be quite slow.

Saving an object file is as simple as calling `saveAsObjectFile` on an RDD. Reading an object file back is also quite simple: the function `objectFile()` on the SparkContext takes in a path and returns an RDD.

With all of these warnings about object files, you might wonder why anyone would use them. The primary reason to use object files is that they require almost no work to save almost arbitrary objects.

Object files are not available in Python, but the Python RDDs and SparkContext support methods called `saveAsPickleFile()` and `pickleFile()` instead. These use Python's `pickle` serialization library. The same caveats for object files apply to pickle files, however: the pickle library can be slow, and old files may not be readable if you change your classes.

Hadoop Input and Output Formats

In addition to the formats Spark has wrappers for, we can also interact with any Hadoop-supported formats. Spark supports both the "old" and "new" Hadoop file APIs, providing a great amount of flexibility.[2]

---

2 Hadoop added a new MapReduce API early in its lifetime, but some libraries still use the old one.

Loading with other Hadoop input formats

To read in a file using the new Hadoop API we need to tell Spark a few things. The newAPIHadoopFile takes a path, and three classes. The first class is the "format" class, which is the class representing our input format. The next class is the class for our key, and the final class is the class of our value. If we need to specify additional Hadoop configuration properties, we can also pass in a conf object. A similar function, hadoopFile(), exists for working with Hadoop input formats implemented with the older API.

One of the simplest Hadoop input formats is the KeyValueTextInputFormat, which can be used for reading in key/value data from text files (see Example 5-24). Each line is processed individually, with the key and value separated by a tab character. This format ships with Hadoop so we don't have to add any extra dependencies to our project to use it.

Example 5-24. Loading KeyValueTextInputFormat() with old-style API in Scala

```
val input = sc.hadoopFile[Text, Text, KeyValueTextInputFormat](inputFile).map{
  case (x, y) => (x.toString, y.toString)
}
```

We looked at loading JSON data by loading the data as a text file and then parsing it, but we can also load JSON data using a custom Hadoop input format. This example requires setting up some extra bits for compression, so feel free to skip it. Twitter's Elephant Bird package (*https://github.com/kevinweil/elephant-bird*) supports a large number of data formats, including JSON, Lucene, Protocol Buffer–related formats, and others. The package also works with both the new and old Hadoop file APIs. To illustrate how to work with the new-style Hadoop APIs from Spark, we'll look at loading LZO-compressed JSON data with Lzo JsonInputFormat in Example 5-25.

Example 5-25. Loading LZO-compressed JSON with Elephant Bird in Scala

```
val input = sc.newAPIHadoopFile(inputFile, classOf[LzoJsonInputFormat],
  classOf[LongWritable], classOf[MapWritable], conf)
// Each MapWritable in "input" represents a JSON object
```

 LZO support requires you to install the hadoop-lzo package and point Spark to its native libraries. If you install the Debian package, adding --driver-library-path /usr/lib/hadoop/lib/native/ --driver-class-path /usr/lib/hadoop/lib/ to your spark-submit invocation should do the trick.

Reading a file using the old Hadoop API is pretty much the same from a usage point of view, except we provide an old-style InputFormat class. Many of Spark's built-in convenience functions (like `sequenceFile()`) are implemented using the old-style Hadoop API.

Saving with Hadoop output formats

We already examined SequenceFiles to some extent, but in Java we don't have the same convenience function for saving from a pair RDD. We will use this as a way to illustrate how to use the old Hadoop format APIs (see Example 5-26); the call for the new one (`saveAsNewAPIHadoopFile`) is similar.

Example 5-26. Saving a SequenceFile in Java

```
public static class ConvertToWritableTypes implements
  PairFunction<Tuple2<String, Integer>, Text, IntWritable> {
  public Tuple2<Text, IntWritable> call(Tuple2<String, Integer> record) {
    return new Tuple2(new Text(record._1), new IntWritable(record._2));
  }
}

JavaPairRDD<String, Integer> rdd = sc.parallelizePairs(input);
JavaPairRDD<Text, IntWritable> result = rdd.mapToPair(new ConvertToWritableTypes());
result.saveAsHadoopFile(fileName, Text.class, IntWritable.class,
  SequenceFileOutputFormat.class);
```

Non-filesystem data sources

In addition to the `hadoopFile()` and `saveAsHadoopFile()` family of functions, you can use `hadoopDataset/saveAsHadoopDataSet` and `newAPIHadoopDataset/saveAsNewAPIHadoopDataset` to access Hadoop-supported storage formats that are not filesystems. For example, many key/value stores, such as HBase and MongoDB, provide Hadoop input formats that read directly from the key/value store. You can easily use any such format in Spark.

The `hadoopDataset()` family of functions just take a `Configuration` object on which you set the Hadoop properties needed to access your data source. You do the configuration the same way as you would configure a Hadoop MapReduce job, so you can follow the instructions for accessing one of these data sources in MapReduce and then pass the object to Spark. For example, "HBase" on page 96 shows how to use `newAPIHadoopDataset` to load data from HBase.

Example: Protocol buffers

Protocol buffers (*https://code.google.com/p/protobuf/*)[3] were first developed at Google for internal remote procedure calls (RPCs) and have since been open sourced. Proto-

---

3 Sometimes called *pbs* or *protobufs*.

col buffers (PBs) are structured data, with the fields and types of fields being clearly defined. They are optimized to be fast for encoding and decoding and also take up the minimum amount of space. Compared to XML, PBs are 3× to 10× smaller and can be 20× to 100× faster to encode and decode. While a PB has a consistent encoding, there are multiple ways to create a file consisting of many PB messages.

Protocol buffers are defined using a domain-specific language, and then the protocol buffer compiler can be used to generate accessor methods in a variety of languages (including all those supported by Spark). Since PBs aim to take up a minimal amount of space they are not "self-describing," as encoding the description of the data would take up additional space. This means that to parse data that is formatted as PB, we need the protocol buffer definition to make sense of it.

PBs consist of fields that can be either optional, required, or repeated. When you're parsing data, a missing optional field does not result in a failure, but a missing required field results in failing to parse the data. Therefore, when you're adding new fields to existing protocol buffers it is good practice to make the new fields optional, as not everyone will upgrade at the same time (and even if they do, you might want to read your old data).

PB fields can be many predefined types, or another PB message. These types include string, int32, enums, and more. This is by no means a complete introduction to protocol buffers, so if you are interested you should consult the Protocol Buffers website (*https://developers.google.com/protocol-buffers*).

In Example 5-27 we will look at loading many VenueResponse objects from a simple protocol buffer format. The sample VenueResponse is a simple format with one repeated field, containing another message with required, optional, and enumeration fields.

Example 5-27. Sample protocol buffer definition

```
message Venue {
  required int32 id = 1;
  required string name = 2;
  required VenueType type = 3;
  optional string address = 4;

  enum VenueType {
    COFFEESHOP = 0;
    WORKPLACE = 1;
    CLUB = 2;
    OMNOMNOM = 3;
    OTHER = 4;
  }
}
```

```
message VenueResponse {
  repeated Venue results = 1;
}
```

Twitter's Elephant Bird library, which we used in the previous section to load JSON data, also supports loading and saving data from protocol buffers. Let's look at writing out some Venues in Example 5-28.

Example 5-28. Elephant Bird protocol buffer writeout in Scala

```
val job = new Job()
val conf = job.getConfiguration
LzoProtobufBlockOutputFormat.setClassConf(classOf[Places.Venue], conf);
val dnaLounge = Places.Venue.newBuilder()
dnaLounge.setId(1);
dnaLounge.setName("DNA Lounge")
dnaLounge.setType(Places.Venue.VenueType.CLUB)
val data = sc.parallelize(List(dnaLounge.build()))
val outputData = data.map{ pb =>
  val protoWritable = ProtobufWritable.newInstance(classOf[Places.Venue]);
  protoWritable.set(pb)
  (null, protoWritable)
}
outputData.saveAsNewAPIHadoopFile(outputFile, classOf[Text],
  classOf[ProtobufWritable[Places.Venue]],
  classOf[LzoProtobufBlockOutputFormat[ProtobufWritable[Places.Venue]]], conf)
```

A full version of this example is available in the source code for this book.

When building your project, make sure to use the same protocol buffer library version as Spark. As of this writing, that is version 2.5.

File Compression

Frequently when working with Big Data, we find ourselves needing to use compressed data to save storage space and network overhead. With most Hadoop output formats, we can specify a compression codec that will compress the data. As we have already seen, Spark's native input formats (textFile and sequenceFile) can automatically handle some types of compression for us. When you're reading in compressed data, there are some compression codecs that can be used to automatically guess the compression type.

These compression options apply only to the Hadoop formats that support compression, namely those that are written out to a filesystem. The database Hadoop formats generally do not implement support for compression, or if they have compressed records that is configured in the database itself.

Choosing an output compression codec can have a big impact on future users of the data. With distributed systems such as Spark, we normally try to read our data in from multiple different machines. To make this possible, each worker needs to be able to find the start of a new record. Some compression formats make this impossible, which requires a single node to read in all of the data and thus can easily lead to a bottleneck. Formats that can be easily read from multiple machines are called "split-table." Table 5-3 lists the available compression options.

Table 5-3. Compression options

Format	Splittable	Average compression speed	Effectiveness on text	Hadoop compression codec	Pure Java	Native	Comments
gzip	N	Fast	High	`org.apache.hadoop.io.com press.GzipCodec`	Y	Y	
lzo	Y[a]	Very fast	Medium	`com.hadoop.compres sion.lzo.LzoCodec`	Y	Y	LZO requires installation on every worker node
bzip2	Y	Slow	Very high	`org.apache.hadoop.io.com press.BZip2Codec`	Y	Y	Uses pure Java for splittable version
zlib	N	Slow	Medium	`org.apache.hadoop.io.com press.DefaultCodec`	Y	Y	Default compression codec for Hadoop
Snappy	N	Very Fast	Low	`org.apache.hadoop.io.com press.SnappyCodec`	N	Y	There is a pure Java port of Snappy but it is not yet available in Spark/Hadoop

[a] Depends on the library used

While Spark's textFile() method *can* handle compressed input, it automatically disables splittable even if the input is compressed such that it could be read in a splittable way. If you find yourself needing to read in a large single-file compressed input, consider skipping Spark's wrapper and instead use either newAPIHadoopFile or hadoopFile and specify the correct compression codec.

Some input formats (like SequenceFiles) allow us to compress only the values in key/value data, which can be useful for doing lookups. Other input formats have their own compression control: for example, many of the formats in Twitter's Elephant Bird package work with LZO compressed data.

Filesystems

Spark supports a large number of filesystems for reading and writing to, which we can use with any of the file formats we want.

Local/"Regular" FS

While Spark supports loading files from the local filesystem, it *requires that the files are available at the same path on all nodes in your cluster.*

Some network filesystems, like NFS, AFS, and MapR's NFS layer, are exposed to the user as a regular filesystem. If your data is already in one of these systems, then you can use it as an input by just specifying a *file://* path; Spark will handle it as long as the filesystem is mounted at the same path on each node (see Example 5-29).

Example 5-29. Loading a compressed text file from the local filesystem in Scala

```
val rdd = sc.textFile("file:///home/holden/happypandas.gz")
```

If your file isn't already on all nodes in the cluster, you can load it locally on the driver without going through Spark and then call parallelize to distribute the contents to workers. This approach can be slow, however, so we recommend putting your files in a shared filesystem like HDFS, NFS, or S3.

Amazon S3

Amazon S3 is an increasingly popular option for storing large amounts of data. S3 is especially fast when your compute nodes are located inside of Amazon EC2, but can easily have much worse performance if you have to go over the public Internet.

To access S3 in Spark, you should first set the AWS_ACCESS_KEY_ID and AWS_SECRET_ACCESS_KEY environment variables to your S3 credentials. You can create these credentials from the Amazon Web Services console. Then pass a path starting with `s3n://` to Spark's file input methods, of the form `s3n://bucket/path-within-bucket`. As with all the other filesystems, Spark supports wildcard paths for S3, such as `s3n://bucket/my-files/*.txt`.

If you get an S3 access permissions error from Amazon, make sure that the account for which you specified an access key has both "read" and "list" permissions on the bucket. Spark needs to be able to list the objects in the bucket to identify the ones you want to read.

HDFS

The Hadoop Distributed File System (HDFS) is a popular distributed filesystem with which Spark works well. HDFS is designed to work on commodity hardware and be resilient to node failure while providing high data throughput. Spark and HDFS can be collocated on the same machines, and Spark can take advantage of this data locality to avoid network overhead.

Using Spark with HDFS is as simple as specifying `hdfs://master:port/path` for your input and output.

The HDFS protocol changes across Hadoop versions, so if you run a version of Spark that is compiled for a different version it will fail. By default Spark is built against Hadoop 1.0.4. If you build from source, you can specify `SPARK_HADOOP_VERSION=` as an environment variable to build against a different version; or you can download a different precompiled version of Spark. You can determine the value by running `hadoop version`.

Structured Data with Spark SQL

Spark SQL is a component added in Spark 1.0 that is quickly becoming Spark's preferred way to work with structured and semistructured data. By structured data, we mean data that has a *schema*—that is, a consistent set of fields across data records. Spark SQL supports multiple structured data sources as input, and because it understands their schema, it can efficiently read only the fields you require from these data sources. We will cover Spark SQL in more detail in Chapter 9, but for now, we show how to use it to load data from a few common sources.

In all cases, we give Spark SQL a SQL query to run on the data source (selecting some fields or a function of the fields), and we get back an RDD of Row objects, one per record. In Java and Scala, the Row objects allow access based on the column number. Each Row has a `get()` method that gives back a general type we can cast, and specific `get()` methods for common basic types (e.g., `getFloat()`, `getInt()`, `getLong()`, `get`

String(), getShort(), and getBoolean()). In Python we can just access the elements with row[column_number] and row.column_name.

Apache Hive

One common structured data source on Hadoop is Apache Hive. Hive can store tables in a variety of formats, from plain text to column-oriented formats, inside HDFS or other storage systems. Spark SQL can load any table supported by Hive.

Hive Interface to Spark

To connect Spark SQL to an existing Hive installation, you need to provide a Hive configuration. You do so by copying your *hive-site.xml* file to Spark's *./conf/* directory. Once you have done this, you create a HiveContext object, which is the entry point to Spark SQL, and you can write Hive Query Language (HQL) queries against your tables to get data back as RDDs of rows. Examples 5-30 through 5-32 demonstrate.

Example 5-30. Creating a HiveContext and selecting data in Python

```
from pyspark.sql import HiveContext

hiveCtx = HiveContext(sc)
rows = hiveCtx.sql("SELECT name, age FROM users")
firstRow = rows.first()
print firstRow.name
```

Using Python to make Hive queries!!

Example 5-31. Creating a HiveContext and selecting data in Scala

```
import org.apache.spark.sql.hive.HiveContext

val hiveCtx = new HiveContext(sc)
val rows = hiveCtx.sql("SELECT name, age FROM users")
val firstRow = rows.first()
println(firstRow.getString(0)) // Field 0 is the name
```

Example 5-32. Creating a HiveContext and selecting data in Java

```
import org.apache.spark.sql.hive.HiveContext;
import org.apache.spark.sql.Row;
import org.apache.spark.sql.SchemaRDD;

HiveContext hiveCtx = new HiveContext(sc);
SchemaRDD rows = hiveCtx.sql("SELECT name, age FROM users");
Row firstRow = rows.first();
System.out.println(firstRow.getString(0)); // Field 0 is the name
```

Using Java to make Hive queries -- relatively simple

We cover loading data from Hive in more detail in "Apache Hive" on page 171.

JSON

If you have JSON data with a consistent schema across records, Spark SQL can infer their schema and load this data as rows as well, making it very simple to pull out the fields you need. To load JSON data, first create a `HiveContext` as when using Hive. (No installation of Hive is needed in this case, though—that is, you don't need a *hive-site.xml* file.) Then use the `HiveContext.jsonFile` method to get an RDD of `Row` objects for the whole file. Apart from using the whole `Row` object, you can also register this RDD as a table and select specific fields from it. For example, suppose that we had a JSON file containing tweets in the format shown in Example 5-33, one per line.

Example 5-33. Sample tweets in JSON

```
{"user": {"name": "Holden", "location": "San Francisco"}, "text": "Nice day out today"}
{"user": {"name": "Matei", "location": "Berkeley"}, "text": "Even nicer here :)"}
```

We could load this data and select just the username and text fields as shown in Examples 5-34 through 5-36.

Example 5-34. JSON loading with Spark SQL in Python

```
tweets = hiveCtx.jsonFile("tweets.json")
tweets.registerTempTable("tweets")
results = hiveCtx.sql("SELECT user.name, text FROM tweets")
```

Example 5-35. JSON loading with Spark SQL in Scala

```
val tweets = hiveCtx.jsonFile("tweets.json")
tweets.registerTempTable("tweets")
val results = hiveCtx.sql("SELECT user.name, text FROM tweets")
```

Example 5-36. JSON loading with Spark SQL in Java

```
SchemaRDD tweets = hiveCtx.jsonFile(jsonFile);
tweets.registerTempTable("tweets");
SchemaRDD results = hiveCtx.sql("SELECT user.name, text FROM tweets");
```

We discuss more about how to load JSON data with Spark SQL and access its schema in "JSON" on page 173. In addition, Spark SQL supports quite a bit more than loading data, including querying the data, combining it in more complex ways with RDDs, and running custom functions over it, which we will cover in Chapter 9.

Databases

Spark can access several popular databases using either their Hadoop connectors or custom Spark connectors. In this section, we will show four common connectors.

Java Database Connectivity

Spark can load data from any relational database that supports Java Database Connectivity (JDBC), including MySQL, Postgres, and other systems. To access this data, we construct an `org.apache.spark.rdd.JdbcRDD` and provide it with our SparkContext and the other parameters. Example 5-37 walks you through using `JdbcRDD` for a MySQL database.

Example 5-37. JdbcRDD in Scala

```scala
def createConnection() = {
  Class.forName("com.mysql.jdbc.Driver").newInstance();
  DriverManager.getConnection("jdbc:mysql://localhost/test?user=holden");
}

def extractValues(r: ResultSet) = {
  (r.getInt(1), r.getString(2))
}

val data = new JdbcRDD(sc,
  createConnection, "SELECT * FROM panda WHERE ? <= id AND id <= ?",
  lowerBound = 1, upperBound = 3, numPartitions = 2, mapRow = extractValues)
println(data.collect().toList)
```

JdbcRDD takes several parameters:

- First, we provide a function to establish a connection to our database. This lets each node create its own connection to load data over, after performing any configuration required to connect.

- Next, we provide a query that can read a range of the data, as well as a `lowerBound` and `upperBound` value for the parameter to this query. These parameters allow Spark to query different ranges of the data on different machines, so we don't get bottlenecked trying to load all the data on a single node.[4]

- The last parameter is a function that converts each row of output from a `java.sql.ResultSet` (*http://bit.ly/1xSi5DQ*) to a format that is useful for manipulating our data. In Example 5-37, we will get (`Int`, `String`) pairs. If this parameter is left out, Spark will automatically convert each row to an array of objects.

As with other data sources, when using `JdbcRDD`, make sure that your database can handle the load of parallel reads from Spark. If you'd like to query the data offline

---

4 If you don't know how many records there are, you can just do a count query manually first and use its result to determine the `upperBound` and `lowerBound`.

rather than the live database, you can always use your database's export feature to export a text file.

Cassandra

Spark's Cassandra support has improved greatly with the introduction of the open source Spark Cassandra connector (*https://github.com/datastax/spark-cassandra-connector*) from DataStax. Since the connector is not currently part of Spark, you will need to add some further dependencies to your build file. Cassandra doesn't yet use Spark SQL, but it returns RDDs of CassandraRow objects, which have some of the same methods as Spark SQL's Row object, as shown in Examples 5-38 and 5-39.The Spark Cassandra connector is currently only available in Java and Scala.

Example 5-38. sbt requirements for Cassandra connector

```
"com.datastax.spark" %% "spark-cassandra-connector" % "1.0.0-rc5",
"com.datastax.spark" %% "spark-cassandra-connector-java" % "1.0.0-rc5"
```

Example 5-39. Maven requirements for Cassandra connector

```
<dependency> <!-- Cassandra -->
  <groupId>com.datastax.spark</groupId>
  <artifactId>spark-cassandra-connector</artifactId>
  <version>1.0.0-rc5</version>
</dependency>
<dependency> <!-- Cassandra -->
  <groupId>com.datastax.spark</groupId>
  <artifactId>spark-cassandra-connector-java</artifactId>
  <version>1.0.0-rc5</version>
</dependency>
```

Much like with Elasticsearch, the Cassandra connector reads a job property to determine which cluster to connect to. We set the spark.cassandra.connection.host to point to our Cassandra cluster and if we have a username and password we can set them with spark.cassandra.auth.username and spark.cassandra.auth.password. Assuming you have only a single Cassandra cluster to connect to, we can set this up when we are creating our SparkContext as shown in Examples 5-40 and 5-41.

Example 5-40. Setting the Cassandra property in Scala

```
val conf = new SparkConf(true)
        .set("spark.cassandra.connection.host", "hostname")

val sc = new SparkContext(conf)
```

Example 5-41. Setting the Cassandra property in Java

```java
SparkConf conf = new SparkConf(true)
  .set("spark.cassandra.connection.host", cassandraHost);
JavaSparkContext sc = new JavaSparkContext(conf);
```

The Datastax Cassandra connector uses implicits in Scala to provide some additional functions on top of the SparkContext and RDDs. Let's import the implicit conversions and try loading some data (Example 5-42).

Example 5-42. Loading the entire table as an RDD with key/value data in Scala

```scala
// Implicits that add functions to the SparkContext & RDDs.
import com.datastax.spark.connector._

// Read entire table as an RDD. Assumes your table test was created as
// CREATE TABLE test.kv(key text PRIMARY KEY, value int);
val data = sc.cassandraTable("test" , "kv")
// Print some basic stats on the value field.
data.map(row => row.getInt("value")).stats()
```

In Java we don't have implicit conversions, so we need to explicitly convert our SparkContext and RDDs for this functionality (Example 5-43).

Example 5-43. Loading the entire table as an RDD with key/value data in Java

```java
import com.datastax.spark.connector.CassandraRow;
import static com.datastax.spark.connector.CassandraJavaUtil.javaFunctions;

// Read entire table as an RDD. Assumes your table test was created as
// CREATE TABLE test.kv(key text PRIMARY KEY, value int);
JavaRDD<CassandraRow> data = javaFunctions(sc).cassandraTable("test" , "kv");
// Print some basic stats.
System.out.println(data.mapToDouble(new DoubleFunction<CassandraRow>() {
  public double call(CassandraRow row) { return row.getInt("value"); }
}).stats());
```

In addition to loading an entire table, we can also query subsets of our data. We can restrict our data by adding a `where` clause to the `cassandraTable()` call—for example, `sc.cassandraTable(…).where("key=?", "panda")`.

The Cassandra connector supports saving to Cassandra from a variety of RDD types. We can directly save RDDs of `CassandraRow` objects, which is useful for copying data between tables. We can save RDDs that aren't in row form as tuples and lists by specifying the column mapping, as Example 5-44 shows.

Example 5-44. Saving to Cassandra in Scala

```scala
val rdd = sc.parallelize(List(Seq("moremagic", 1)))
rdd.saveToCassandra("test" , "kv", SomeColumns("key", "value"))
```

This section only briefly introduced the Cassandra connector. For more information, check out the connector's GitHub page (*https://github.com/datastax/spark-cassandra-connector*).

HBase

Spark can access HBase through its Hadoop input format, implemented in the org.apache.hadoop.hbase.mapreduce.TableInputFormat class. This input format returns key/value pairs where the key is of type org.apache.hadoop.hbase.io.Immu tableBytesWritable and the value is of type org.apache.hadoop.hbase.cli ent.Result. The Result class includes various methods for getting values based on their column family, as described in its API documentation (*http://bit.ly/1xSllPI*).

To use Spark with HBase, you can call SparkContext.newAPIHadoopRDD with the correct input format, as shown for Scala in Example 5-45.

Example 5-45. Scala example of reading from HBase

```scala
import org.apache.hadoop.hbase.HBaseConfiguration
import org.apache.hadoop.hbase.client.Result
import org.apache.hadoop.hbase.io.ImmutableBytesWritable
import org.apache.hadoop.hbase.mapreduce.TableInputFormat

val conf = HBaseConfiguration.create()
conf.set(TableInputFormat.INPUT_TABLE, "tablename")  // which table to scan

val rdd = sc.newAPIHadoopRDD(
  conf, classOf[TableInputFormat], classOf[ImmutableBytesWritable], classOf[Result])
```

To optimize reading from HBase, TableInputFormat includes multiple settings such as limiting the scan to just one set of columns and limiting the time ranges scanned. You can find these options in the TableInputFormat API documentation (*http://bit.ly/1xSlz9B*) and set them on your HBaseConfiguration before passing it to Spark.

Elasticsearch

Spark can both read and write data from Elasticsearch using Elasticsearch-Hadoop (*https://github.com/elasticsearch/elasticsearch-hadoop*). Elasticsearch is a new open source, Lucene-based search system.

The Elasticsearch connector is a bit different than the other connectors we have examined, since it ignores the path information we provide and instead depends on setting up configuration on our SparkContext. The Elasticsearch `OutputFormat` connector also doesn't quite have the types to use Spark's wrappers, so we instead use `saveAsHadoopDataSet`, which means we need to set more properties by hand. Let's look at how to read/write some simple data to Elasticsearch in Examples 5-46 and 5-47.

The latest Elasticsearch Spark connector is even easier to use, supporting returning Spark SQL rows. This connector is still covered, as the row conversion doesn't yet support all of the native types in Elasticsearch.

Example 5-46. Elasticsearch output in Scala

```scala
val jobConf = new JobConf(sc.hadoopConfiguration)
jobConf.set("mapred.output.format.class", "org.elasticsearch.hadoop.mr.EsOutputFormat")
jobConf.setOutputCommitter(classOf[FileOutputCommitter])
jobConf.set(ConfigurationOptions.ES_RESOURCE_WRITE, "twitter/tweets")
jobConf.set(ConfigurationOptions.ES_NODES, "localhost")
FileOutputFormat.setOutputPath(jobConf, new Path("-"))
output.saveAsHadoopDataset(jobConf)
```

Example 5-47. Elasticsearch input in Scala

```scala
def mapWritableToInput(in: MapWritable): Map[String, String] = {
  in.map{case (k, v) => (k.toString, v.toString)}.toMap
}

val jobConf = new JobConf(sc.hadoopConfiguration)
jobConf.set(ConfigurationOptions.ES_RESOURCE_READ, args(1))
jobConf.set(ConfigurationOptions.ES_NODES, args(2))
val currentTweets = sc.hadoopRDD(jobConf,
  classOf[EsInputFormat[Object, MapWritable]], classOf[Object],
  classOf[MapWritable])
// Extract only the map
// Convert the MapWritable[Text, Text] to Map[String, String]
val tweets = currentTweets.map{ case (key, value) => mapWritableToInput(value) }
```

Compared to some of our other connectors, this is a bit convoluted, but it serves as a useful reference for how to work with these types of connectors.

On the write side, Elasticsearch can do mapping inference, but this can occasionally infer the types incorrectly, so it can be a good idea to explicitly set a mapping (*http://bit.ly/1xSmeaS*) if you are storing data types other than strings.

Conclusion

With the end of this chapter you should now be able to get your data into Spark to work with and store the result of your computation in a format that is useful for you. We have examined a number of different formats we can use for our data, as well as compression options and their implications on how data can be consumed. Subsequent chapters will examine ways to write more effective and powerful Spark programs now that we can load and save large datasets.

## CHAPTER 6

Advanced Spark Programming

Introduction

This chapter introduces a variety of advanced Spark programming features that we didn't get to cover in the previous chapters. We introduce two types of shared variables: *accumulators* to aggregate information and *broadcast variables* to efficiently distribute large values. Building on our existing transformations on RDDs, we introduce batch operations for tasks with high setup costs, like querying a database. To expand the range of tools accessible to us, we cover Spark's methods for interacting with external programs, such as scripts written in R.

Throughout this chapter we build an example using ham radio operators' call logs as the input. These logs, at the minimum, include the call signs of the stations contacted. Call signs are assigned by country, and each country has its own range of call signs so we can look up the countries involved. Some call logs also include the physical location of the operators, which we can use to determine the distance involved. We include a sample log entry in Example 6-1. The book's sample repo includes a list of call signs to look up the call logs for and process the results.

Example 6-1. Sample call log entry in JSON, with some fields removed

```
{"address":"address here", "band":"40m","callsign":"KK6JLK","city":"SUNNYVALE",
"contactlat":"37.384733","contactlong":"-122.032164",
"county":"Santa Clara","dxcc":"291","fullname":"MATTHEW McPherrin",
"id":57779,"mode":"FM","mylat":"37.751952821","mylong":"-122.4208688735",...}
```

The first set of Spark features we'll look at are shared variables, which are a special type of variable you can use in Spark tasks. In our example we use Spark's shared variables to count nonfatal error conditions and distribute a large lookup table.

When our task involves a large setup time, such as creating a database connection or random-number generator, it is useful to share this setup work across multiple data items. Using a remote call sign lookup database, we examine how to reuse setup work by operating on a per-partition basis.

In addition to the languages directly supported by Spark, the system can call into programs written in other languages. This chapter introduces how to use Spark's language-agnostic pipe() method to interact with other programs through standard input and output. We will use the pipe() method to access an R library for computing the distance of a ham radio operator's contacts.

Finally, similar to its tools for working with key/value pairs, Spark has methods for working with numeric data. We demonstrate these methods by removing outliers from the distances computed with our ham radio call logs.

Accumulators

When we normally pass functions to Spark, such as a map() function or a condition for filter(), they can use variables defined outside them in the driver program, but each task running on the cluster gets a new copy of each variable, and updates from these copies are not propagated back to the driver. Spark's shared variables, *accumulators* and *broadcast variables*, relax this restriction for two common types of communication patterns: aggregation of results and broadcasts.

Our first type of shared variable, accumulators, provides a simple syntax for aggregating values from worker nodes back to the driver program. One of the most common uses of accumulators is to count events that occur during job execution for debugging purposes. For example, say that we are loading a list of all of the call signs for which we want to retrieve logs from a file, but we are also interested in how many lines of the input file were blank (perhaps we do not expect to see many such lines in valid input). Examples 6-2 through 6-4 demonstrate this scenario.

Example 6-2. Accumulator empty line count in Python

```
file = sc.textFile(inputFile)
# Create Accumulator[Int] initialized to 0
blankLines = sc.accumulator(0)

def extractCallSigns(line):
    global blankLines  # Make the global variable accessible
    if (line == ""):
        blankLines += 1
    return line.split(" ")

callSigns = file.flatMap(extractCallSigns)
```

```
callSigns.saveAsTextFile(outputDir + "/callsigns")
print "Blank lines: %d" % blankLines.value
```

Example 6-3. Accumulator empty line count in Scala

```scala
val file = sc.textFile("file.txt")

val blankLines = sc.accumulator(0)  // Create an Accumulator[Int] initialized to 0

val callSigns = file.flatMap(line => {
  if (line == "") {
    blankLines += 1 // Add to the accumulator
  }
  line.split(" ")
})

callSigns.saveAsTextFile("output.txt")
println("Blank lines: " + blankLines.value)
```

Example 6-4. Accumulator empty line count in Java

```java
JavaRDD<String> rdd = sc.textFile(args[1]);

final Accumulator<Integer> blankLines = sc.accumulator(0);
JavaRDD<String> callSigns = rdd.flatMap(
  new FlatMapFunction<String, String>() { public Iterable<String> call(String line) {
    if (line.equals("")) {
      blankLines.add(1);
    }
    return Arrays.asList(line.split(" "));
  }});

callSigns.saveAsTextFile("output.txt")
System.out.println("Blank lines: "+ blankLines.value());
```

In these examples, we create an `Accumulator[Int]` called `blankLines`, and then add 1 to it whenever we see a blank line in the input. After evaluating the transformation, we print the value of the counter. Note that we will see the right count only *after* we run the `saveAsTextFile()` action, because the transformation above it, `map()`, is lazy, so the side-effect incrementing of the accumulator will happen only when the lazy `map()` transformation is forced to occur by the `saveAsTextFile()` action.

Of course, it is possible to aggregate values from an entire RDD back to the driver program using actions like `reduce()`, but sometimes we need a simple way to aggregate values that, in the process of transforming an RDD, are generated at different scale or granularity than that of the RDD itself. In the previous example, accumulators let us count errors as we load the data, without doing a separate `filter()` or `reduce()`.

To summarize, accumulators work as follows:

- We create them in the driver by calling the `SparkContext.accumulator(initial Value)` method, which produces an accumulator holding an initial value. The return type is an `org.apache.spark.Accumulator[T]` object, where `T` is the type of `initialValue`.

- Worker code in Spark closures can add to the accumulator with its `+=` method (or `add` in Java).

- The driver program can call the `value` property on the accumulator to access its value (or call `value()` and `setValue()` in Java).

Note that tasks on worker nodes cannot access the accumulator's `value()`—from the point of view of these tasks, accumulators are *write-only* variables. This allows accumulators to be implemented efficiently, without having to communicate every update.

The type of counting shown here becomes especially handy when there are multiple values to keep track of or when the same value needs to increase at multiple places in the parallel program (for example, you might be counting calls to a JSON parsing library throughout your program). For instance, often we expect some percentage of our data to be corrupted or allow for the backend to fail some number of times. To prevent producing garbage output when there are too many errors, we can use a counter for valid records and a counter for invalid records. The value of our accumulators is available only in the driver program, so that is where we place our checks.

Continuing from our last example, we can now validate the call signs and write the output only if most of the input is valid. The ham radio call sign format is specified in Article 19 by the International Telecommunication Union, from which we construct a regular expression to verify conformance, shown in Example 6-5.

Example 6-5. Accumulator error count in Python

```python
# Create Accumulators for validating call signs
validSignCount = sc.accumulator(0)
invalidSignCount = sc.accumulator(0)

def validateSign(sign):
    global validSignCount, invalidSignCount
    if re.match(r"\A\d?[a-zA-Z]{1,2}\d{1,4}[a-zA-Z]{1,3}\Z", sign):
        validSignCount += 1
        return True
    else:
        invalidSignCount += 1
        return False
```

```
# Count the number of times we contacted each call sign
validSigns = callSigns.filter(validateSign)
contactCount = validSigns.map(lambda sign: (sign, 1)).reduceByKey(lambda (x, y): x + y)

# Force evaluation so the counters are populated
contactCount.count()
if invalidSignCount.value < 0.1 * validSignCount.value:
    contactCount.saveAsTextFile(outputDir + "/contactCount")
else:
    print "Too many errors: %d, %d valid" %
        (invalidSignCount.value, validSignCount.value)
```

Accumulators and Fault Tolerance

Spark automatically deals with failed or slow machines by re-executing failed or slow tasks. For example, if the node running a partition of a map() operation crashes, Spark will rerun it on another node; and even if the node does not crash but is simply much slower than other nodes, Spark can preemptively launch a "speculative" copy of the task on another node, and take its result if that finishes. Even if no nodes fail, Spark may have to rerun a task to rebuild a cached value that falls out of memory. The net result is therefore that the same function may run multiple times on the same data depending on what happens on the cluster.

How does this interact with accumulators? The end result is that *for accumulators used in actions, Spark applies each task's update to each accumulator only once.* Thus, if we want a reliable absolute value counter, regardless of failures or multiple evaluations, we must put it inside an action like foreach().

For accumulators used in RDD transformations instead of actions, this guarantee does not exist. An accumulator update within a transformation can occur more than once. One such case of a probably unintended multiple update occurs when a cached but infrequently used RDD is first evicted from the LRU cache and is then subsequently needed. This forces the RDD to be recalculated from its lineage, with the unintended side effect that calls to update an accumulator within the transformations in that lineage are sent again to the driver. Within transformations, accumulators should, consequently, be used only for debugging purposes.

While future versions of Spark may change this behavior to count the update only once, the current version (1.3.0) does have the multiple update behavior, so accumulators in transformations are recommended only for debugging purposes.

Custom Accumulators

So far we've seen how to use one of Spark's built-in accumulator types: integers (Accumulator[Int]) with addition. Out of the box, Spark supports accumulators of type Double, Long, and Float. In addition to these, Spark also includes an API to define custom accumulator types and custom aggregation operations (e.g., finding the maximum of the accumulated values instead of adding them). Custom accumulators need to extend `AccumulatorParam`, which is covered in the Spark API documentation (*http://bit.ly/1xSpy5N*). Beyond adding to a numeric value, we can use any operation for add, provided that operation is commutative and associative. For example, instead of adding to track the total we could keep track of the maximum value seen so far.

An operation *op* is commutative if *a op b = b op a* for all values *a*, *b*.

An operation *op* is associative if *(a op b) op c = a op (b op c)* for all values *a*, *b*, and *c*.

For example, `sum` and `max` are commutative and associative operations that are commonly used in Spark accumulators.

Broadcast Variables

Spark's second type of shared variable, *broadcast variables*, allows the program to efficiently send a large, read-only value to all the worker nodes for use in one or more Spark operations. They come in handy, for example, if your application needs to send a large, read-only lookup table to all the nodes, or even a large feature vector in a machine learning algorithm.

Recall that Spark automatically sends all variables referenced in your closures to the worker nodes. While this is convenient, it can also be inefficient because (1) the default task launching mechanism is optimized for small task sizes, and (2) you might, in fact, use the same variable in *multiple* parallel operations, but Spark will send it separately for each operation. As an example, say that we wanted to write a Spark program that looks up countries by their call signs by prefix matching in an array. This is useful for ham radio call signs since each country gets its own prefix, although the prefixes are not uniform in length. If we wrote this naively in Spark, the code might look like Example 6-6.

Example 6-6. Country lookup in Python

```
# Look up the locations of the call signs on the
# RDD contactCounts. We load a list of call sign
# prefixes to country code to support this lookup.
signPrefixes = loadCallSignTable()

def processSignCount(sign_count, signPrefixes):
    country = lookupCountry(sign_count[0], signPrefixes)
    count = sign_count[1]
    return (country, count)
```

```
countryContactCounts = (contactCounts
                        .map(processSignCount)
                        .reduceByKey((lambda x, y: x+ y)))
```

This program would run, but if we had a larger table (say, with IP addresses instead of call signs), the signPrefixes could easily be several megabytes in size, making it expensive to send that Array from the master alongside each task. In addition, if we used the same signPrefixes object later (maybe we next ran the same code on *file2.txt*), it would be sent *again* to each node.

We can fix this by making signPrefixes a broadcast variable. A broadcast variable is simply an object of type spark.broadcast.Broadcast[T], which wraps a value of type T. We can access this value by calling value on the Broadcast object in our tasks. The value is sent to each node only once, using an efficient, BitTorrent-like communication mechanism.

Using broadcast variables, our previous example looks like Examples 6-7 through 6-9.

Example 6-7. Country lookup with Broadcast values in Python

```
# Look up the locations of the call signs on the
# RDD contactCounts. We load a list of call sign
# prefixes to country code to support this lookup.
signPrefixes = sc.broadcast(loadCallSignTable())

def processSignCount(sign_count, signPrefixes):
    country = lookupCountry(sign_count[0], signPrefixes.value)
    count = sign_count[1]
    return (country, count)

countryContactCounts = (contactCounts
                        .map(processSignCount)
                        .reduceByKey((lambda x, y: x+ y)))

countryContactCounts.saveAsTextFile(outputDir + "/countries.txt")
```

Example 6-8. Country lookup with Broadcast values in Scala

```
// Look up the countries for each call sign for the
// contactCounts RDD.  We load an array of call sign
// prefixes to country code to support this lookup.
val signPrefixes = sc.broadcast(loadCallSignTable())
val countryContactCounts = contactCounts.map{case (sign, count) =>
  val country = lookupInArray(sign, signPrefixes.value)
  (country, count)
}.reduceByKey((x, y) => x + y)
countryContactCounts.saveAsTextFile(outputDir + "/countries.txt")
```

Example 6-9. Country lookup with Broadcast values in Java

```java
// Read in the call sign table
// Look up the countries for each call sign in the
// contactCounts RDD
final Broadcast<String[]> signPrefixes = sc.broadcast(loadCallSignTable());
JavaPairRDD<String, Integer> countryContactCounts = contactCounts.mapToPair(
  new PairFunction<Tuple2<String, Integer>, String, Integer> (){
    public Tuple2<String, Integer> call(Tuple2<String, Integer> callSignCount) {
      String sign = callSignCount._1();
      String country = lookupCountry(sign, signPrefixes.value());
      return new Tuple2(country, callSignCount._2());
    }}).reduceByKey(new SumInts());
countryContactCounts.saveAsTextFile(outputDir + "/countries.txt");
```

As shown in these examples, the process of using broadcast variables is simple:

1. Create a `Broadcast[T]` by calling `SparkContext.broadcast` on an object of type T. Any type works as long as it is also `Serializable`.

2. Access its value with the `value` property (or `value()` method in Java).

3. The variable will be sent to each node only once, and should be treated as read-only (updates will *not* be propagated to other nodes).

The easiest way to satisfy the *read-only* requirement is to broadcast a primitive value or a reference to an immutable object. In such cases, you won't be able to change the value of the broadcast variable except within the driver code. However, sometimes it can be more convenient or more efficient to broadcast a mutable object. If you do that, it is up to you to maintain the read-only condition. As we did with our call sign prefix table of `Array[String]`, we must make sure that the code we run on our worker nodes does not try to do something like val `theArray` = broadcastAr ray.value; theArray(0) = newValue. When run in a worker node, that line will assign newValue to the first array element only in the copy of the array local to the worker node running the code; it will not change the contents of broadcastAr ray.value on any of the other worker nodes.

Optimizing Broadcasts

When we are broadcasting large values, it is important to choose a data serialization format that is both fast and compact, because the time to send the value over the network can quickly become a bottleneck if it takes a long time to either serialize a value or to send the serialized value over the network. In particular, Java Serialization, the default serialization library used in Spark's Scala and Java APIs, can be very inefficient out of the box for anything except arrays of primitive types. You can optimize serialization by selecting a different serialization library using the `spark.serializer` property (Chapter 8 will describe how to use *Kryo*, a faster serialization library), or by implementing your own serialization routines for your data types (e.g., using the `java.io.Externalizable` interface for Java Serialization, or using the `reduce()` method to define custom serialization for Python's pickle library).

Working on a Per-Partition Basis

Working with data on a per-partition basis allows us to avoid redoing setup work for each data item. Operations like opening a database connection or creating a random-number generator are examples of setup steps that we wish to avoid doing for each element. Spark has *per-partition* versions of `map` and `foreach` to help reduce the cost of these operations by letting you run code only once for each partition of an RDD.

Going back to our example with call signs, there is an online database of ham radio call signs we can query for a public list of their logged contacts. By using partition-based operations, we can share a connection pool to this database to avoid setting up many connections, and reuse our JSON parser. As Examples 6-10 through 6-12 show, we use the `mapPartitions()` function, which gives us an iterator of the elements in each partition of the input RDD and expects us to return an iterator of our results.

Example 6-10. Shared connection pool in Python

```python
def processCallSigns(signs):
    """Lookup call signs using a connection pool"""
    # Create a connection pool
    http = urllib3.PoolManager()
    # the URL associated with each call sign record
    urls = map(lambda x: "http://73s.com/qsos/%s.json" % x, signs)
    # create the requests (non-blocking)
    requests = map(lambda x: (x, http.request('GET', x)), urls)
    # fetch the results
    result = map(lambda x: (x[0], json.loads(x[1].data)), requests)
    # remove any empty results and return
    return filter(lambda x: x[1] is not None, result)

def fetchCallSigns(input):
    """Fetch call signs"""
    return input.mapPartitions(lambda callSigns : processCallSigns(callSigns))

contactsContactList = fetchCallSigns(validSigns)
```

Example 6-11. Shared connection pool and JSON parser in Scala

```scala
val contactsContactLists = validSigns.distinct().mapPartitions{
  signs =>
  val mapper = createMapper()
  val client = new HttpClient()
  client.start()
  // create http request
```

```
    signs.map {sign =>
      createExchangeForSign(sign)
  // fetch responses
    }.map{ case (sign, exchange) =>
      (sign, readExchangeCallLog(mapper, exchange))
    }.filter(x => x._2 != null) // Remove empty CallLogs
}
```

Example 6-12. Shared connection pool and JSON parser in Java

```java
// Use mapPartitions to reuse setup work.
JavaPairRDD<String, CallLog[]> contactsContactLists =
  validCallSigns.mapPartitionsToPair(
  new PairFlatMapFunction<Iterator<String>, String, CallLog[]>() {
    public Iterable<Tuple2<String, CallLog[]>> call(Iterator<String> input) {
      // List for our results.
      ArrayList<Tuple2<String, CallLog[]>> callsignLogs = new ArrayList<>();
      ArrayList<Tuple2<String, ContentExchange>> requests = new ArrayList<>();
      ObjectMapper mapper = createMapper();
      HttpClient client = new HttpClient();
      try {
        client.start();
        while (input.hasNext()) {
          requests.add(createRequestForSign(input.next(), client));
        }
        for (Tuple2<String, ContentExchange> signExchange : requests) {
          callsignLogs.add(fetchResultFromRequest(mapper, signExchange));
        }
      } catch (Exception e) {
      }
      return callsignLogs;
    }});
System.out.println(StringUtils.join(contactsContactLists.collect(), ","));
```

When operating on a per-partition basis, Spark gives our function an `Iterator` of the elements in that partition. To return values, we return an `Iterable`. In addition to `mapPartitions()`, Spark has a number of other per-partition operators, listed in Table 6-1.

Table 6-1. Per-partition operators

Function name	We are called with	We return	Function signature on RDD[T]
mapPartitions()	Iterator of the elements in that partition	Iterator of our return elements	f: (Iterator[T]) → Iterator[U]
mapPartitionsWithIndex()	Integer of partition number, and Iterator of the elements in that partition	Iterator of our return elements	f: (Int, Iterator[T]) → Iterator[U]

Function name	We are called with	We return	Function signature on RDD[T]
foreachPartition()	Iterator of the elements	Nothing	f: (Iterator[T]) → Unit

In addition to avoiding setup work, we can sometimes use `mapPartitions()` to avoid object creation overhead. Sometimes we need to make an object for aggregating the result that is of a different type. Thinking back to Chapter 3, where we computed the average, one of the ways we did this was by converting our RDD of numbers to an RDD of tuples so we could track the number of elements processed in our reduce step. Instead of doing this for each element, we can instead create the tuple once per partition, as shown in Examples 6-13 and 6-14.

Example 6-13. Average without mapPartitions() in Python

```python
def combineCtrs(c1, c2):
    return (c1[0] + c2[0], c1[1] + c2[1])

def basicAvg(nums):
    """Compute the average"""
    nums.map(lambda num: (num, 1)).reduce(combineCtrs)
```

Example 6-14. Average with mapPartitions() in Python

```python
def partitionCtr(nums):
    """Compute sumCounter for partition"""
    sumCount = [0, 0]
    for num in nums:
        sumCount[0] += num
        sumCount[1] += 1
    return [sumCount]

def fastAvg(nums):
    """Compute the avg"""
    sumCount = nums.mapPartitions(partitionCtr).reduce(combineCtrs)
    return sumCount[0] / float(sumCount[1])
```

Piping to External Programs

With three language bindings to choose from out of the box, you may have all the options you need for writing Spark applications. However, if none of Scala, Java, or Python does what you need, then Spark provides a general mechanism to pipe data to programs in other languages, like R scripts.

Spark provides a `pipe()` method on RDDs. Spark's `pipe()` lets us write parts of jobs using any language we want as long as it can read and write to Unix standard streams. With `pipe()`, you can write a transformation of an RDD that reads each

RDD element from standard input as a `String`, manipulates that `String` however you like, and then writes the result(s) as `Strings` to standard output. The interface and programming model is restrictive and limited, but sometimes it's just what you need to do something like make use of a native code function within a map or filter operation.

Most likely, you'd want to pipe an RDD's content through some external program or script because you've already got complicated software built and tested that you'd like to reuse with Spark. A lot of data scientists have code in R,[1] and we can interact with R programs using `pipe()`.

In Example 6-15 we use an R library to compute the distance for all of the contacts. Each element in our RDD is written out by our program with newlines as separators, and every line that the program outputs is a string element in the resulting RDD. To make it easy for our R program to parse the input we will reformat our data to be `mylat`, `mylon`, `theirlat`, `theirlon`. Here we have a comma as the separator.

Example 6-15. R distance program

```
#!/usr/bin/env Rscript
library("Imap")
f <- file("stdin")
open(f)
while(length(line <- readLines(f,n=1)) > 0) {
  # process line
  contents <- Map(as.numeric, strsplit(line, ","))
  mydist <- gdist(contents[[1]][1], contents[[1]][2],
                  contents[[1]][3], contents[[1]][4],
                  units="m", a=6378137.0, b=6356752.3142, verbose = FALSE)
  write(mydist, stdout())
}
```

If that is written to an executable file named *./src/R/finddistance.R*, then it looks like this in use:

```
$ ./src/R/finddistance.R
37.75889318222431,-122.42683635321838,37.7614213,-122.4240097
349.2602
coffee
NA
ctrl-d
```

So far, so good—we've now got a way to transform every line from `stdin` into output on `stdout`. Now we need to make `finddistance.R` available to each of our worker

---

[1] The SparkR (*http://amplab-extras.github.io/SparkR-pkg/*) project also provides a lightweight frontend to use Spark from within R.

nodes and to actually transform our RDD with our shell script. Both tasks are easy to accomplish in Spark, as you can see in Examples 6-16 through 6-18.

Example 6-16. Driver program using pipe() to call finddistance.R in Python

```
# Compute the distance of each call using an external R program
distScript = "./src/R/finddistance.R"
distScriptName = "finddistance.R"
sc.addFile(distScript)
def hasDistInfo(call):
    """Verify that a call has the fields required to compute the distance"""
    requiredFields = ["mylat", "mylong", "contactlat", "contactlong"]
    return all(map(lambda f: call[f], requiredFields))
def formatCall(call):
    """Format a call so that it can be parsed by our R program"""
    return "{0},{1},{2},{3}".format(
        call["mylat"], call["mylong"],
        call["contactlat"], call["contactlong"])

pipeInputs = contactsContactList.values().flatMap(
    lambda calls: map(formatCall, filter(hasDistInfo, calls)))
distances = pipeInputs.pipe(SparkFiles.get(distScriptName))
print distances.collect()
```

Example 6-17. Driver program using pipe() to call finddistance.R in Scala

```
// Compute the distance of each call using an external R program
// adds our script to a list of files for each node to download with this job
val distScript = "./src/R/finddistance.R"
val distScriptName = "finddistance.R"
sc.addFile(distScript)
val distances = contactsContactLists.values.flatMap(x => x.map(y =>
  s"${y.contactlay},${y.contactlong},${y.mylat},${y.mylong}")).pipe(Seq(
    SparkFiles.get(distScriptName)))
println(distances.collect().toList)
```

Example 6-18. Driver program using pipe() to call finddistance.R in Java

```
// Compute the distance of each call using an external R program
// adds our script to a list of files for each node to download with this job
String distScript = "./src/R/finddistance.R";
String distScriptName = "finddistance.R";
sc.addFile(distScript);
JavaRDD<String> pipeInputs = contactsContactLists.values()
  .map(new VerifyCallLogs()).flatMap(
  new FlatMapFunction<CallLog[], String>() {
    public Iterable<String> call(CallLog[] calls) {
      ArrayList<String> latLons = new ArrayList<String>();
      for (CallLog call: calls) {
        latLons.add(call.mylat + "," + call.mylong +
```

```
                        "," + call.contactlat + "," + call.contactlong);
    }
    return latLons;
  }
});
JavaRDD<String> distances = pipeInputs.pipe(SparkFiles.get(distScriptName));
System.out.println(StringUtils.join(distances.collect(), ","));
```

With SparkContext.addFile(path), we can build up a list of files for each of the
worker nodes to download with a Spark job. These files can come from the driver's
local filesystem (as we did in these examples), from HDFS or other Hadoop-
supported filesystems, or from an HTTP, HTTPS, or FTP URI. When an action is
run in the job, the files will be downloaded by each of the nodes. The files can then be
found on the worker nodes in SparkFiles.getRootDirectory, or located with Spark
Files.get(filename). Of course, this is only one way to make sure that pipe() can
find a script on each worker node. You could use another remote copying tool to
place the script file in a knowable location on each node.

> All the files added with SparkContext.addFile(path) are stored
> in the same directory, so it's important to use unique names.

Once the script is available, the pipe() method on RDDs makes it easy to pipe the
elements of an RDD through the script. Perhaps a smarter version of findDistance
would accept SEPARATOR as a command-line argument. In that case, either of these
would do the job, although the first is preferred:

- rdd.pipe(Seq(SparkFiles.get("finddistance.R"), ","))
- rdd.pipe(SparkFiles.get("finddistance.R") + " ,")

In the first option, we are passing the command invocation as a sequence of positional arguments (with the command itself at the zero-offset position); in the second,
we're passing it as a single command string that Spark will then break down into
positional arguments.

We can also specify shell environment variables with pipe() if we desire. Simply pass
in a map of environment variables to values as the second parameter to pipe(), and
Spark will set those values.

You should now at least have an understanding of how to use pipe() to process the
elements of an RDD through an external command, and of how to distribute such
command scripts to the cluster in a way that the worker nodes can find them.

Numeric RDD Operations

Spark provides several descriptive statistics operations on RDDs containing numeric data. These are in addition to the more complex statistical and machine learning methods we will describe later in Chapter 11.

Spark's numeric operations are implemented with a streaming algorithm that allows for building up our model one element at a time. The descriptive statistics are all computed in a single pass over the data and returned as a StatsCounter object by calling stats(). Table 6-2 lists the methods available on the StatsCounter object.

Table 6-2. Summary statistics available from StatsCounter

Method	Meaning
count()	Number of elements in the RDD
mean()	Average of the elements
sum()	Total
max()	Maximum value
min()	Minimum value
variance()	Variance of the elements
sampleVariance()	Variance of the elements, computed for a sample
stdev()	Standard deviation
sampleStdev()	Sample standard deviation

If you want to compute only one of these statistics, you can also call the corresponding method directly on an RDD—for example, rdd.mean() or rdd.sum().

In Examples 6-19 through 6-21, we will use summary statistics to remove some outliers from our data. Since we will be going over the same RDD twice (once to compute the summary statistics and once to remove the outliers), we may wish to cache the RDD. Going back to our call log example, we can remove the contact points from our call log that are too far away.

Example 6-19. Removing outliers in Python

```python
# Convert our RDD of strings to numeric data so we can compute stats and
# remove the outliers.
distanceNumerics = distances.map(lambda string: float(string))
stats = distanceNumerics.stats()
stddev = stats.stdev()
mean = stats.mean()
reasonableDistances = distanceNumerics.filter(
  lambda x: math.fabs(x - mean) < 3 * stddev)
print reasonableDistances.collect()
```

Example 6-20. Removing outliers in Scala

```scala
// Now we can go ahead and remove outliers since those may have misreported locations
// first we need to take our RDD of strings and turn it into doubles.
val distanceDouble = distance.map(string => string.toDouble)
val stats = distanceDoubles.stats()
val stddev = stats.stdev
val mean = stats.mean
val reasonableDistances = distanceDoubles.filter(x => math.abs(x-mean) < 3 * stddev)
println(reasonableDistance.collect().toList)
```

Example 6-21. Removing outliers in Java

```java
// First we need to convert our RDD of String to a DoubleRDD so we can
// access the stats function
JavaDoubleRDD distanceDoubles = distances.mapToDouble(new DoubleFunction<String>() {
    public double call(String value) {
      return Double.parseDouble(value);
    }});
final StatCounter stats = distanceDoubles.stats();
final Double stddev = stats.stdev();
final Double mean = stats.mean();
JavaDoubleRDD reasonableDistances =
  distanceDoubles.filter(new Function<Double, Boolean>() {
    public Boolean call(Double x) {
      return (Math.abs(x-mean) < 3 * stddev);}});
System.out.println(StringUtils.join(reasonableDistance.collect(), ","));
```

With that final piece we have completed our sample application, which uses accumulators and broadcast variables, per-partition processing, interfaces with external programs, and summary statistics. The entire source code is available in *src/python/ChapterSixExample.py*, *src/main/scala/com/oreilly/learningsparkexamples/scala/ChapterSixExample.scala*, and *src/main/java/com/oreilly/learningsparkexamples/java/ChapterSixExample.java*, respectively.

Conclusion

In this chapter, you have been introduced to some of the more advanced Spark programming features that you can use to make your programs more efficient or expressive. Subsequent chapters cover deploying and tuning Spark applications, as well as built-in libraries for SQL and streaming and machine learning. We'll also start seeing more complex and more complete sample applications that make use of much of the functionality described so far, and that should help guide and inspire your own usage of Spark.

## CHAPTER 7

Running on a Cluster

Introduction

Up to now, we've focused on learning Spark by using the Spark shell and examples that run in Spark's local mode. One benefit of writing applications on Spark is the ability to scale computation by adding more machines and running in cluster mode. The good news is that writing applications for parallel cluster execution uses the same API you've already learned in this book. The examples and applications you've written so far will run on a cluster "out of the box." This is one of the benefits of Spark's higher level API: users can rapidly prototype applications on smaller datasets locally, then run unmodified code on even very large clusters.

This chapter first explains the runtime architecture of a distributed Spark application, then discusses options for running Spark in distributed clusters. Spark can run on a wide variety of cluster managers (Hadoop YARN, Apache Mesos, and Spark's own built-in Standalone cluster manager) in both on-premise and cloud deployments. We'll discuss the trade-offs and configurations required for running in each case. Along the way we'll also cover the "nuts and bolts" of scheduling, deploying, and configuring a Spark application. After reading this chapter you'll have everything you need to run a distributed Spark program. The following chapter will cover tuning and debugging applications.

Spark Runtime Architecture

Before we dive into the specifics of running Spark on a cluster, it's helpful to understand the architecture of Spark in distributed mode (illustrated in Figure 7-1).

In distributed mode, Spark uses a master/slave architecture with one central coordinator and many distributed workers. The central coordinator is called the *driver*. The driver communicates with a potentially large number of distributed workers called *executors*. The driver runs in its own Java process and each executor is a separate Java process. A driver and its executors are together termed a Spark *application*.

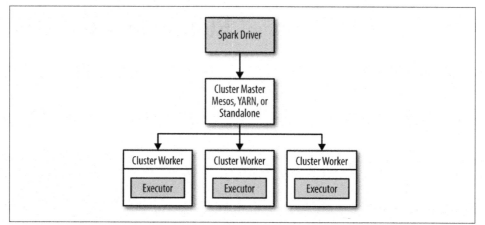

Figure 7-1. The components of a distributed Spark application

A Spark application is launched on a set of machines using an external service called a *cluster manager*. As noted, Spark is packaged with a built-in cluster manager called the Standalone cluster manager. Spark also works with Hadoop YARN and Apache Mesos, two popular open source cluster managers.

The Driver

The driver is the process where the `main()` method of your program runs. It is the process running the user code that creates a SparkContext, creates RDDs, and performs transformations and actions. When you launch a Spark shell, you've created a driver program (if you remember, the Spark shell comes preloaded with a SparkContext called `sc`). Once the driver terminates, the application is finished.

When the driver runs, it performs two duties:

Converting a user program into tasks

The Spark driver is responsible for converting a user program into units of physical execution called *tasks*. At a high level, all Spark programs follow the same structure: they create RDDs from some input, derive new RDDs from those using transformations, and perform actions to collect or save data. A Spark program implicitly creates a logical *directed acyclic graph* (DAG) of operations. When the driver runs, it converts this logical graph into a physical execution plan.

Spark performs several optimizations, such as "pipelining" map transformations together to merge them, and converts the execution graph into a set of *stages*. Each stage, in turn, consists of multiple *tasks*. The tasks are bundled up and prepared to be sent to the cluster. Tasks are the smallest unit of work in Spark; a typical user program can launch hundreds or thousands of individual tasks.

Scheduling tasks on executors

Given a physical execution plan, a Spark driver must coordinate the scheduling of individual tasks on executors. When executors are started they register themselves with the driver, so it has a complete view of the application's executors at all times. Each executor represents a process capable of running tasks and storing RDD data.

The Spark driver will look at the current set of executors and try to schedule each task in an appropriate location, based on data placement. When tasks execute, they may have a side effect of storing cached data. The driver also tracks the location of cached data and uses it to schedule future tasks that access that data.

The driver exposes information about the running Spark application through a web interface, which by default is available at port 4040. For instance, in local mode, this UI is available at *http://localhost:4040*. We'll cover Spark's web UI and its scheduling mechanisms in more detail in Chapter 8.

Executors

Spark executors are worker processes responsible for running the individual tasks in a given Spark job. Executors are launched once at the beginning of a Spark application and typically run for the entire lifetime of an application, though Spark applications can continue if executors fail. Executors have two roles. First, they run the tasks that make up the application and return results to the driver. Second, they provide in-memory storage for RDDs that are cached by user programs, through a service called the Block Manager that lives within each executor. Because RDDs are cached directly inside of executors, tasks can run alongside the cached data.

Drivers and Executors in Local Mode

For most of this book, you've run examples in Spark's local mode. In this mode, the Spark driver runs along with an executor in the same Java process. This is a special case; executors typically each run in a dedicated process.

Cluster Manager

So far we've discussed drivers and executors in somewhat abstract terms. But how do drivers and executor processes initially get launched? Spark depends on a cluster manager to launch executors and, in certain cases, to launch the driver. The cluster manager is a pluggable component in Spark. This allows Spark to run on top of different external managers, such as YARN and Mesos, as well as its built-in Standalone cluster manager.

 Spark's documentation consistently uses the terms *driver* and *executor* when describing the processes that execute each Spark application. The terms *master* and *worker* are used to describe the centralized and distributed portions of the cluster manager. It's easy to confuse these terms, so pay close attention. For instance, Hadoop YARN runs a master daemon (called the Resource Manager) and several worker daemons called Node Managers. Spark can run both drivers and executors on the YARN worker nodes.

Launching a Program

No matter which cluster manager you use, Spark provides a single script you can use to submit your program to it called `spark-submit`. Through various options, `spark-submit` can connect to different cluster managers and control how many resources your application gets. For some cluster managers, `spark-submit` can run the driver within the cluster (e.g., on a YARN worker node), while for others, it can run it only on your local machine. We'll cover `spark-submit` in more detail in the next section.

Summary

To summarize the concepts in this section, let's walk through the exact steps that occur when you run a Spark application on a cluster:

1. The user submits an application using `spark-submit`.

2. `spark-submit` launches the driver program and invokes the `main()` method specified by the user.

3. The driver program contacts the cluster manager to ask for resources to launch executors.

4. The cluster manager launches executors on behalf of the driver program.

5. The driver process runs through the user application. Based on the RDD actions and transformations in the program, the driver sends work to executors in the form of tasks.

6. Tasks are run on executor processes to compute and save results.

7. If the driver's `main()` method exits or it calls `SparkContext.stop()`, it will terminate the executors and release resources from the cluster manager.

Deploying Applications with spark-submit

As you've learned, Spark provides a single tool for submitting jobs across all cluster managers, called spark-submit. In Chapter 2 you saw a simple example of submitting a Python program with spark-submit, repeated here in Example 7-1.

Example 7-1. Submitting a Python application

```
bin/spark-submit my_script.py
```

When spark-submit is called with nothing but the name of a script or JAR, it simply runs the supplied Spark program locally. Let's say we wanted to submit this program to a Spark Standalone cluster. We can provide extra flags with the address of a Standalone cluster and a specific size of each executor process we'd like to launch, as shown in Example 7-2.

Example 7-2. Submitting an application with extra arguments

```
bin/spark-submit --master spark://host:7077 --executor-memory 10g my_script.py
```

The --master flag specifies a *cluster URL* to connect to; in this case, the *spark://* URL means a cluster using Spark's Standalone mode (see Table 7-1). We will discuss other URL types later.

Table 7-1. Possible values for the --master flag in spark-submit

Value	Explanation
spark:// host:port	Connect to a Spark Standalone cluster at the specified port. By default Spark Standalone masters use port 7077.
mesos:// host:port	Connect to a Mesos cluster master at the specified port. By default Mesos masters listen on port 5050.
yarn	Connect to a YARN cluster. When running on YARN you'll need to set the HADOOP_CONF_DIR environment variable to point the location of your Hadoop configuration directory, which contains information about the cluster.
local	Run in local mode with a single core.
local[N]	Run in local mode with N cores.
local[*]	Run in local mode and use as many cores as the machine has.

Apart from a cluster URL, spark-submit provides a variety of options that let you control specific details about a particular run of your application. These options fall roughly into two categories. The first is scheduling information, such as the amount of resources you'd like to request for your job (as shown in Example 7-2). The second is information about the runtime dependencies of your application, such as libraries or files you want to deploy to all worker machines.

The general format for `spark-submit` is shown in Example 7-3.

Example 7-3. General format for spark-submit

```
bin/spark-submit [options] <app jar | python file> [app options]
```

`[options]` are a list of flags for `spark-submit`. You can enumerate all possible flags by running `spark-submit --help`. A list of common flags is enumerated in Table 7-2.

`<app jar | python file>` refers to the JAR or Python script containing the entry point into your application.

`[app options]` are options that will be passed onto your application. If the `main()` method of your program parses its calling arguments, it will see only `[app options]` and not the flags specific to `spark-submit`.

Table 7-2. Common flags for spark-submit

Flag	Explanation
`--master`	Indicates the cluster manager to connect to. The options for this flag are described in Table 7-1.
`--deploy-mode`	Whether to launch the driver program locally ("client") or on one of the worker machines inside the cluster ("cluster"). In client mode `spark-submit` will run your driver on the same machine where `spark-submit` is itself being invoked. In cluster mode, the driver will be shipped to execute on a worker node in the cluster. The default is client mode.
`--class`	The "main" class of your application if you're running a Java or Scala program.
`--name`	A human-readable name for your application. This will be displayed in Spark's web UI.
`--jars`	A list of JAR files to upload and place on the classpath of your application. If your application depends on a small number of third-party JARs, you can add them here.
`--files`	A list of files to be placed in the working directory of your application. This can be used for data files that you want to distribute to each node.
`--py-files`	A list of files to be added to the PYTHONPATH of your application. This can contain *.py*, *.egg*, or *.zip* files.

Flag	Explanation
--executor-memory	The amount of memory to use for executors, in bytes. Suffixes can be used to specify larger quantities such as "512m" (512 megabytes) or "15g" (15 gigabytes).
--driver-memory	The amount of memory to use for the driver process, in bytes. Suffixes can be used to specify larger quantities such as "512m" (512 megabytes) or "15g" (15 gigabytes).

spark-submit also allows setting arbitrary SparkConf configuration options using either the --conf prop=value flag or providing a properties file through --properties-file that contains key/value pairs. Chapter 8 will discuss Spark's configuration system.

Example 7-4 shows a few longer-form invocations of spark-submit using various options.

Example 7-4. Using spark-submit with various options

```
# Submitting a Java application to Standalone cluster mode
$ ./bin/spark-submit \
  --master spark://hostname:7077 \
  --deploy-mode cluster \
  --class com.databricks.examples.SparkExample \
  --name "Example Program" \
  --jars dep1.jar,dep2.jar,dep3.jar \
  --total-executor-cores 300 \
  --executor-memory 10g \
  myApp.jar "options" "to your application" "go here"

# Submitting a Python application in YARN client mode
$ export HADOP_CONF_DIR=/opt/hadoop/conf
$ ./bin/spark-submit \
  --master yarn \
  --py-files somelib-1.2.egg,otherlib-4.4.zip,other-file.py \
  --deploy-mode client \
  --name "Example Program" \
  --queue exampleQueue \
  --num-executors 40 \
  --executor-memory 10g \
  my_script.py "options" "to your application" "go here"
```

Packaging Your Code and Dependencies

Throughout most of this book we've provided example programs that are self-contained and had no library dependencies outside of Spark. More often, user programs depend on third-party libraries. If your program imports any libraries that are not in the org.apache.spark package or part of the language library, you need to ensure that all your dependencies are present at the runtime of your Spark application.

For Python users, there are a few ways to install third-party libraries. Since PySpark uses the existing Python installation on worker machines, you can install dependency libraries directly on the cluster machines using standard Python package managers (such as pip or easy_install), or via a manual installation into the *site-packages/* directory of your Python installation. Alternatively, you can submit individual libraries using the --py-files argument to spark-submit and they will be added to the Python interpreter's path. Adding libraries manually is more convenient if you do not have access to install packages on the cluster, but do keep in mind potential conflicts with existing packages already installed on the machines.

What About Spark Itself?

When you are bundling an application, you should never include Spark itself in the list of submitted dependencies. spark-submit automatically ensures that Spark is present in the path of your program.

For Java and Scala users, it is also possible to submit individual JAR files using the --jars flag to spark-submit. This can work well if you have a very simple dependency on one or two libraries and they themselves don't have any other dependencies. It is more common, however, for users to have Java or Scala projects that depend on several libraries. When you submit an application to Spark, it must ship with its entire *transitive dependency graph* to the cluster. This includes not only the libraries you directly depend on, but also their dependencies, their dependencies' dependencies, and so on. Manually tracking and submitting this set of JAR files would be extremely cumbersome. Instead, it's common practice to rely on a build tool to produce a single large JAR containing the entire transitive dependency graph of an application. This is often called an *uber JAR* or an *assembly JAR*, and most Java or Scala build tools can produce this type of artifact.

The most popular build tools for Java and Scala are Maven and sbt (Scala build tool). Either tool can be used with either language, but Maven is more often used for Java projects and sbt for Scala projects. Here, we'll give examples of Spark application builds using both tools. You can use these as templates for your own Spark projects.

A Java Spark Application Built with Maven

Let's look at an example Java project with multiple dependencies that produces an uber JAR. Example 7-5 provides a Maven *pom.xml* file containing a build definition. This example doesn't show the actual Java code or project directory structure, but

Maven expects user code to be in a *src/main/java* directory relative to the project root (the root should contain the *pom.xml* file).

Example 7-5. pom.xml file for a Spark application built with Maven

```
<project>
  <modelVersion>4.0.0</modelVersion>

  <!-- Information about your project -->
  <groupId>com.databricks</groupId>
  <artifactId>example-build</artifactId>
  <name>Simple Project</name>
  <packaging>jar</packaging>
  <version>1.0</version>

  <dependencies>
    <!-- Spark dependency -->
    <dependency>
      <groupId>org.apache.spark</groupId>
      <artifactId>spark-core_2.10</artifactId>
      <version>1.3.0</version>
      <scope>provided</scope>
    </dependency>
    <!-- Third-party library -->
    <dependency>
      <groupId>net.sf.jopt-simple</groupId>
      <artifactId>jopt-simple</artifactId>
      <version>4.3</version>
    </dependency>
    <!-- Third-party library -->
    <dependency>
      <groupId>joda-time</groupId>
      <artifactId>joda-time</artifactId>
      <version>2.0</version>
    </dependency>
  </dependencies>

  <build>
    <plugins>
      <!-- Maven shade plug-in that creates uber JARs -->
      <plugin>
        <groupId>org.apache.maven.plugins</groupId>
        <artifactId>maven-shade-plugin</artifactId>
        <version>2.3</version>
        <executions>
          <execution>
            <phase>package</phase>
            <goals>
              <goal>shade</goal>
            </goals>
          </execution>
```

```
        </executions>
      </plugin>
    </plugins>
  </build>
</project>
```

This project declares two transitive dependencies: jopt-simple, a Java library to perform option parsing, and joda-time, a library with utilities for time and date conversion. It also depends on Spark, but Spark is marked as provided to ensure that Spark
is never packaged with the application artifacts. The build includes the maven-shade-
plugin to create an uber JAR containing all of its dependencies. You enable this by
asking Maven to execute the shade goal of the plug-in every time a package phase
occurs. With this build configuration, an uber JAR is created automatically when mvn
package is run (see Example 7-6).

Example 7-6. Packaging a Spark application built with Maven

```
$ mvn package
# In the target directory, we'll see an uber JAR and the original package JAR
$ ls target/
example-build-1.0.jar
original-example-build-1.0.jar
# Listing the uber JAR will reveal classes from dependency libraries
$ jar tf target/example-build-1.0.jar
...
joptsimple/HelpFormatter.class
...
org/joda/time/tz/UTCProvider.class
...
# An uber JAR can be passed directly to spark-submit
$ /path/to/spark/bin/spark-submit --master local ... target/example-build-1.0.jar
```

A Scala Spark Application Built with sbt

sbt is a newer build tool most often used for Scala projects. sbt assumes a similar
project layout to Maven. At the root of your project you create a build file called
build.sbt and your source code is expected to live in *src/main/scala*. sbt build files are
written in a configuration language where you assign values to specific keys in order
to define the build for your project. For instance, there is a key called name, which
contains the project name, and a key called libraryDependencies, which contains a
list of dependencies of your project. Example 7-7 gives a full sbt build file for a simple
application that depends on Spark along with a few other third-party libraries. This
build file works with sbt 0.13. Since sbt evolves quickly, you may want to read its
most recent documentation for any formatting changes in the build file format.

Example 7-7. build.sbt file for a Spark application built with sbt 0.13

```
import AssemblyKeys._

name := "Simple Project"

version := "1.0"

organization := "com.databricks"

scalaVersion := "2.10.3"

libraryDependencies ++= Seq(
    // Spark dependency
    "org.apache.spark" % "spark-core_2.10" % "1.3.0" % "provided",
    // Third-party libraries
    "net.sf.jopt-simple" % "jopt-simple" % "4.3",
    "joda-time" % "joda-time" % "2.0"
)

// This statement includes the assembly plug-in capabilities
assemblySettings

// Configure JAR used with the assembly plug-in
jarName in assembly := "my-project-assembly.jar"

// A special option to exclude Scala itself from our assembly JAR, since Spark
// already bundles Scala.
assemblyOption in assembly :=
  (assemblyOption in assembly).value.copy(includeScala = false)
```

The first line in this build file imports some functionality from an sbt build plug-in that supports creating project assembly JARs. To enable this plug-in we have to also include a small file in a *project/* directory that lists the dependency on the plug-in. Simply create a file called *project/assembly.sbt* and add the following to it: addSbtPlugin("com.eed3si9n" % "sbt-assembly" % "0.11.2"). The exact version of sbt-assembly you use might differ if you build with a newer version of sbt. Example 7-8 works with sbt 0.13.

Example 7-8. Adding the assembly plug-in to an sbt project build

```
# Display contents of project/assembly.sbt
$ cat project/assembly.sbt
addSbtPlugin("com.eed3si9n" % "sbt-assembly" % "0.11.2")
```

Now that we have a well-defined build, we can create a fully assembled Spark application JAR (Example 7-9).

Example 7-9. Packaging a Spark application built with sbt

```
$ sbt assembly
# In the target directory, we'll see an assembly JAR
$ ls target/scala-2.10/
my-project-assembly.jar
# Listing the assembly JAR will reveal classes from dependency libraries
$ jar tf target/scala-2.10/my-project-assembly.jar
...
joptsimple/HelpFormatter.class
...
org/joda/time/tz/UTCProvider.class
...
# An assembly JAR can be passed directly to spark-submit
$ /path/to/spark/bin/spark-submit --master local ...
  target/scala-2.10/my-project-assembly.jar
```

Dependency Conflicts

One occasionally disruptive issue is dealing with dependency conflicts in cases where a user application and Spark itself both depend on the same library. This comes up relatively rarely, but when it does, it can be vexing for users. Typically, this will manifest itself when a NoSuchMethodError, a ClassNotFoundException, or some other JVM exception related to class loading is thrown during the execution of a Spark job. There are two solutions to this problem. The first is to modify your application to depend on the same version of the third-party library that Spark does. The second is to modify the packaging of your application using a procedure that is often called "shading." The Maven build tool supports shading through advanced configuration of the plug-in shown in Example 7-5 (in fact, the shading capability is why the plug-in is named maven-shade-plugin). Shading allows you to make a second copy of the conflicting package under a different namespace and rewrites your application's code to use the renamed version. This somewhat brute-force technique is quite effective at resolving runtime dependency conflicts. For specific instructions on how to shade dependencies, see the documentation for your build tool.

Scheduling Within and Between Spark Applications

The example we just walked through involves a single user submitting a job to a cluster. In reality, many clusters are shared between multiple users. Shared environments have the challenge of scheduling: what happens if two users both launch Spark applications that each want to use the entire cluster's worth of resources? Scheduling policies help ensure that resources are not overwhelmed and allow for prioritization of workloads.

For scheduling in multitenant clusters, Spark primarily relies on the cluster manager to share resources between Spark applications. When a Spark application asks for executors from the cluster manager, it may receive more or fewer executors depending on availability and contention in the cluster. Many cluster managers offer the ability to define queues with different priorities or capacity limits, and Spark will then submit jobs to such queues. See the documentation of your specific cluster manager for more details.

One special case of Spark applications are those that are *long lived*, meaning that they are never intended to terminate. An example of a long-lived Spark application is the JDBC server bundled with Spark SQL. When the JDBC server launches it acquires a set of executors from the cluster manager, then acts as a permanent gateway for SQL queries submitted by users. Since this single application is scheduling work for multiple users, it needs a finer-grained mechanism to enforce sharing policies. Spark provides such a mechanism through configurable intra-application scheduling policies. Spark's internal *Fair Scheduler* lets long-lived applications define queues for prioritizing scheduling of tasks. A detailed review of these is beyond the scope of this book; the official documentation on the Fair Scheduler (*http://spark.apache.org/docs/latest/job-scheduling.html*) provides a good reference.

Cluster Managers

Spark can run over a variety of *cluster managers* to access the machines in a cluster. If you only want to run Spark by itself on a set of machines, the built-in Standalone mode is the easiest way to deploy it. However, if you have a cluster that you'd like to share with other distributed applications (e.g., both Spark jobs and Hadoop MapReduce jobs), Spark can also run over two popular cluster managers: Hadoop YARN and Apache Mesos. Finally, for deploying on Amazon EC2, Spark comes with built-in scripts that launch a Standalone cluster and various supporting services. In this section, we'll cover how to run Spark in each of these environments.

Standalone Cluster Manager

Spark's Standalone manager offers a simple way to run applications on a cluster. It consists of a *master* and multiple *workers*, each with a configured amount of memory and CPU cores. When you submit an application, you can choose how much memory its executors will use, as well as the total number of cores across all executors.

Launching the Standalone cluster manager

You can start the Standalone cluster manager either by starting a master and workers by hand, or by using launch scripts in Spark's *sbin* directory. The launch scripts are the simplest option to use, but require SSH access between your machines and are currently (as of Spark 1.1) available only on Mac OS X and Linux. We will cover these first, then show how to launch a cluster manually on other platforms.

To use the cluster launch scripts, follow these steps:

1. Copy a compiled version of Spark to the same location on all your machines—for example, */home/yourname/spark*.

2. Set up password-less SSH access from your master machine to the others. This requires having the same user account on all the machines, creating a private SSH key for it on the master via ssh-keygen, and adding this key to the *.ssh/ authorized_keys* file of all the workers. If you have not set this up before, you can follow these commands:

```
# On master: run ssh-keygen accepting default options
$ ssh-keygen -t dsa
Enter file in which to save the key (/home/you/.ssh/id_dsa): [ENTER]
Enter passphrase (empty for no passphrase): [EMPTY]
Enter same passphrase again: [EMPTY]

# On workers:
# copy ~/.ssh/id_dsa.pub from your master to the worker, then use:
$ cat ~/.ssh/id_dsa.pub >> ~/.ssh/authorized_keys
$ chmod 644 ~/.ssh/authorized_keys
```

3. Edit the *conf/slaves* file on your master and fill in the workers' hostnames.

4. To start the cluster, run sbin/start-all.sh on your master (it is important to run it there rather than on a worker). If everything started, you should get no prompts for a password, and the cluster manager's web UI should appear at *http://masternode:8080* and show all your workers.

5. To stop the cluster, run sbin/stop-all.sh on your master node.

If you are not on a UNIX system or would like to launch the cluster manually, you can also start the master and workers by hand, using the spark-class script in Spark's *bin/* directory. On your master, type:

```
bin/spark-class org.apache.spark.deploy.master.Master
```

Then on workers:

```
bin/spark-class org.apache.spark.deploy.worker.Worker spark://masternode:7077
```

(where masternode is the hostname of your master). On Windows, use \ instead of /.

By default, the cluster manager will automatically allocate the amount of CPUs and memory on each worker and pick a suitable default to use for Spark. More details on configuring the Standalone cluster manager are available in Spark's official documentation (*http://spark.apache.org/docs/latest/spark-standalone.html*).

Submitting applications

To submit an application to the Standalone cluster manager, pass `spark://master node:7077` as the master argument to `spark-submit`. For example:

```
spark-submit --master spark://masternode:7077 yourapp
```

This cluster URL is also shown in the Standalone cluster manager's web UI, at *http://masternode:8080*. Note that the hostname and port used during submission must *exactly match* the URL present in the UI. This can trip up users who try to encode an IP address, for instance, instead of a hostname. Even if the IP address is associated with the same host, submission will fail if the naming doesn't match exactly. Some administrators might configure Spark to use a different port than 7077. To ensure consistency of host and port components, one safe bet is to just copy and paste the URL directly from the UI of the master node.

You can also launch `spark-shell` or `pyspark` against the cluster in the same way, by passing the `--master` parameter:

```
spark-shell --master spark://masternode:7077
pyspark --master spark://masternode:7077
```

To check that your application or shell is running, look at the cluster manager's web UI *http://masternode:8080* and make sure that (1) your application is connected (i.e., it appears under Running Applications) and (2) it is listed as having more than 0 cores and memory.

 A common pitfall that might prevent your application from running is requesting more memory for executors (with the `--executor-memory` flag to `spark-submit`) than is available in the cluster. In this case, the Standalone cluster manager will never allocate executors for the application. Make sure that the value your application is requesting can be satisfied by the cluster.

Finally, the Standalone cluster manager supports two *deploy modes* for where the driver program of your application runs. In client mode (the default), the driver runs on the machine where you executed `spark-submit`, as part of the `spark-submit` command. This means that you can directly see the output of your driver program, or send input to it (e.g., for an interactive shell), but it requires the machine from which your application was submitted to have fast connectivity to the workers and to stay available for the duration of your application. In contrast, in cluster mode, the driver is launched within the Standalone cluster, as another process on one of the worker nodes, and then it connects back to request executors. In this mode `spark-submit` is "fire-and-forget" in that you can close your laptop while the application is running. You will still be able to access logs for the application through the cluster manager's web UI. You can switch to cluster mode by passing `--deploy-mode cluster` to `spark-submit`.

Configuring resource usage

When sharing a Spark cluster among multiple applications, you will need to decide how to allocate resources between the executors. The Standalone cluster manager has a basic scheduling policy that allows capping the usage of each application so that multiple ones may run concurrently. Apache Mesos supports more dynamic sharing while an application is running, while YARN has a concept of queues that allows you to cap usage for various sets of applications.

In the Standalone cluster manager, resource allocation is controlled by two settings:

Executor memory
> You can configure this using the `--executor-memory` argument to `spark-submit`. Each application will have at most one executor on each worker, so this setting controls how much of that worker's memory the application will claim. By default, this setting is 1 GB—you will likely want to increase it on most servers.

The maximum number of total cores
> This is the total number of cores used across all executors for an application. By default, this is unlimited; that is, the application will launch executors on every available node in the cluster. For a multiuser workload, you should instead ask users to cap their usage. You can set this value through the `--total-executor-cores` argument to `spark-submit`, or by configuring `spark.cores.max` in your Spark configuration file.

To verify the settings, you can always see the current resource allocation in the Standalone cluster manager's web UI, *http://masternode:8080*.

Finally, the Standalone cluster manager works by spreading out each application across the maximum number of executors by default. For example, suppose that you have a 20-node cluster with 4-core machines, and you submit an application with `--executor-memory 1G` and `--total-executor-cores 8`. Then Spark will launch eight executors, each with 1 GB of RAM, on different machines. Spark does this by default to give applications a chance to achieve data locality for distributed filesystems running on the same machines (e.g., HDFS), because these systems typically have data spread out across all nodes. If you prefer, you can instead ask Spark to consolidate executors on as few nodes as possible, by setting the config property `spark.deploy.spreadOut` to `false` in *conf/spark-defaults.conf*. In this case, the preceding application would get only two executors, each with 1 GB RAM and four cores. This setting affects *all* applications on the Standalone cluster and must be configured before you launch the Standalone cluster manager.

High availability

When running in production settings, you will want your Standalone cluster to be available to accept applications even if individual nodes in your cluster go down. Out of the box, the Standalone mode will gracefully support the failure of worker nodes. If you also want the master of the cluster to be highly available, Spark supports using Apache ZooKeeper (a distributed coordination system) to keep multiple standby masters and switch to a new one when any of them fails. Configuring a Standalone cluster with ZooKeeper is outside the scope of the book, but is described in the official Spark documentation (*http://bit.ly/1BQCEOO*).

Hadoop YARN

YARN is a cluster manager introduced in Hadoop 2.0 that allows diverse data processing frameworks to run on a shared resource pool, and is typically installed on the same nodes as the Hadoop filesystem (HDFS). Running Spark on YARN in these environments is useful because it lets Spark access HDFS data quickly, on the same nodes where the data is stored.

Using YARN in Spark is straightforward: you set an environment variable that points to your Hadoop configuration directory, then submit jobs to a special master URL with spark-submit.

The first step is to figure out your Hadoop configuration directory, and set it as the environment variable HADOOP_CONF_DIR. This is the directory that contains *yarn-site.xml* and other config files; typically, it is *HADOOP_HOME/conf* if you installed Hadoop in *HADOOP_HOME*, or a system path like */etc/hadoop/conf*. Then, submit your application as follows:

```
export HADOOP_CONF_DIR="..."
spark-submit --master yarn yourapp
```

As with the Standalone cluster manager, there are two modes to connect your application to the cluster: client mode, where the driver program for your application runs on the machine that you submitted the application from (e.g., your laptop), and cluster mode, where the driver also runs inside a YARN container. You can set the mode to use via the --deploy-mode argument to spark-submit.

Spark's interactive shell and pyspark both work on YARN as well; simply set HADOOP_CONF_DIR and pass --master yarn to these applications. Note that these will run only in client mode since they need to obtain input from the user.

Configuring resource usage

When running on YARN, Spark applications use a fixed number of executors, which you can set via the --num-executors flag to spark-submit, spark-shell, and so on. By default, this is only two, so you will likely need to increase it. You can also set the memory used by each executor via --executor-memory and the number of cores it claims from YARN via --executor-cores. On a given set of hardware resources, Spark will usually run better with a smaller number of larger executors (with multiple cores and more memory), since it can optimize communication within each executor. Note, however, that some clusters have a limit on the maximum size of an executor (8 GB by default), and will not let you launch larger ones.

Some YARN clusters are configured to schedule applications into multiple "queues" for resource management purposes. Use the --queue option to select your queue name.

Finally, further information on configuration options for YARN is available in the official Spark documentation (*http://bit.ly/1yCkxNf*).

Apache Mesos

Apache Mesos is a general-purpose cluster manager that can run both analytics workloads and long-running services (e.g., web applications or key/value stores) on a cluster. To use Spark on Mesos, pass a *mesos://* URI to spark-submit:

```
spark-submit --master mesos://masternode:5050 yourapp
```

You can also configure Mesos clusters to use ZooKeeper to elect a master when running in multimaster mode. In this case, use a *mesos://zk://* URI pointing to a list of ZooKeeper nodes. For example, if you have three ZooKeeper nodes (node1, node2, and node3) on which ZooKeeper is running on port 2181, use the following URI:

```
mesos://zk://node1:2181/mesos,node2:2181/mesos,node3:2181/mesos
```

Mesos scheduling modes

Unlike the other cluster managers, Mesos offers two modes to share resources between executors on the same cluster. In "fine-grained" mode, which is the default, executors scale up and down the number of CPUs they claim from Mesos as they execute tasks, and so a machine running multiple executors can dynamically share CPU resources between them. In "coarse-grained" mode, Spark allocates a fixed number of CPUs to each executor in advance and never releases them until the application ends, even if the executor is not currently running tasks. You can enable coarse-grained mode by passing --conf spark.mesos.coarse=true to spark-submit.

The fine-grained Mesos mode is attractive when multiple users share a cluster to run interactive workloads such as shells, because applications will scale down their number of cores when they're not doing work and still allow other users' programs to use the cluster. The downside, however, is that scheduling tasks through fine-grained mode adds more latency (so very low-latency applications like Spark Streaming may suffer), and that applications may need to wait some amount of time for CPU cores to become free to "ramp up" again when the user types a new command. Note, however, that you can use a mix of scheduling modes in the same Mesos cluster (i.e., some of your Spark applications might have `spark.mesos.coarse` set to `true` and some might not).

Client and cluster mode

As of Spark 1.2, Spark on Mesos supports running applications only in the "client" deploy mode—that is, with the driver running on the machine that submitted the application. If you would like to run your driver in the Mesos cluster as well, frameworks like Aurora (*http://aurora.incubator.apache.org*) and Chronos (*http://airbnb.github.io/chronos*) allow you to submit arbitrary scripts to run on Mesos and monitor them. You can use one of these to launch the driver for your application.

Configuring resource usage

You can control resource usage on Mesos through two parameters to `spark-submit`: `--executor-memory`, to set the memory for each executor, and `--total-executor-cores`, to set the maximum number of CPU cores for the application to claim (across all executors). By default, Spark will launch each executor with as many cores as possible, consolidating the application to the smallest number of executors that give it the desired number of cores. If you do not set `--total-executor-cores`, it will try to use all available cores in the cluster.

Amazon EC2

Spark comes with a built-in script to launch clusters on Amazon EC2. This script launches a set of nodes and then installs the Standalone cluster manager on them, so once the cluster is up, you can use it according to the Standalone mode instructions in the previous section. In addition, the EC2 script sets up supporting services such as HDFS, Tachyon, and Ganglia to monitor your cluster.

The Spark EC2 script is called `spark-ec2`, and is located in the *ec2* folder of your Spark installation. It requires Python 2.6 or higher. You can download Spark and run the EC2 script without compiling Spark beforehand.

The EC2 script can manage multiple named *clusters*, identifying them using EC2 security groups. For each cluster, the script will create a security group called `clustername-master` for the master node, and `clustername-slaves` for the workers.

Launching a cluster

To launch a cluster, you should first create an Amazon Web Services (AWS) account and obtain an access key ID and secret access key. Then export these as environment variables:

```
export AWS_ACCESS_KEY_ID="..."
export AWS_SECRET_ACCESS_KEY="..."
```

In addition, create an EC2 SSH key pair and download its private key file (usually called *keypair.pem*) so that you can SSH into the machines.

Next, run the `launch` command of the `spark-ec2` script, giving it your key pair name, private key file, and a name for the cluster. By default, this will launch a cluster with one master and one slave, using `m1.xlarge` EC2 instances:

```
cd /path/to/spark/ec2
./spark-ec2 -k mykeypair -i mykeypair.pem launch mycluster
```

You can also configure the instance types, number of slaves, EC2 region, and other factors using options to `spark-ec2`. For example:

```
# Launch a cluster with 5 slaves of type m3.xlarge
./spark-ec2 -k mykeypair -i mykeypair.pem -s 5 -t m3.xlarge launch mycluster
```

For a full list of options, run `spark-ec2 --help`. Some of the most common ones are listed in Table 7-3.

Table 7-3. Common options to spark-ec2

Option	Meaning
`-k KEYPAIR`	Name of key pair to use
`-i IDENTITY_FILE`	Private key file (ending in *.pem*)
`-s NUM_SLAVES`	Number of slave nodes
`-t INSTANCE_TYPE`	Amazon instance type to use
`-r REGION`	Amazon region to use (e.g., `us-west-1`)
`-z ZONE`	Availability zone (e.g., `us-west-1b`)
`--spot-price=PRICE`	Use spot instances at the given spot price (in US dollars)

Once you launch the script, it usually takes about five minutes to launch the machines, log in to them, and set up Spark.

Logging in to a cluster

You can log in to a cluster by SSHing into its master node with the *.pem* file for your keypair. For convenience, `spark-ec2` provides a `login` command for this purpose:

```
./spark-ec2 -k mykeypair -i mykeypair.pem login mycluster
```

Alternatively, you can find the master's hostname by running:

```
./spark-ec2 get-master mycluster
```

Then SSH into it yourself using `ssh -i keypair.pem root@masternode`.

Once you are in the cluster, you can use the Spark installation in */root/spark* to run programs. This is a Standalone cluster installation, with the master URL *spark://masternode:7077*. If you launch an application with `spark-submit`, it will come correctly configured to submit your application to this cluster automatically. You can view the cluster's web UI at *http://masternode:8080*.

Note that only programs launched from the cluster will be able to submit jobs to it with `spark-submit`; the firewall rules will prevent external hosts from submitting them for security reasons. To run a prepackaged application on the cluster, first copy it over using SCP:

```
scp -i mykeypair.pem app.jar root@masternode:~
```

Destroying a cluster

To destroy a cluster launched by `spark-ec2`, run:

```
./spark-ec2 destroy mycluster
```

This will terminate all the instances associated with the cluster (i.e., all instances in its two security groups, `mycluster-master` and `mycluster-slaves`).

Pausing and restarting clusters

In addition to outright terminating clusters, `spark-ec2` lets you stop the Amazon instances running your cluster and then start them again later. Stopping instances shuts them down and makes them lose all data on the "ephemeral" disks, which are configured with an installation of HDFS for `spark-ec2` (see "Storage on the cluster" on page 138). However, the stopped instances retain all data in their root directory (e.g., any files you uploaded there), so you'll be able to quickly return to work.

To stop a cluster, use:

```
./spark-ec2 stop mycluster
```

Then, later, to start it up again:

```
./spark-ec2 -k mykeypair -i mykeypair.pem start mycluster
```

While the Spark EC2 script does not provide commands to resize clusters, you can resize them by adding or removing machines to the `mycluster-slaves` security group. To add machines, first stop the cluster, then use the AWS management console to right-click one of the slave nodes and select "Launch more like this." This will create more instances in the same security group. Then use `spark-ec2 start` to start your cluster. To remove machines, simply terminate them from the AWS console (though beware that this destroys data on the cluster's HDFS installations).

Storage on the cluster

Spark EC2 clusters come configured with two installations of the Hadoop filesystem that you can use for scratch space. This can be handy to save datasets in a medium that's faster to access than Amazon S3. The two installations are:

- An "ephemeral" HDFS installation using the ephemeral drives on the nodes. Most Amazon instance types come with a substantial amount of local space attached on "ephemeral" drives that go away if you stop the instance. This installation of HDFS uses this space, giving you a significant amount of scratch space, but it loses all data when you stop and restart the EC2 cluster. It is installed in the */root/ephemeral-hdfs* directory on the nodes, where you can use the `bin/hdfs` command to access and list files. You can also view the web UI and HDFS URL for it at *http://masternode:50070*.

- A "persistent" HDFS installation on the root volumes of the nodes. This instance persists data even through cluster restarts, but is generally smaller and slower to access than the ephemeral one. It is good for medium-sized datasets that you do not wish to download multiple times. It is installed in */root/persistent-hdfs*, and you can view the web UI and HDFS URL for it at *http://masternode:60070*.

Apart from these, you will most likely be accessing data from Amazon S3, which you can do using the *s3n://* URI scheme in Spark. Refer to "Amazon S3" on page 89 for details.

Which Cluster Manager to Use?

The cluster managers supported in Spark offer a variety of options for deploying applications. If you are starting a new deployment and looking to choose a cluster manager, we recommend the following guidelines:

- Start with a Standalone cluster if this is a new deployment. Standalone mode is the easiest to set up and will provide almost all the same features as the other cluster managers if you are running only Spark.

- If you would like to run Spark alongside other applications, or to use richer resource scheduling capabilities (e.g., queues), both YARN and Mesos provide these features. Of these, YARN will likely be preinstalled in many Hadoop distributions.

- One advantage of Mesos over both YARN and Standalone mode is its fine-grained sharing option, which lets interactive applications such as the Spark shell scale down their CPU allocation between commands. This makes it attractive in environments where multiple users are running interactive shells.

- In all cases, it is best to run Spark on the same nodes as HDFS for fast access to storage. You can install Mesos or the Standalone cluster manager on the same nodes manually, or most Hadoop distributions already install YARN and HDFS together.

Finally, keep in mind that cluster management is a fast-moving space—by the time this book comes out, there might be more features available for Spark under the current cluster managers, as well as new cluster managers. The methods of submitting applications described here will not change, but you can check the official documentation (*http://spark.apache.org/docs/latest/*) for your Spark release to see the latest options.

Conclusion

This chapter described the runtime architecture of a Spark application, composed of a driver process and a distributed set of executor processes. We then covered how to build, package, and submit Spark applications. Finally, we outlined the common deployment environments for Spark, including its built-in cluster manager, running Spark with YARN or Mesos, and running Spark on Amazon's EC2 cloud. In the next chapter we'll dive into more advanced operational concerns, with a focus on tuning and debugging production Spark applications.

## CHAPTER 8

Tuning and Debugging Spark

This chapter describes how to configure a Spark application and gives an overview of how to tune and debug production Spark workloads. Spark is designed so that default settings work "out of the box" in many cases; however, there are still some configurations users might want to modify. This chapter outlines Spark's configuration mechanisms and highlights some options users might want to tweak. Configuration is also useful for tuning an application's performance; the second part of this chapter covers the fundamentals necessary for understanding the performance of a Spark application, along with the associated configuration settings and design patterns for writing high performance applications. We also cover information about Spark's user interface, instrumentation, and logging mechanisms. These are all useful when you are performance tuning or troubleshooting issues.

Configuring Spark with SparkConf

Tuning Spark often simply means changing the Spark application's runtime configuration. The primary configuration mechanism in Spark is the SparkConf class. A SparkConf instance is required when you are creating a new SparkContext, as shown in Examples 8-1 through 8-3.

Example 8-1. Creating an application using a SparkConf in Python

```
# Construct a conf
conf = new SparkConf()
conf.set("spark.app.name", "My Spark App")
conf.set("spark.master", "local[4]")
conf.set("spark.ui.port", "36000") # Override the default port

# Create a SparkContext with this configuration
sc = SparkContext(conf)
```

Example 8-2. Creating an application using a SparkConf in Scala

```
// Construct a conf
val conf = new SparkConf()
conf.set("spark.app.name", "My Spark App")
conf.set("spark.master", "local[4]")
conf.set("spark.ui.port", "36000") // Override the default port

// Create a SparkContext with this configuration
val sc = new SparkContext(conf)
```

Example 8-3. Creating an application using a SparkConf in Java

```
// Construct a conf
SparkConf conf = new SparkConf();
conf.set("spark.app.name", "My Spark App");
conf.set("spark.master", "local[4]");
conf.set("spark.ui.port", "36000"); // Override the default port

// Create a SparkContext with this configuration
JavaSparkContext sc = JavaSparkContext(conf);
```

The SparkConf class is quite simple: a SparkConf instance contains key/value pairs of configuration options the user would like to override. Every configuration option in Spark is based on a string key and value. To use a SparkConf object you create one, call set() to add configuration values, and then supply it to the SparkContext constructor. In addition to set(), the SparkConf class includes a small number of utility methods for setting common parameters. In the preceding three examples, you could also call setAppName() and setMaster() to set the spark.app.name and the spark.master configurations, respectively.

In these examples, the SparkConf values are set programmatically in the application code. In many cases, it is more convenient to populate configurations dynamically for a given application. Spark allows setting configurations dynamically through the spark-submit tool. When an application is launched with spark-submit, it injects configuration values into the environment. These are detected and automatically filled in when a new SparkConf is constructed. Therefore, user applications can simply construct an "empty" SparkConf and pass it directly to the SparkContext constructor if you are using spark-submit.

The spark-submit tool provides built-in flags for the most common Spark configuration parameters and a generic --conf flag that accepts any Spark configuration value. These are demonstrated in Example 8-4.

Example 8-4. Setting configuration values at runtime using flags

```
$ bin/spark-submit \
  --class com.example.MyApp \
  --master local[4] \
  --name "My Spark App" \
  --conf spark.ui.port=36000 \
  myApp.jar
```

spark-submit also supports loading configuration values from a file. This can be useful to set environmental configuration, which may be shared across multiple users, such as a default master. By default, spark-submit will look for a file called *conf/spark-defaults.conf* in the Spark directory and attempt to read whitespace-delimited key/value pairs from this file. You can also customize the exact location of the file using the --properties-file flag to spark-submit, as you can see in Example 8-5.

Example 8-5. Setting configuration values at runtime using a defaults file

```
$ bin/spark-submit \
  --class com.example.MyApp \
  --properties-file my-config.conf \
  myApp.jar

## Contents of my-config.conf ##
spark.master     local[4]
spark.app.name   "My Spark App"
spark.ui.port    36000
```

> The SparkConf associated with a given application is immutable once it is passed to the SparkContext constructor. That means that all configuration decisions must be made before a SparkContext is instantiated.

In some cases, the same configuration property might be set in multiple places. For instance, a user might call setAppName() directly on a SparkConf object and also pass the --name flag to spark-submit. In these cases Spark has a specific precedence order. The highest priority is given to configurations declared explicitly in the user's code using the set() function on a SparkConf object. Next are flags passed to spark-submit, then values in the properties file, and finally default values. If you want to know which configurations are in place for a given application, you can examine a list of active configurations displayed through the application web UI discussed later in this chapter.

Several common configurations were listed in Table 7-2. Table 8-1 outlines a few additional configuration options that might be of interest. For the full list of configuration options, see the Spark documentation (*http://bit.ly/1yClm8O*).

Table 8-1. Common Spark configuration values

Option(s)	Default	Explanation
spark.executor.memory (--executor-memory)	512m	Amount of memory to use per executor process, in the same format as JVM memory strings (e.g., 512m, 2g). See "Hardware Provisioning" on page 158 for more detail on this option.
spark.executor.cores(--executor-cores) spark.cores.max(--total-executor-cores)	1 (none)	Configurations for bounding the number of cores used by the application. In YARN mode spark.executor.cores will assign a specific number of cores to each executor. In standalone and Mesos modes, you can upper-bound the total number of cores across all executors using spark.cores.max. Refer to "Hardware Provisioning" on page 158 for more detail.
spark.speculation	false	Setting to true will enable speculative execution of tasks. This means tasks that are running slowly will have a second copy launched on another node. Enabling this can help cut down on straggler tasks in large clusters.
spark.storage.blockManagerTimeoutIntervalMs	45000	An internal timeout used for tracking the liveness of executors. For jobs that have long garbage collection pauses, tuning this to be 100 seconds (a value of 100000) or higher can prevent thrashing. In future versions of Spark this may be replaced with a general timeout setting, so check current documentation.
spark.executor.extraJavaOptions spark.executor.extraClassPath spark.executor.extraLibraryPath	(empty)	These three options allow you to customize the launch behavior of executor JVMs. The three flags add extra Java options, classpath entries, or path entries for the JVM library path. These parameters should be specified as strings (e.g., spark.executor.extraJavaOptions="-XX:+PrintGCDetails-XX:+PrintGCTimeStamps"). Note that while this allows you to manually augment the executor classpath, the recommended way to add dependencies is through the --jars flag to spark-submit (not using this option).

Option(s)	Default	Explanation
`spark.serializer`	`org.apache.spark.seri` `alizer.JavaSerializer`	Class to use for serializing objects that will be sent over the network or need to be cached in serialized form. The default of Java Serialization works with any serializable Java object but is quite slow, so we recommend using `org.apache.spark.seri` `alizer.KryoSerializer` and configuring Kryo serialization when speed is necessary. Can be any subclass of `org.apache.spark.Serial` `izer`.
`spark.[X].port`	(random/purpose-specific)	Allows setting integer port values to be used by a running Spark applications. This is useful in clusters where network access is secured. The possible values of X are `driver`, `fileserver`, `broad` `cast`, `replClassServer`, `blockManager`, `ui` and `executor`.
`spark.eventLog.enabled`	`false`	Set to `true` to enable event logging, which allows completed Spark jobs to be viewed using a history server. For more information about Spark's history server, see the official documentation.
`spark.eventLog.dir`	`file:///tmp/spark-` `events`	The storage location used for event logging, if enabled. This needs to be in a globally visible filesystem such as HDFS.

Almost all Spark configurations occur through the `SparkConf` construct, but one important option doesn't. To set the local storage directories for Spark to use for shuffle data (necessary for standalone and Mesos modes), you export the `SPARK_LOCAL_DIRS` environment variable inside of *conf/spark-env.sh* to a comma-separated list of storage locations. `SPARK_LOCAL_DIRS` is described in detail in "Hardware Provisioning" on page 158. This is specified differently from other Spark configurations because its value may be different on different physical hosts.

Components of Execution: Jobs, Tasks, and Stages

A first step in tuning and debugging Spark is to have a deeper understanding of the system's internal design. In previous chapters you saw the "logical" representation of RDDs and their partitions. When executing, Spark translates this logical representation into a physical execution plan by merging multiple operations into tasks. Understanding every aspect of Spark's execution is beyond the scope of this book, but an appreciation for the steps involved along with the relevant terminology can be helpful when tuning and debugging jobs.

To demonstrate Spark's phases of execution, we'll walk through an example application and see how user code compiles down to a lower-level execution plan. The application we'll consider is a simple bit of log analysis in the Spark shell. For input data, we'll use a text file that consists of log messages of varying degrees of severity, along with some blank lines interspersed (Example 8-6).

Example 8-6. input.txt, the source file for our example

```
## input.txt ##
INFO This is a message with content
INFO This is some other content
(empty line)
INFO Here are more messages
WARN This is a warning
(empty line)
ERROR Something bad happened
WARN More details on the bad thing
INFO back to normal messages
```

We want to open this file in the Spark shell and compute how many log messages appear at each level of severity. First let's create a few RDDs that will help us answer this question, as shown in Example 8-7.

Example 8-7. Processing text data in the Scala Spark shell

```
// Read input file
scala> val input = sc.textFile("input.txt")
// Split into words and remove empty lines
scala> val tokenized = input.
     |   filter(line => line.size > 0).
     |   map(line => line.split(" ")).
// Extract the first word from each line (the log level) and do a count
scala> val counts = tokenized.
     |   map(words => (words(0), 1)).
     | reduceByKey{ (a, b) => a + b }
```

This sequence of commands results in an RDD, counts, that will contain the number of log entries at each level of severity. After executing these lines in the shell, the program has not performed any actions. Instead, it has implicitly defined a directed acyclic graph (DAG) of RDD objects that will be used later once an action occurs. Each RDD maintains a pointer to one or more parents along with metadata about what type of relationship they have. For instance, when you call val b = a.map() on an RDD, the RDD b keeps a reference to its parent a. These pointers allow an RDD to be traced to all of its ancestors.

To display the lineage of an RDD, Spark provides a toDebugString() method. In Example 8-8, we'll look at some of the RDDs we created in the preceding example.

Example 8-8. Visualizing RDDs with toDebugString() in Scala

```
scala> input.toDebugString
res85: String =
(2) input.text MappedRDD[292] at textFile at <console>:13
 |  input.text HadoopRDD[291] at textFile at <console>:13

scala> counts.toDebugString
res84: String =
(2) ShuffledRDD[296] at reduceByKey at <console>:17
+-(2) MappedRDD[295] at map at <console>:17
    |  FilteredRDD[294] at filter at <console>:15
    |  MappedRDD[293] at map at <console>:15
    |  input.text MappedRDD[292] at textFile at <console>:13
    |  input.text HadoopRDD[291] at textFile at <console>:13
```

The first visualization shows the input RDD. We created this RDD by calling sc.textFile(). The lineage gives us some clues as to what sc.textFile() does since it reveals which RDDs were created in the textFile() function. We can see that it creates a HadoopRDD and then performs a map on it to create the returned RDD. The lineage of counts is more complicated. That RDD has several ancestors, since there are other operations that were performed on top of the input RDD, such as additional maps, filtering, and reduction. The lineage of counts shown here is also displayed graphically on the left side of Figure 8-1.

Before we perform an action, these RDDs simply store metadata that will help us compute them later. To trigger computation, let's call an action on the counts RDD by collect()ing it to the driver, as shown in Example 8-9.

Example 8-9. Collecting an RDD

```
scala> counts.collect()
res86: Array[(String, Int)] = Array((ERROR,1), (INFO,4), (WARN,2))
```

Spark's scheduler creates a physical execution plan to compute the RDDs needed for performing the action. Here when we call collect() on the RDD, every partition of the RDD must be materialized and then transferred to the driver program. Spark's scheduler starts at the final RDD being computed (in this case, counts) and works backward to find what it must compute. It visits that RDD's parents, its parents' parents, and so on, recursively to develop a physical plan necessary to compute all ancestor RDDs. In the simplest case, the scheduler outputs a computation *stage* for each RDD in this graph where the stage has *tasks* for each partition in that RDD. Those stages are then executed in reverse order to compute the final required RDD.

In more complex cases, the physical set of stages will not be an exact 1:1 correspondence to the RDD graph. This can occur when the scheduler performs *pipelining*, or collapsing of multiple RDDs into a single stage. Pipelining occurs when RDDs can be computed from their parents without data movement. The lineage output shown in Example 8-8 uses indentation levels to show where RDDs are going to be pipelined together into physical stages. RDDs that exist at the same level of indentation as their parents will be pipelined during physical execution. For instance, when we are computing counts, even though there are a large number of parent RDDs, there are only two levels of indentation shown. This indicates that the physical execution will require only two stages. The pipelining in this case is because there are several filter and map operations in sequence. The right half of Figure 8-1 shows the two stages of execution that are required to compute the counts RDD.

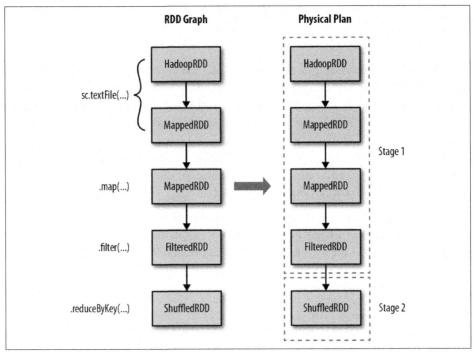

Figure 8-1. RDD transformations pipelined into physical stages

If you visit the application's web UI, you will see that two stages occur in order to fulfill the collect() action. The Spark UI can be found at *http://localhost:4040* if you are running this example on your own machine. The UI is discussed in more detail later in this chapter, but you can use it here to quickly see what stages are executing during this program.

In addition to pipelining, Spark's internal scheduler may truncate the lineage of the RDD graph if an existing RDD has already been persisted in cluster memory or on disk. Spark can "short-circuit" in this case and just begin computing based on the persisted RDD. A second case in which this truncation can happen is when an RDD is already materialized as a side effect of an earlier shuffle, even if it was not explicitly persist()ed. This is an under-the-hood optimization that takes advantage of the fact that Spark shuffle outputs are written to disk, and exploits the fact that many times portions of the RDD graph are recomputed.

To see the effects of caching on physical execution, let's cache the counts RDD and see how that truncates the execution graph for future actions (Example 8-10). If you revisit the UI, you should see that caching reduces the number of stages required when executing future computations. Calling collect() a few more times will reveal only one stage executing to perform the action.

Example 8-10. Computing an already cached RDD

```
// Cache the RDD
scala> counts.cache()
// The first subsequent execution will again require 2 stages
scala> counts.collect()
res87: Array[(String, Int)] = Array((ERROR,1), (INFO,4), (WARN,2), (##,1),
((empty,2))
// This execution will only require a single stage
scala> counts.collect()
res88: Array[(String, Int)] = Array((ERROR,1), (INFO,4), (WARN,2), (##,1),
((empty,2))
```

The set of stages produced for a particular action is termed a *job*. In each case when we invoke actions such as count(), we are creating a job composed of one or more stages.

Once the stage graph is defined, tasks are created and dispatched to an internal scheduler, which varies depending on the deployment mode being used. Stages in the physical plan can depend on each other, based on the RDD lineage, so they will be executed in a specific order. For instance, a stage that outputs shuffle data must occur before one that relies on that data being present.

A physical stage will launch tasks that each do the same thing but on specific partitions of data. Each task internally performs the same steps:

1. Fetching its input, either from data storage (if the RDD is an input RDD), an existing RDD (if the stage is based on already cached data), or shuffle outputs.

2. Performing the operation necessary to compute RDD(s) that it represents. For instance, executing filter() or map() functions on the input data, or performing grouping or reduction.

3. Writing output to a shuffle, to external storage, or back to the driver (if it is the final RDD of an action such as count()).

Most logging and instrumentation in Spark is expressed in terms of stages, tasks, and shuffles. Understanding how user code compiles down into the bits of physical execution is an advanced concept, but one that will help you immensely in tuning and debugging applications.

To summarize, the following phases occur during Spark execution:

User code defines a DAG (directed acyclic graph) of RDDs
Operations on RDDs create new RDDs that refer back to their parents, thereby creating a graph.

Actions force translation of the DAG to an execution plan
When you call an action on an RDD it must be computed. This requires computing its parent RDDs as well. Spark's scheduler submits a *job* to compute all needed RDDs. That job will have one or more *stages*, which are parallel waves of computation composed of *tasks*. Each stage will correspond to one or more RDDs in the DAG. A single stage can correspond to multiple RDDs due to *pipelining*.

Tasks are scheduled and executed on a cluster
Stages are processed in order, with individual tasks launching to compute segments of the RDD. Once the final stage is finished in a job, the action is complete.

In a given Spark application, this entire sequence of steps may occur many times in a continuous fashion as new RDDs are created.

Finding Information

Spark records detailed progress information and performance metrics as applications execute. These are presented to the user in two places: the Spark web UI and the logfiles produced by the driver and executor processes.

Spark Web UI

The first stop for learning about the behavior and performance of a Spark application is Spark's built-in web UI. This is available on the machine where the driver is running at port 4040 by default. One caveat is that in the case of the YARN cluster mode, where the application driver runs inside the cluster, you should access the UI through the YARN ResourceManager, which proxies requests directly to the driver.

The Spark UI contains several different pages, and the exact format may differ across Spark versions. As of Spark 1.2, the UI is composed of four different sections, which we'll cover next.

Jobs: Progress and metrics of stages, tasks, and more

The jobs page, shown in Figure 8-2, contains detailed execution information for active and recently completed Spark jobs. One very useful piece of information on this page is the progress of running jobs, stages, and tasks. Within each stage, this page provides several metrics that you can use to better understand physical execution.

The jobs page was only added in Spark 1.2, so you may not see it in earlier versions of Spark.

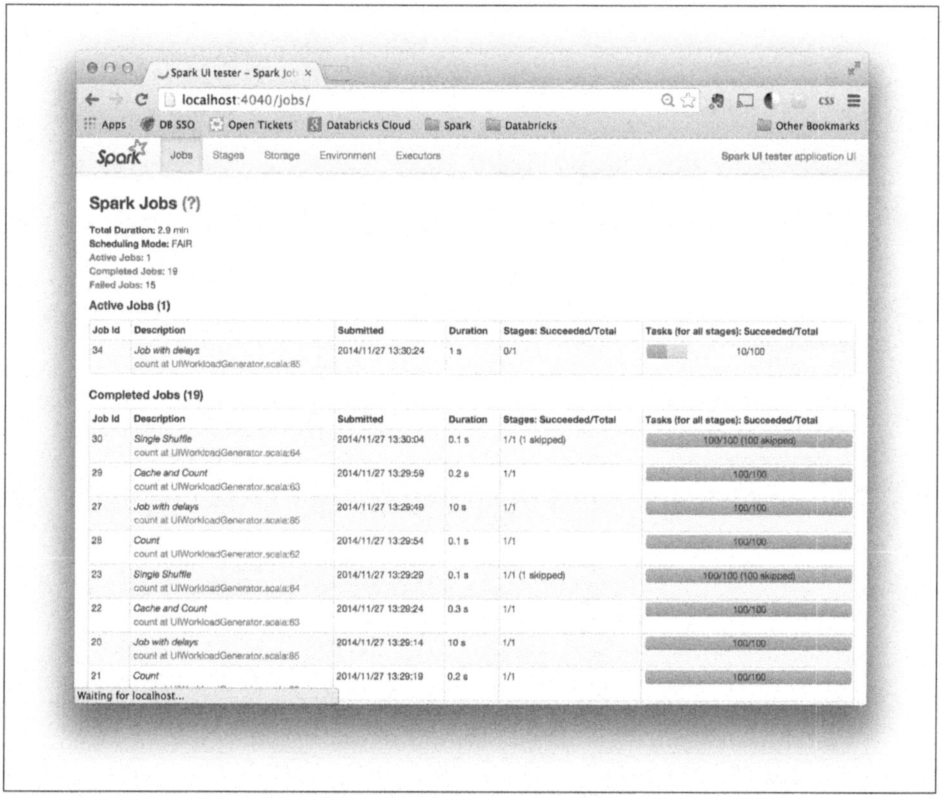

Figure 8-2. The Spark application UI's jobs index page

A common use for this page is to assess the performance of a job. A good first step is to look through the stages that make up a job and see whether some are particularly slow or vary significantly in response time across multiple runs of the same job. If you have an especially expensive stage, you can click through and better understand what user code the stage is associated with.

Once you've narrowed down a stage of interest, the stage page, shown in Figure 8-3, can help isolate performance issues. In data-parallel systems such as Spark, a common source of performance issues is *skew*, which occurs when a small number of tasks take a very large amount of time compared to others. The stage page can help you identify skew by looking at the distribution of different metrics over all tasks. A good starting point is the runtime of the task; do a few tasks take much more time than others? If this is the case, you can dig deeper and see what is causing the tasks to be slow. Do a small number of tasks read or write much more data than others? Are tasks running on certain nodes very slow? These are useful first steps when you're debugging a job.

Details for Stage 3

Total task time across all tasks: 3 s

▸ Show additional metrics

Summary Metrics for 100 Completed Tasks

Metric	Min	25th percentile	Median	75th percentile	Max
Duration	2 ms	3 ms	4 ms	8 ms	0.3 s
Scheduler Delay	3 ms	6 ms	11 ms	28 ms	0.1 s
Task Deserialization Time	0 ms	1 ms	1 ms	2 ms	26 ms
GC Time	0 ms	0 ms	0 ms	0 ms	12 ms
Result Serialization Time	0 ms	0 ms	0 ms	0 ms	4 ms
Getting Result Time	0 ms	0 ms	0 ms	0 ms	0 ms

Aggregated Metrics by Executor

Executor ID	Address	Task Time	Total Tasks	Failed Tasks	Succeeded Tasks	Input	Output	Shuffle Read	Shuffle Write	Shuffle Spill (Memory)	Shuffle Spill (Disk)
<driver>	localhost:53242	5 s	100	0	100	0.0 B	0.0 B	0.0 B	0.0 B	0.0 B	0.0 B

Tasks

Index	ID	Attempt	Status	Locality Level	Executor ID / Host	Launch Time	Duration	Scheduler Delay	Task Deserialization Time	GC Time	Result Serialization Time	Getting Result Time	Errors
0	300	0	SUCCESS	PROCESS_LOCAL	<driver> / localhost	2014/11/27 13:27:44	0.2 s	33 ms	1 ms	12 ms	0 ms	0 ms	
1	301	0	SUCCESS	PROCESS_LOCAL	<driver> / localhost	2014/11/27 13:27:44	0.3 s	11 ms	0 ms	12 ms	0 ms	0 ms	
2	302	0	SUCCESS	PROCESS_LOCAL	<driver> / localhost	2014/11/27 13:27:44	0.3 s	17 ms	1 ms	12 ms	0 ms	0 ms	

Figure 8-3. The Spark application UI's stage detail page

In addition to looking at task skew, it can be helpful to identify how much time tasks are spending in each of the phases of the task lifecycle: reading, computing, and writing. If tasks spend very little time reading or writing data, but take a long time overall, it might be the case that the user code itself is expensive (for an example of user code optimizations, see "Working on a Per-Partition Basis" on page 107). Some tasks may spend almost all of their time reading data from an external storage system, and will not benefit much from additional optimization in Spark since they are bottlenecked on input read.

Storage: Information for RDDs that are persisted

The storage page contains information about persisted RDDs. An RDD is persisted if someone called `persist()` on the RDD *and* it was later computed in some job. In some cases, if many RDDs are cached, older ones will fall out of memory to make space for newer ones. This page will tell you exactly what fraction of each RDD is cached and the quantity of data cached in various storage media (disk, memory, etc.). It can be helpful to scan this page and understand whether important datasets are fitting into memory or not.

Executors: A list of executors present in the application

This page lists the active executors in the application along with some metrics around the processing and storage on each executor. One valuable use of this page is to confirm that your application has the amount of resources you were expecting. A good first step when debugging issues is to scan this page, since a misconfiguration resulting in fewer executors than expected can, for obvious reasons, affect performance. It can also be useful to look for executors with anomalous behaviors, such as a very large ratio of failed to successful tasks. An executor with a high failure rate could indicate a misconfiguration or failure on the physical host in question. Simply removing that host from the cluster can improve performance.

Another feature in the executors page is the ability to collect a stack trace from executors using the Thread Dump button (this feature was introduced in Spark 1.2). Visualizing the thread call stack of an executor can show exactly what code is executing at an instant in time. If an executor is sampled several times in a short time period with this feature, you can identify "hot spots," or expensive sections, in user code. This type of informal profiling can often detect inefficiencies in user code.

Environment: Debugging Spark's configuration

This page enumerates the set of active properties in the environment of your Spark application. The configuration here represents the "ground truth" of your application's configuration. It can be helpful if you are debugging which configuration flags are enabled, especially if you are using multiple configuration mechanisms. This page will also enumerate JARs and files you've added to your application, which can be useful when you're tracking down issues such as missing dependencies.

Driver and Executor Logs

In certain cases users can learn more information from Spark by inspecting the logs produced directly by the driver program and executors. Logs contain more detailed traces of anomalous events such as internal warnings or detailed exceptions from user code. This data can help when you're troubleshooting errors or unexpected behavior.

The exact location of Spark's logfiles depends on the deployment mode:

- In Spark's Standalone mode, application logs are directly displayed in the standalone master's web UI. They are stored by default in the *work/* directory of the Spark distribution on each worker.

- In Mesos, logs are stored in the *work/* directory of a Mesos slave, and accessible from the Mesos master UI.

- In YARN mode, the easiest way to collect logs is to use YARN's log collection tool (running `yarn logs -applicationId <app ID>`) to produce a report containing logs from your application. This will work only after an application has fully finished, since YARN must first aggregate these logs together. For viewing logs of a running application in YARN, you can click through the ResourceManager UI to the Nodes page, then browse to a particular node, and from there, a particular container. YARN will give you the logs associated with output produced by Spark in that container. This process is likely to become less roundabout in a future version of Spark with direct links to the relevant logs.

By default Spark outputs a healthy amount of logging information. It is also possible to customize the logging behavior to change the logging level or log output to non-standard locations. Spark's logging subsystem is based on log4j, a widely used Java logging library, and uses log4j's configuration format. An example log4j configuration file is bundled with Spark at *conf/log4j.properties.template*. To customize Spark's logging, first copy the example to a file called *log4j.properties*. You can then modify behavior such as the root logging level (the threshold level for logging output). By default, it is INFO. For less log output, it can be set to WARN or ERROR. Once you've tweaked the logging to match your desired level or format, you can add the *log4j.properties* file using the `--files` flag of `spark-submit`. If you have trouble setting the log level in this way, make sure that you are not including any JARs that themselves contain *log4j.properties* files with your application. Log4j works by scanning the classpath for the first properties file it finds, and will ignore your customization if it finds properties somewhere else first.

Key Performance Considerations

At this point you know a bit about how Spark works internally, how to follow the progress of a running Spark application, and where to go for metrics and log information. This section takes the next step and discusses common performance issues you might encounter in Spark applications along with tips for tuning your application to get the best possible performance. The first three subsections cover code-level changes you can make in order to improve performance, while the last subsection discusses tuning the cluster and environment in which Spark runs.

Level of Parallelism

The logical representation of an RDD is a single collection of objects. During physical execution, as discussed already a few times in this book, an RDD is divided into a set of partitions with each partition containing some subset of the total data. When Spark schedules and runs tasks, it creates a single task for data stored in one partition, and that task will require, by default, a single core in the cluster to execute. Out of the box, Spark will infer what it thinks is a good degree of parallelism for RDDs, and this is sufficient for many use cases. Input RDDs typically choose parallelism based on the underlying storage systems. For example, HDFS input RDDs have one partition for each block of the underlying HDFS file. RDDs that are derived from shuffling other RDDs will have parallelism set based on the size of their parent RDDs.

The degree of parallelism can affect performance in two ways. First, if there is too little parallelism, Spark might leave resources idle. For example, if your application has 1,000 cores allocated to it, and you are running a stage with only 30 tasks, you might be able to increase the level of parallelism to utilize more cores. If there is too much parallelism, small overheads associated with each partition can add up and become significant. A sign of this is that you have tasks that complete almost instantly—in a few milliseconds—or tasks that do not read or write any data.

Spark offers two ways to tune the degree of parallelism for operations. The first is that, during operations that shuffle data, you can always give a degree of parallelism for the produced RDD as a parameter. The second is that any existing RDD can be redistributed to have more or fewer partitions. The `repartition()` operator will randomly shuffle an RDD into the desired number of partitions. If you know you are shrinking the RDD, you can use the `coalesce()` operator; this is more efficient than `repartition()` since it avoids a shuffle operation. If you think you have too much or too little parallelism, it can help to redistribute your data with these operators.

As an example, let's say we are reading a large amount of data from S3, but then immediately performing a `filter()` operation that is likely to exclude all but a tiny fraction of the dataset. By default the RDD returned by `filter()` will have the same size as its parent and might have many empty or small partitions. In this case you can improve the application's performance by coalescing down to a smaller RDD, as shown in Example 8-11.

Example 8-11. Coalescing a large RDD in the PySpark shell

```
# Wildcard input that may match thousands of files
>>> input = sc.textFile("s3n://log-files/2014/*.log")
>>> input.getNumPartitions()
35154
# A filter that excludes almost all data
>>> lines = input.filter(lambda line: line.startswith("2014-10-17"))
>>> lines.getNumPartitions()
35154
# We coalesce the lines RDD before caching
>>> lines = lines.coalesce(5).cache()
>>> lines.getNumPartitions()
5
# Subsequent analysis can operate on the coalesced RDD...
>>> lines.count()
```

Serialization Format

When Spark is transferring data over the network or spilling data to disk, it needs to serialize objects into a binary format. This comes into play during shuffle operations, where potentially large amounts of data are transferred. By default Spark will use Java's built-in serializer. Spark also supports the use of Kryo (*https://github.com/ EsotericSoftware/kryo*), a third-party serialization library that improves on Java's serialization by offering both faster serialization times and a more compact binary representation, but cannot serialize all types of objects "out of the box." Almost all applications will benefit from shifting to Kryo for serialization.

To use Kryo serialization, you can set the `spark.serializer` setting to `org.apache.spark.serializer.KryoSerializer`. For best performance, you'll also want to register classes with Kryo that you plan to serialize, as shown in Example 8-12. Registering a class allows Kryo to avoid writing full class names with individual objects, a space savings that can add up over thousands or millions of serialized records. If you want to force this type of registration, you can set `spark.kryo.registrationRequired` to `true`, and Kryo will throw errors if it encounters an unregistered class.

Example 8-12. Using the Kryo serializer and registering classes

```
val conf = new SparkConf()
conf.set("spark.serializer", "org.apache.spark.serializer.KryoSerializer")
// Be strict about class registration
conf.set("spark.kryo.registrationRequired", "true")
conf.registerKryoClasses(Array(classOf[MyClass], classOf[MyOtherClass]))
```

Whether using Kryo or Java's serializer, you may encounter a `NotSerializableExcep tion` if your code refers to a class that does not extend Java's Serializable interface. It can be difficult to track down which class is causing the problem in this case, since many different classes can be referenced from user code. Many JVMs support a special option to help debug this situation: `"-Dsun.io.serialization.extended Debu gInfo=true"`. You can enable this option using the `--driver-java-options` and `-- executor-java-options` flags to `spark-submit`. Once you've found the class in question, the easiest solution is to simply modify it to implement Serializable. If you cannot modify the class in question you'll need to use more advanced workarounds, such as creating a subclass of the type in question that implements Java's Externalizable interface (*http://bit.ly/1yC15BJ*) or customizing the serialization behavior using Kryo.

Memory Management

Spark uses memory in different ways, so understanding and tuning Spark's use of memory can help optimize your application. Inside of each executor, memory is used for a few purposes:

RDD storage
When you call `persist()` or `cache()` on an RDD, its partitions will be stored in memory buffers. Spark will limit the amount of memory used when caching to a certain fraction of the JVM's overall heap, set by `spark.storage.memoryFrac tion`. If this limit is exceeded, older partitions will be dropped from memory.

Shuffle and aggregation buffers
When performing shuffle operations, Spark will create intermediate buffers for storing shuffle output data. These buffers are used to store intermediate results of aggregations in addition to buffering data that is going to be directly output as part of the shuffle. Spark will attempt to limit the total amount of memory used in shuffle-related buffers to `spark.shuffle.memoryFraction`.

User code
Spark executes arbitrary user code, so user functions can themselves require substantial memory. For instance, if a user application allocates large arrays or other objects, these will contend for overall memory usage. User code has access to

everything left in the JVM heap after the space for RDD storage and shuffle storage are allocated.

By default Spark will leave 60% of space for RDD storage, 20% for shuffle memory, and the remaining 20% for user programs. In some cases users can tune these options for better performance. If your user code is allocating very large objects, it might make sense to decrease the storage and shuffle regions to avoid running out of memory.

In addition to tweaking memory regions, you can improve certain elements of Spark's default caching behavior for some workloads. Spark's default cache() operation persists memory using the MEMORY_ONLY storage level. This means that if there is not enough space to cache new RDD partitions, old ones will simply be deleted and, if they are needed again, they will be recomputed. It is sometimes better to call per sist() with the MEMORY_AND_DISK storage level, which instead drops RDD partitions to disk and simply reads them back to memory from a local store if they are needed again. This can be much cheaper than recomputing blocks and can lead to more predictable performance. This is particularly useful if your RDD partitions are very expensive to recompute (for instance, if you are reading data from a database). The full list of possible storage levels is given in Table 3-6.

A second improvement on the default caching policy is to cache serialized objects instead of raw Java objects, which you can accomplish using the MEMORY_ONLY_SER or MEMORY_AND_DISK_SER storage levels. Caching serialized objects will slightly slow down the cache operation due to the cost of serializing objects, but it can substantially reduce time spent on garbage collection in the JVM, since many individual records can be stored as a single serialized buffer. This is because the cost of garbage collection scales with the number of objects on the heap, not the number of bytes of data, and this caching method will take many objects and serialize them into a single giant buffer. Consider this option if you are caching large amounts of data (e.g., gigabytes) as objects and/or seeing long garbage collection pauses. Such pauses would be visible in the application UI under the GC Time column for each task.

Hardware Provisioning

The hardware resources you give to Spark will have a significant effect on the completion time of your application. The main parameters that affect cluster sizing are the amount of memory given to each executor, the number of cores for each executor, the total number of executors, and the number of local disks to use for scratch data.

In all deployment modes, executor memory is set with spark.executor.memory or the --executor-memory flag to spark-submit. The options for number and cores of executors differ depending on deployment mode. In YARN you can set spark.execu tor.cores or the --executor-cores flag and the --num-executors flag to determine the total count. In Mesos and Standalone mode, Spark will greedily acquire as many cores and executors as are offered by the scheduler. However, both Mesos and Standalone mode support setting spark.cores.max to limit the total number of cores across all executors for an application. Local disks are used for scratch storage during shuffle operations.

Broadly speaking, Spark applications will benefit from having more memory and cores. Spark's architecture allows for linear scaling; adding twice the resources will often make your application run twice as fast. An additional consideration when sizing a Spark application is whether you plan to cache intermediate datasets as part of your workload. If you do plan to use caching, the more of your cached data can fit in memory, the better the performance will be. The Spark storage UI will give details about what fraction of your cached data is in memory. One approach is to start by caching a subset of your data on a smaller cluster and extrapolate the total memory you will need to fit larger amounts of the data in memory.

In addition to memory and cores, Spark uses local disk volumes to store intermediate data required during shuffle operations along with RDD partitions that are spilled to disk. Using a larger number of local disks can help accelerate the performance of Spark applications. In YARN mode, the configuration for local disks is read directly from YARN, which provides its own mechanism for specifying scratch storage directories. In Standalone mode, you can set the SPARK_LOCAL_DIRS environment variable in spark-env.sh when deploying the Standalone cluster and Spark applications will inherit this config when they are launched. In Mesos mode, or if you are running in another mode and want to override the cluster's default storage locations, you can set the spark.local.dir option. In all cases you specify the local directories using a single comma-separated list. It is common to have one local directory for each disk volume available to Spark. Writes will be evenly striped across all local directories provided. Larger numbers of disks will provide higher overall throughput.

One caveat to the "more is better" guideline is when sizing memory for executors. Using very large heap sizes can cause garbage collection pauses to hurt the throughput of a Spark job. It can sometimes be beneficial to request smaller executors (say, 64 GB or less) to mitigate this issue. Mesos and YARN can, out of the box, support packing multiple, smaller executors onto the same physical host, so requesting smaller executors doesn't mean your application will have fewer overall resources. In Spark's Standalone mode, you need to launch multiple workers (determined using SPARK_WORKER_INSTANCES) for a single application to run more than one executor on a host. This limitation will likely be removed in a later version of Spark. In addition to using smaller executors, storing data in serialized form (see "Memory Management" on page 157) can also help alleviate garbage collection.

Conclusion

If you've made it through this chapter, you are well poised to tackle a production Spark use case. We covered Spark's configuration management, instrumentation and metrics in Spark's UI, and common tuning techniques for production workloads. To dive deeper into tuning Spark, visit the tuning guide (*http://spark.apache.org/docs/ latest/tuning.html*) in the official documentation.

## CHAPTER 9

Spark SQL

This chapter introduces Spark SQL, Spark's interface for working with structured and semistructured data. Structured data is any data that has a *schema*—that is, a known set of fields for each record. When you have this type of data, Spark SQL makes it both easier and more efficient to load and query. In particular, Spark SQL provides three main capabilities (illustrated in Figure 9-1):

1. It provides a DataFrame abstraction in Python, Java, and Scala that simplifies working with structured datasets. DataFrames are similar to tables in a relational database.

2. It can read and write data in a variety of structured formats (e.g., JSON, Hive Tables, and Parquet).

3. It lets you query the data using SQL, both inside a Spark program and from external tools that connect to Spark SQL through standard database connectors (JDBC/ODBC), such as business intelligence tools like Tableau.

Under the hood, Spark SQL is based on an extension of the RDD model called a DataFrame. A DataFrame contains an RDD of Row objects, each representing a record. A DataFrame also knows the schema (i.e., data fields) of its rows. DataFrames store data in a more efficient manner than native RDDs, taking advantage of their schema. In addition, they provide new operations not available on RDDs, such as the ability to run SQL queries. DataFrames can be created from external data sources, from the results of queries, or from regular RDDs.

DataFrames are an evolution of SchemaRDDs available in earlier (1.0-1.2) versions of Spark. For users upgrading from 1.0-1.2 to 1.3 there is a type alias in Scala between SchemaRDD and DataFrame. While a type alias does exist, DataFrames no longer inherit from the RDD base class so they have a different API.

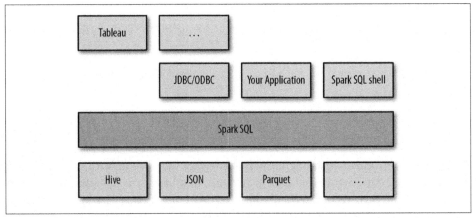

Figure 9-1. Spark SQL usage

In this chapter, we'll start by showing how to use DataFrames inside regular Spark programs, to load and query structured data. We'll then describe the Spark SQL JDBC server, which lets you run Spark SQL on a shared server and connect either SQL shells or visualization tools like Tableau to it. Finally, we'll discuss some advanced features. Spark SQL is a newer component of Spark and it will evolve substantially in future versions, so consult the most recent documentation for the latest information on Spark SQL and DataFrames.

As we move through this chapter, we'll use Spark SQL to explore a JSON file with tweets. If you don't have any tweets on hand, you can use the Databricks reference application (*http://bit.ly/1yC32hs*) to download some, or you can use *files/test-weet.json* in the book's Git repo.

Linking with Spark SQL

As with the other Spark libraries, including Spark SQL in our application requires some additional dependencies. This allows Spark Core to be built without depending on a large number of additional packages.

Spark SQL can be built with or without support for Apache Hive, the Hadoop SQL engine. Spark SQL with Hive support allows us to access Hive tables, UDFs (user-defined functions), SerDes (serialization and deserialization formats), and the Hive query language (HiveQL). It is important to note that including the Hive libraries does not require an existing Hive installation. In general, it is best to build Spark SQL with Hive support to access these features. If you download Spark in binary form, it should already be built with Hive support. If you are building Spark from source, you should run `sbt/sbt -Phive assembly`.

If you have dependency conflicts with Hive that you cannot solve through exclusions or shading, you can also build and link to Spark SQL without Hive. In that case you link to a separate Maven artifact.

In Java and Scala, the Maven coordinates to link to Spark SQL with Hive are shown in Example 9-1.

Example 9-1. Maven coordinates for Spark SQL with Hive support

```
groupId = org.apache.spark
artifactId = spark-hive_2.10
version = 1.3.0
```

If you can't include the Hive dependencies, use the artifact ID `spark-sql_2.10` instead of `spark-hive_2.10`.

As with the other Spark libraries, in Python no changes to your build are required.

When programming against Spark SQL we have two entry points depending on whether we need Hive support. The recommended entry point is the `HiveContext` to provide access to HiveQL and other Hive-dependent functionality. The more basic `SQLContext` provides a subset of the Spark SQL support that does not depend on Hive. The separation exists for users who might have conflicts with including all of the Hive dependencies. Using a `HiveContext` does not require an existing Hive setup.

HiveQL is the recommended query language for working with Spark SQL. Many resources have been written on HiveQL, including *Programming Hive* and the online Hive Language Manual (*http://bit.ly/1yC3goM*). In Spark 1.0 and 1.1, Spark SQL is based on Hive 0.12, whereas in Spark 1.2 and 1.3 it also supports Hive 0.13. If you already know standard SQL, using HiveQL should feel very similar.

 Spark SQL is a newer and fast moving component of Spark. The set of compatible Hive versions may change in the future, so consult the most recent documentation for more details.

Finally, to connect Spark SQL to an existing Hive installation, you must copy your *hive-site.xml* file to Spark's configuration directory (*$SPARK_HOME/conf*). If you don't have an existing Hive installation, Spark SQL will still run.

Note that if you don't have an existing Hive installation, Spark SQL will create its own Hive metastore (metadata DB) in your program's work directory, called `meta store_db`. In addition, if you attempt to create tables using HiveQL's `CREATE TABLE` statement (not `CREATE EXTERNAL TABLE`), they will be placed in the */user/hive/warehouse* directory on your default filesystem (either your local filesystem, or HDFS if you have a *hdfs-site.xml* on your classpath).

Using Spark SQL in Applications

The most powerful way to use Spark SQL is inside a Spark application. This gives us the power to easily load data and query it with SQL while simultaneously combining it with "regular" program code in Python, Java, or Scala.

To use Spark SQL this way, we construct a HiveContext (or SQLContext for those wanting a stripped-down version) based on our SparkContext. This context provides additional functions for querying and interacting with Spark SQL data. Using the HiveContext, we can build DataFrames, which represent our structure data, and operate on them with SQL or with normal RDD operations like `map()`.

Initializing Spark SQL

To get started with Spark SQL we need to add a few imports to our programs, as shown in Example 9-2.

Example 9-2. Scala SQL imports

```
// Import Spark SQL
import org.apache.spark.sql.hive.HiveContext
// Or if you can't have the hive dependencies
import org.apache.spark.sql.SQLContext
```

Scala users should note that we don't import `HiveContext._`, like we do with the SparkContext, to get access to implicits. These implicits are used to convert RDDs with the required type information into Spark SQL's specialized RDDs for querying. Instead, once we have constructed an instance of the `HiveContext` we can then import the implicits by adding the code shown in Example 9-3. The imports for Java and Python are shown in Examples 9-4 and 9-5, respectively.

Example 9-3. Scala SQL implicits

```
// Create a Spark SQL HiveContext
val hiveCtx = ...
// Import the implicit conversions
import hiveCtx.implicits._
```

Prior versions of Spark SQL had the implicits directly in the hiveCtx/sqlCtx.

Example 9-4. Java SQL imports

```
// Import Spark SQL
import org.apache.spark.sql.hive.HiveContext;
// Or if you can't have the hive dependencies
import org.apache.spark.sql.SQLContext;
// Import the JavaSchemaRDD
import org.apache.spark.sql.DataFrame;
import org.apache.spark.sql.Row;
```

Example 9-5. Python SQL imports

```
# Import Spark SQL
from pyspark.sql import HiveContext, Row
# Or if you can't include the hive requirements
from pyspark.sql import SQLContext, Row
```

Once we've added our imports, we need to create a HiveContext, or a SQLContext if we cannot bring in the Hive dependencies (see Examples 9-6 through 9-8). Both of these classes take a SparkContext to run on.

Example 9-6. Constructing a SQL context in Scala

```
val sc = new SparkContext(...)
val hiveCtx = new HiveContext(sc)
```

Example 9-7. Constructing a SQL context in Java

```
JavaSparkContext ctx = new JavaSparkContext(...);
HiveContext sqlCtx = new HiveContext(ctx);
```

Example 9-8. Constructing a SQL context in Python

```
sc = SparkContext(...)
hiveCtx = HiveContext(sc)
```

Now that we have a HiveContext or SQLContext, we are ready to load our data and query it.

Basic Query Example

To make a query against a table, we call the `sql()` method on the HiveContext or SQLContext. The first thing we need to do is tell Spark SQL about some data to query. In this case we will load some Twitter data from JSON, and give it a name by registering it as a "temporary table" so we can query it with SQL. (We will go over more details on loading in "Loading and Saving Data" on page 170.) Then we can select the top tweets by `retweetCount`. See Examples 9-9 through 9-11.

Example 9-9. Loading and quering tweets in Scala

```
val input = hiveCtx.jsonFile(inputFile)
// Register the input schema RDD
input.registerTempTable("tweets")
// Select tweets based on the retweetCount
val topTweets = hiveCtx.sql("SELECT text, retweetCount FROM
  tweets ORDER BY retweetCount LIMIT 10")
```

Example 9-10. Loading and quering tweets in Java

```
DataFrame input = hiveCtx.jsonFile(inputFile);
// Register the input schema RDD
input.registerTempTable("tweets");
// Select tweets based on the retweetCount
DataFrame topTweets = hiveCtx.sql("SELECT text, retweetCount FROM
  tweets ORDER BY retweetCount LIMIT 10");
```

Example 9-11. Loading and quering tweets in Python

```
input = hiveCtx.jsonFile(inputFile)
# Register the input DataFrame
input.registerTempTable("tweets")
# Select tweets based on the retweetCount
topTweets = hiveCtx.sql("""SELECT text, retweetCount  FROM
  tweets ORDER BY retweetCount LIMIT 10""")
```

 If you have an existing Hive installation, and have copied your *hive-site.xml* file to *$SPARK_HOME/conf*, you can also just run `hiveCtx.sql` to query your existing Hive tables.

DataFrames

Both loading data and executing queries return DataFrames. DataFrames are similar to tables in a traditional database. Under the hood, a DataFrame contains an RDD composed of Row objects with additional schema information of the types in each column. Row objects are just wrappers around arrays of basic types (e.g., integers and strings), and we'll cover them in more detail in the next section.

In earlier versions of Spark, the precursor to DataFrames were called SchemaRDDs. This renaming happened in version 1.3. Unlike DataFrames SchemaRDDs extend the RDD class so map/ filter operations are available directly on the SchemaRDD.

DataFrames also provide a way to access the RDD (by calling rdd()), so you can operate on them using existing RDD transformations like map() and filter(). However, they provide several additional capabilities. Most importantly, you can register any DataFrame as a temporary table to query it via *HiveContext.sql* or *SQLContext.sql*. You do so using the DataFrame's registerTempTable() method, as in Examples 9-9 through 9-11.

Temp tables are local to the HiveContext or SQLContext being used, and go away when your application exits.

DataFrames also provide a number of transformations that operate directly on the DataFrame, without having to register as a temporary table or manipulate the underlying RDD. Similar to collect() on RDDs, show() brings the DataFrame back to the local machine and displays the results. The other functions behave much like their SQL counterparts, such as df.select(columns). For more details on this API, you can consult the API docs for the DataFrame class of the language you are working in (Python (*http://bit.ly/1KnJjVh*), Java (*http://bit.ly/1HOiYkU*), or Scala (*http://bit.ly/1A5LGpn*)).

Table 9-1. Basic DataFrame operations on an DataFrame with Name, Age {Row("Bear", None), Row("Databricks", 1)}

Function name	Purpose	Example
show()	Show the contents of the DataFrame	df.show()
select()	Select the specified fields/ functions	df.select("name", df("age")+1)
filter()	Select only the rows meeting the criteria	df.filter(df("age") > 19)
groupBy()	Group together on a column, needs to be followed by an aggergation like min(), max(), mean() or agg().	df.groupBy(df("name")).min()

DataFrames can store several basic types, as well as structures and arrays of these types. They use the HiveQL syntax (*http://bit.ly/1yC5nJ7*) for type definitions. Table 9-2 shows the supported types.

Table 9-2. Types stored by DataFrames

Spark SQL/HiveQL type	Scala type	Java type	Python
TINYINT	Byte	Byte/byte	int/Long (in range of −128 to 127)
SMALLINT	Short	Short/short	int/Long (in range of −32768 to 32767)
INT	Int	Int/int	int or long
BIGINT	Long	Long/long	long
FLOAT	Float	Float/float	float
DOUBLE	Double	Double/double	float
DECIMAL	scala.math.BigDecimal	java.math.BigDecimal	decimal.Decimal
STRING	String	String	string
BINARY	Array[Byte]	byte[]	bytearray
BOOLEAN	Boolean	Boolean/boolean	bool
TIMESTAMP	java.sql.Timestamp	java.sql.Timestamp	datetime.datetime
ARRAY<DATA_TYPE>	Seq	List	list, tuple, or array
MAP<KEY_TYPE, VAL_TYPE>	Map	Map	dict
STRUCT<COL1: COL1_TYPE, ...>	Row	Row	Row

The last type, structures, is simply represented as other Rows in Spark SQL. All of these types can also be nested within each other; for example, you can have arrays of structs, or maps that contain structs.

Converting between DataFrames and RDDs

Row objects represent records inside DataFrames, and are simply fixed-length arrays of fields. In Scala/Java, Row objects have a number of getter functions to obtain the value of each field given its index. The standard getter, get (or apply in Scala), takes a column number and returns an Object type (or Any in Scala) that we are responsible for casting to the correct type. For Boolean, Byte, Double, Float, Int, Long, Short, and String, there is a getType() method, which returns that type. For example, get String(0) would return field 0 as a string, as you can see in Examples 9-12 and 9-13.

Example 9-12. Accessing the text column (also first column) in the topTweets DataFrame in Scala

```
val topTweetText = topTweets.rdd().map(row => row.getString(0))
```

Example 9-13. Accessing the text column (also first column) in the topTweets DataFrame in Java

```
JavaRDD<String> topTweetText = topTweets.toJavaRDD().map(new Function<Row, String>() {
    public String call(Row row) {
      return row.getString(0);
    }});
```

In Python, Row objects are a bit different since we don't have explicit typing. We just access the *i*th element using row[i]. In addition, Python Rows support named access to their fields, of the form row.*column_name*, as you can see in Example 9-14. If you are uncertain of what the column names are, we illustrate printing the schema in "JSON" on page 173.

Example 9-14. Accessing the text column in the topTweets DataFrame in Python

```
topTweetText = topTweets.rdd().map(lambda row: row.text)
```

Once we've performed our transformations, we can convert the our RDD by to a DataFrame which we cover in "From RDDs" on page 175.

Caching

Caching in Spark SQL works a bit differently. Since we know the types of each column, Spark is able to more efficiently store the data. To make sure that we cache using the memory efficient representation, rather than the full objects, we should use the special hiveCtx.cacheTable("tableName") method. When caching a table Spark SQL represents the data in an in-memory columnar format. This cached table will remain in memory only for the life of our driver program, so if it exits we will need to recache our data. As with RDDs, we cache tables when we expect to run multiple tasks or queries against the same data.

 In Spark 1.2+, the regular cache() method on SchemaRDDs and DataFrames also results in a cacheTable().

You can also cache tables using HiveQL/SQL statements. To cache or uncache a table simply run CACHE TABLE *tableName* or UNCACHE TABLE *tableName*. This is most commonly used with command-line clients to the JDBC server.

Cached DataFrames show up in the Spark application UI much like other RDDs, as shown in Figure 9-2.

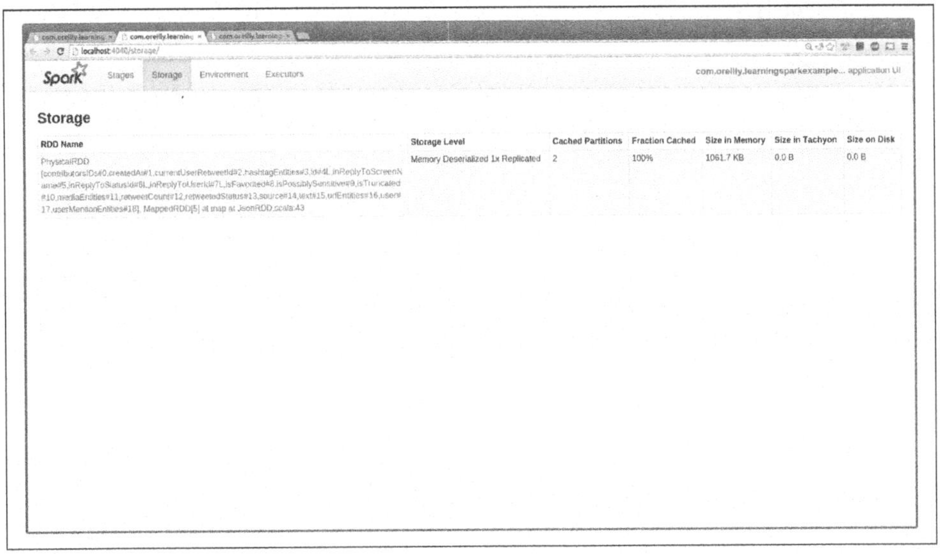

Figure 9-2. Spark SQL UI of DataFrame

We discuss more about how Spark SQL caching performance works in "Spark SQL Performance" on page 181.

Loading and Saving Data

Spark SQL supports a number of structured data sources out of the box, letting you get Row objects from them without any complicated loading process. These sources include Hive tables, JSON, and Parquet files. In addition, if you query these sources using SQL and select only a subset of the fields, Spark SQL can smartly scan only the subset of the data for those fields, instead of scanning all the data like a naive `Spark Context.hadoopFile` might.

Spark SQL also has a DataSource API which allows others to integrate with Spark SQL. Some notable implementations of the DataSource API include Avro, Apache HBase, Elasticsearch, Cassandra, and more. Many of these can be found on the community index of packages for Spark, Spark Packages at *http://www.spark-packages.org*.

Apart from these data sources, you can also convert regular RDDs in your program to DataFrames by assigning them a schema. This makes it easy to write SQL queries even when your underlying data is Python or Java objects. Often, SQL queries are more concise when you're computing many quantities at once (e.g., if you wanted to compute the average age, max age, and count of distinct user IDs in one pass). In addition, you can easily join these RDDs with DataFrames from any other Spark SQL data source. In this section, we'll cover the external sources as well as this way of using RDDs.

Apache Hive

When loading data from Hive, Spark SQL supports any Hive-supported storage formats (SerDes), including text files, RCFiles, ORC, Parquet, Avro, and Protocol Buffers.

To connect Spark SQL to an existing Hive installation, you need to provide a Hive configuration. You do so by copying your *hive-site.xml* file to Spark's *./conf/* directory. If you just want to explore, a local Hive metastore will be used if no *hive-site.xml* is set, and we can easily load data into a Hive table to query later on.

Examples 9-15 through 9-17 illustrate querying a Hive table. Our example Hive table has two columns, key (which is an integer) and value (which is a string). We show how to create such a table later in this chapter.

Example 9-15. Hive load in Python

```
from pyspark.sql import HiveContext

hiveCtx = HiveContext(sc)
rows = hiveCtx.sql("SELECT key, value FROM mytable")
keys = rows.map(lambda row: row[0])
```

Example 9-16. Hive load in Scala

```
import org.apache.spark.sql.hive.HiveContext

val hiveCtx = new HiveContext(sc)
```

```
val rows = hiveCtx.sql("SELECT key, value FROM mytable")
val keys = rows.map(row => row.getInt(0))
```

Example 9-17. Hive load in Java

```java
import org.apache.spark.sql.hive.HiveContext;
import org.apache.spark.sql.Row;
import org.apache.spark.sql.DataFrame;

HiveContext hiveCtx = new HiveContext(sc);
DataFrame rows = hiveCtx.sql("SELECT key, value FROM mytable");
JavaRDD<Integer> keys = rdd.toJavaRDD().map(new Function<Row, Integer>() {
  public Integer call(Row row) { return row.getInt(0); }
});
```

DataFrames can also be written back to Hive through the `saveAsTable("tblName")` function. This creates a persistent table.

Data Sources/Parquet

To support data sources beyond Hive, Spark SQL has a pluggable data source API. Data source implementations can provide automatic mapping from the schema and type system of different storage platforms to Spark SQL's data model. Spark includes a handful of data source implementations, but the vast majority are hosted by third-party repositories. To find third-party data source integrations, visit Spark Packages at *http://www.spark-packages.org*.

One built-in data source is support for Parquet (*http://parquet.incubator.apache.org*), a popular column-oriented storage format that can store records with nested fields efficiently. It is often used with tools in the Hadoop ecosystem, and it supports all of the data types in Spark SQL. Spark SQL provides methods for reading data directly to and from Parquet files.

In earlier versions of Spark, to load data, you can use `HiveCon text.parquetFile` or `SQLContext.parquetFile`.

Example 9-18. Parquet load in Python

```python
# Load some data in from a Parquet file with field's name and favouriteAnimal
rows = hiveCtx.load(parquetFile, "parquet")
names = rows.map(lambda row: row.name)
print "Everyone"
print names.collect()
```

You can also register a Parquet file as a Spark SQL temp table and write queries against it. Example 9-19 continues from Example 9-18 where we loaded the data.

Example 9-19. Parquet query in Python

```
# Find the panda lovers
tbl = rows.registerTempTable("people")
pandaFriends = hiveCtx.sql("SELECT name FROM people WHERE favouriteAnimal = \"panda\"")
print "Panda friends"
print pandaFriends.map(lambda row: row.name).collect()
```

In older versions of Spark SQL you can save the contents of a Data-Frame to Parquet with saveAsParquetFile().

Example 9-20. Parquet file save in Python

```
pandaFriends.save("hdfs://...", "parquet")
```

If we wanted to use Apache Avro instead of Parquet, we would only need to include the Spark Avro package (*https://github.com/databricks/spark-avro*) with our project and change "parquet" to "com.databricks.spark.avro" in our previous examples.

JSON

If you have a JSON file with records fitting the same schema, Spark SQL can infer the schema by scanning the file and let you access fields by name (Example 9-21). If you have ever found yourself staring at a huge directory of JSON records, Spark SQL's schema inference is a very effective way to start working with the data without writing any special loading code.

To load our JSON data, all we need to do is call the jsonFile() function on our hiveCtx, as shown in Examples 9-22 through 9-24. If you are curious about what the inferred schema for your data is, you can call printSchema on the resulting Data-Frame (Example 9-25).

Example 9-21. Input records

```
{"name": "Holden"}
{"name":"Sparky The Bear", "lovesPandas":true, "knows":{"friends": ["holden"]}}
```

Example 9-22. Loading JSON with Spark SQL in Python

```
input = hiveCtx.jsonFile(inputFile)
```

Example 9-23. Loading JSON with Spark SQL in Scala

```scala
val input = hiveCtx.jsonFile(inputFile)
```

Example 9-24. Loading JSON with Spark SQL in Java

```java
DataFrame input = hiveCtx.jsonFile(jsonFile);
```

Example 9-25. Resulting schema from printSchema()

```
root
 |-- knows: struct (nullable = true)
 |    |-- friends: array (nullable = true)
 |    |    |-- element: string (containsNull = false)
 |-- lovesPandas: boolean (nullable = true)
 |-- name: string (nullable = true)
```

You can also look at the schema generated for some tweets, as in Example 9-26.

Example 9-26. Partial schema of tweets

```
root
 |-- contributorsIDs: array (nullable = true)
 |    |-- element: string (containsNull = false)
 |-- createdAt: string (nullable = true)
 |-- currentUserRetweetId: integer (nullable = true)
 |-- hashtagEntities: array (nullable = true)
 |    |-- element: struct (containsNull = false)
 |    |    |-- end: integer (nullable = true)
 |    |    |-- start: integer (nullable = true)
 |    |    |-- text: string (nullable = true)
 |-- id: long (nullable = true)
 |-- inReplyToScreenName: string (nullable = true)
 |-- inReplyToStatusId: long (nullable = true)
 |-- inReplyToUserId: long (nullable = true)
 |-- isFavorited: boolean (nullable = true)
 |-- isPossiblySensitive: boolean (nullable = true)
 |-- isTruncated: boolean (nullable = true)
 |-- mediaEntities: array (nullable = true)
 |    |-- element: struct (containsNull = false)
 |    |    |-- displayURL: string (nullable = true)
 |    |    |-- end: integer (nullable = true)
 |    |    |-- expandedURL: string (nullable = true)
 |    |    |-- id: long (nullable = true)
 |    |    |-- mediaURL: string (nullable = true)
 |    |    |-- mediaURLHttps: string (nullable = true)
 |    |    |-- sizes: struct (nullable = true)
 |    |    |    |-- 0: struct (nullable = true)
 |    |    |    |    |-- height: integer (nullable = true)
 |    |    |    |    |-- resize: integer (nullable = true)
 |    |    |    |    |-- width: integer (nullable = true)
```

```
|   |   |   |-- 1: struct (nullable = true)
|   |   |   |   |-- height: integer (nullable = true)
|   |   |   |   |-- resize: integer (nullable = true)
|   |   |   |   |-- width: integer (nullable = true)
|   |   |   |-- 2: struct (nullable = true)
|   |   |   |   |-- height: integer (nullable = true)
|   |   |   |   |-- resize: integer (nullable = true)
|   |   |   |   |-- width: integer (nullable = true)
|   |   |   |-- 3: struct (nullable = true)
|   |   |   |   |-- height: integer (nullable = true)
|   |   |   |   |-- resize: integer (nullable = true)
|   |   |   |   |-- width: integer (nullable = true)
|   |   |-- start: integer (nullable = true)
|   |   |-- type: string (nullable = true)
|   |   |-- url: string (nullable = true)
|-- retweetCount: integer (nullable = true)
...
```

As you look at these schemas, a natural question is how to access nested fields and array fields. Both in Python and when we register a table, we can access nested elements by using the . for each level of nesting (e.g., *toplevel.nextlevel*). You can access array elements in SQL by specifying the index with [*element*], as shown in Example 9-27.

Example 9-27. SQL query nested and array elements

```
select hashtagEntities[0].text from tweets LIMIT 1;
```

From RDDs

In addition to loading data, we can also create a DataFrame from an RDD. In Scala, RDDs with case classes are implicitly converted into DataFrames.

For Python we create an RDD of Row objects and then call inferSchema(), as shown in Example 9-28.

Example 9-28. Creating a DataFrame using Row and named tuple in Python

```
happyPeopleRDD = sc.parallelize([Row(name="holden", favouriteBeverage="coffee")])
happyPeopleDataFrame = hiveCtx.inferSchema(happyPeopleRDD)
happyPeopleDataFrame.registerTempTable("happy_people")
```

With Scala, our old friend implicit conversions handles the inference of the schema for us (Example 9-29).

Example 9-29. Creating a DataFrame from case class in Scala

```
case class HappyPerson(handle: String, favouriteBeverage: String)
...
// Create a person and turn it into a Schema RDD
val happyPeopleRDD = sc.parallelize(List(HappyPerson("holden", "coffee")))
// Note: there is an implicit conversion
// that is equivalent to sqlCtx.createDataFrame(happyPeopleRDD)
happyPeopleRDD.registerTempTable("happy_people")
```

With Java, we can turn an RDD consisting of a serializable class with public getters and setters into a schema RDD by calling `applySchema()`, as Example 9-30 shows.

Example 9-30. Creating a DataFrame from a JavaBean in Java

```
class HappyPerson implements Serializable {
  private String name;
  private String favouriteBeverage;
  public HappyPerson() {}
  public HappyPerson(String n, String b) {
    name = n; favouriteBeverage = b;
  }
  public String getName() { return name; }
  public void setName(String n) { name = n; }
  public String getFavouriteBeverage() { return favouriteBeverage; }
  public void setFavouriteBeverage(String b) { favouriteBeverage = b; }
};
...
ArrayList<HappyPerson> peopleList = new ArrayList<HappyPerson>();
peopleList.add(new HappyPerson("holden", "coffee"));
JavaRDD<HappyPerson> happyPeopleRDD = sc.parallelize(peopleList);
DataFrame happyPeopleDataFrame = hiveCtx.createDataFrame(happyPeopleRDD,
  HappyPerson.class);
happyPeopleDataFrame.registerTempTable("happy_people");
```

JDBC/ODBC Server

Spark SQL also provides JDBC connectivity, which is useful for connecting business intelligence (BI) tools to a Spark cluster and for sharing a cluster across multiple users. The JDBC server runs as a standalone Spark driver program that can be shared by multiple clients. Any client can cache tables in memory, query them, and so on, and the cluster resources and cached data will be shared among all of them.

Spark SQL's JDBC server corresponds to the HiveServer2 in Hive. It is also known as the "Thrift server" since it uses the Thrift communication protocol. Note that the JDBC server requires Spark be built with Hive support.

The server can be launched with `sbin/start-thriftserver.sh` in your Spark directory (Example 9-31). This script takes many of the same options as `spark-submit`. By default it listens on `localhost:10000`, but we can change these with either environment variables (`HIVE_SERVER2_THRIFT_PORT` and `HIVE_SERVER2_THRIFT_BIND_HOST`), or with Hive configuration properties (`hive.server2.thrift.port` and `hive.server2.thrift.bind.host`). You can also specify Hive properties on the command line with `--hiveconf property=value`.

Example 9-31. Launching the JDBC server

```
./sbin/start-thriftserver.sh --master sparkMaster
```

Spark also ships with the Beeline (*http://bit.ly/1BQmMvF*) client program we can use to connect to our JDBC server, as shown in Example 9-32 and Figure 9-3. This is a simple SQL shell that lets us run commands on the server.

Example 9-32. Connecting to the JDBC server with Beeline

```
holden@hmbp2:~/repos/spark$ ./bin/beeline -u jdbc:hive2://localhost:10000
Spark assembly has been built with Hive, including Datanucleus jars on classpath
scan complete in 1ms
Connecting to jdbc:hive2://localhost:10000
Connected to: Spark SQL (version 1.2.0-SNAPSHOT)
Driver: spark-assembly (version 1.2.0-SNAPSHOT)
Transaction isolation: TRANSACTION_REPEATABLE_READ
Beeline version 1.2.0-SNAPSHOT by Apache Hive
0: jdbc:hive2://localhost:10000> show tables;
+----------+
| result   |
+----------+
| pokes    |
+----------+
1 row selected (1.182 seconds)
0: jdbc:hive2://localhost:10000>
```

When we start the JDBC server, it goes into the background and directs all of its output to a logfile. If you encounter issues with queries you run against the JDBC server, check out the logs for more complete error messages.

Many external tools can also connect to Spark SQL via its ODBC driver. The Spark SQL ODBC driver is produced by Simba (*http://www.simba.com*) and can be downloaded from various Spark vendors (e.g., Databricks Cloud, Datastax, and MapR). It is commonly used by business intelligence (BI) tools such as Microstrategy or Tableau; check with your tool about how it can connect to Spark SQL. In addition, most BI tools that have connectors to Hive can also connect to Spark SQL using their existing Hive connector, because it uses the same query language and server.

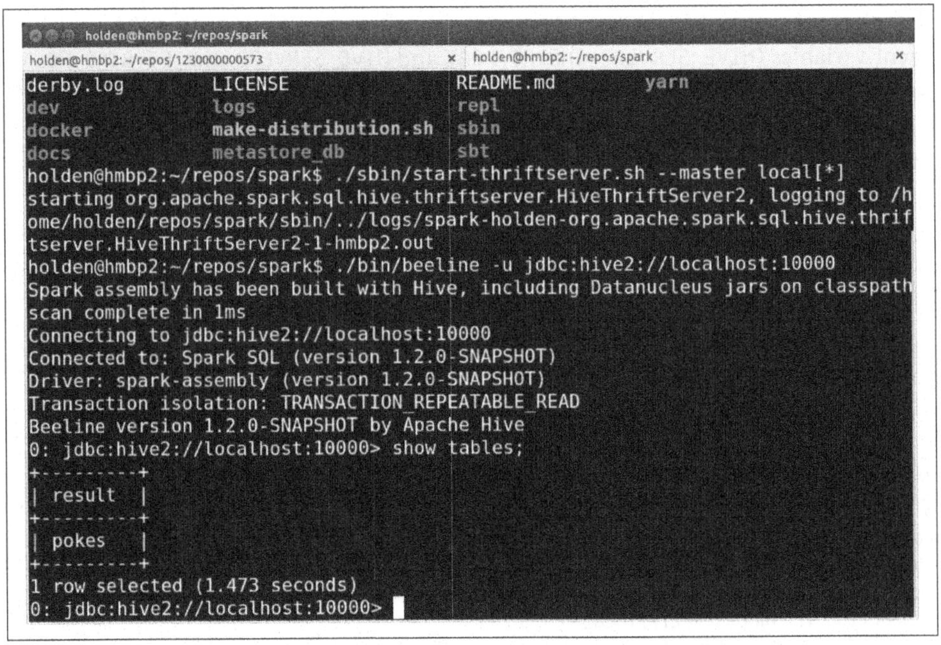

Figure 9-3. Launching the JDBC server and connecting a Beeline client

Working with Beeline

Within the Beeline client, you can use standard HiveQL commands to create, list, and query tables. You can find the full details of HiveQL in the Hive Language Manual (*http://bit.ly/1yC3goM*), but here, we show a few common operations.

First, to create a table from local data, we can use the CREATE TABLE command, followed by LOAD DATA. Hive easily supports loading text files with a fixed delimiter such as CSVs, as well as other files, as shown in Example 9-33.

Example 9-33. Load table

```
> CREATE TABLE IF NOT EXISTS mytable (key INT, value STRING)
  ROW FORMAT DELIMITED FIELDS TERMINATED BY ',';
> LOAD DATA LOCAL INPATH 'learning-spark-examples/files/int_string.csv'
  INTO TABLE mytable;
```

To list tables, you can use the SHOW TABLES statement (Example 9-34). You can also describe each table's schema with DESCRIBE *tableName*.

Example 9-34. Show tables

```
> SHOW TABLES;
mytable
Time taken: 0.052 seconds
```

If you'd like to cache tables, use CACHE TABLE *tableName*. You can later uncache tables with UNCACHE TABLE *tableName*. Note that the cached tables are shared across all clients of this JDBC server, as explained earlier.

Finally, Beeline makes it easy to view query plans. You can run EXPLAIN on a given query to see what the execution plan will be, as shown in Example 9-35.

Example 9-35. Spark SQL shell EXPLAIN

```
spark-sql> EXPLAIN SELECT * FROM mytable where key = 1;
== Physical Plan ==
Filter (key#16 = 1)
 HiveTableScan [key#16,value#17], (MetastoreRelation default, mytable, None), None
Time taken: 0.551 seconds
```

In this specific query plan, Spark SQL is applying a filter on top of a HiveTableScan.

From here you can also write SQL to query the data. The Beeline shell is great for quick data exploration on cached tables shared by multiple users.

Long-Lived Tables and Queries

One of the advantages of using Spark SQL's JDBC server is we can share cached tables between multiple programs. This is possible since the JDBC Thrift server is a single driver program. To do this, you only need to register the table and then run the CACHE command on it, as shown in the previous section.

Standalone Spark SQL Shell

Apart from its JDBC server, Spark SQL also supports a simple shell you can use as a single process, available through *./bin/spark-sql*. This shell connects to the Hive metastore you have set in *conf/hive-site.xml*, if one exists, or creates one locally. It is most useful for local development; in a shared cluster, you should instead use the JDBC server and have users connect with beeline.

User-Defined Functions

User-defined functions, or UDFs, allow you to register custom functions in Python, Java, and Scala to call within SQL. They are a very popular way to expose advanced functionality to SQL users in an organization, so that these users can call into it without writing code. Spark SQL makes it especially easy to write UDFs. It supports both its own UDF interface and existing Apache Hive UDFs.

Spark SQL UDFs

Spark SQL offers a built-in method to easily register UDFs by passing in a function in your programming language. In Scala and Python, we can use the native function and lambda syntax of the language, and in Java we need only extend the appropriate UDF class. Our UDFs can work on a variety of types, and we can return a different type than the one we are called with.

In Python and Java we also need to specify the return type using one of the Data-Frame types, listed in Table 9-2. In Java these types are found in org.apache.spark.sql.api.java.DataType and in Python we import the DataType.

In Examples 9-36 and 9-37, a very simple UDF computes the string length, which we can use to find out the length of the tweets we're using.

Example 9-36. Python string length UDF

```
# Import the IntegerType we are returning
from pyspark.sql.types import IntegerType
# Make a UDF to tell us how long some text is
hiveCtx.registerFunction("strLenPython", lambda x: len(x), IntegerType())
lengthDataFrame = hiveCtx.sql("SELECT strLenPython('text') FROM tweets LIMIT 10")
```

 In version of Spark prior to 1.3, registering a function was done directly on the HiveContext or SQLContext rather than through sqlCtx.udf.

Example 9-37. Scala string length UDF

```
hiveCtx.udf.register("strLenScala", (_: String).length)
val tweetLength = hiveCtx.sql("SELECT strLenScala('tweet') FROM tweets LIMIT 10")
```

There are some additional imports for Java to define UDFs. As with the functions we defined for RDDs we extend a special class. Depending on the number of parameters we extend UDF[N], as shown in Examples 9-38 and 9-39.

Example 9-38. Java UDF imports

```
// Import UDF function class and DataTypes
// Note: these import paths may change in a future release
import org.apache.spark.sql.api.java.UDF1;
import org.apache.spark.sql.types.DataTypes;
```

Example 9-39. Java string length UDF

```
hiveCtx.udf().register("stringLengthJava", new UDF1<String, Integer>() {
    @Override
      public Integer call(String str) throws Exception {
      return str.length();
    }
  }, DataTypes.IntegerType);
DataFrame tweetLength = hiveCtx.sql(
  "SELECT stringLengthJava('text') FROM tweets LIMIT 10");
```

Hive UDFs

Spark SQL can also use existing Hive UDFs. The standard Hive UDFs are already automatically included. If you have a custom UDF, it is important to make sure that the JARs for your UDF are included with your application. If we run the JDBC server, note that we can add this with the `--jars` command-line flag. Developing Hive UDFs is beyond the scope of this book, so we will instead introduce how to use existing Hive UDFs.

Using a Hive UDF requires that we use the HiveContext instead of a regular SQLContext. To make a Hive UDF available, simply call `hiveCtx.sql("CREATE TEM PORARY FUNCTION name AS `*`class.function`*`")`.

Spark SQL Performance

As alluded to in the introduction, Spark SQL's higher-level query language and additional type information allows Spark SQL to be more efficient.

Spark SQL is for more than just users who are familiar with SQL. Spark SQL makes it very easy to perform conditional aggregate operations, like counting the sum of multiple columns (as shown in Example 9-40), without having to construct special objects as we discussed in Chapter 6.

Example 9-40. Spark SQL multiple sums

```
SELECT SUM(user.favouritesCount), SUM(retweetCount), user.id FROM tweets
  GROUP BY user.id
```

Spark SQL is able to use the knowledge of types to more efficiently represent our data. When caching data, Spark SQL uses an in-memory columnar storage. This not only takes up less space when cached, but if our subsequent queries depend only on subsets of the data, Spark SQL minimizes the data read.

Predicate push-down allows Spark SQL to move some parts of our query "down" to the engine we are querying. If we wanted to read only certain records in Spark, the standard way to handle this would be to read in the entire dataset and then execute a filter on it. However, in Spark SQL, if the underlying data store supports retrieving only subsets of the key range, or another restriction, Spark SQL is able to push the restrictions in our query down to the data store, resulting in potentially much less data being read.

Performance Tuning Options

There are a number of different performance tuning options with Spark SQL; they're listed in Table 9-3.

Table 9-3. Performance options in Spark SQL

Option	Default	Usage
spark.sql.codegen	false	When true, Spark SQL will compile each query to Java bytecode on the fly. This can improve performance for large queries, but codegen can slow down very short queries.
spark.sql.inMemoryColumnarStorage.com pressed	true	Compress the in-memory columnar storage automatically. Previously defaulted to false.
spark.sql.inMemoryColumnarStorage.batch Size	1000	The batch size for columnar caching. Larger values may cause out-of-memory problems
spark.sql.parquet.compression.codec	snappy	Which compression codec to use. Possible options include uncompressed, snappy, gzip, and lzo.

Using the JDBC connector, and the Beeline shell, we can set these performance options, and other options, with the **set** command, as shown in Example 9-41.

Example 9-41. Beeline command for enabling codegen

```
beeline> set spark.sql.codegen=true;
SET spark.sql.codegen=true
spark.sql.codegen=true
Time taken: 1.196 seconds
```

In a traditional Spark SQL application we can set these Spark properties on our Spark configuration instead, as shown in Example 9-42.

Example 9-42. Scala code for enabling codegen

```
conf.set("spark.sql.codegen", "true")
```

A few options warrant special attention. First is `spark.sql.codegen`, which causes Spark SQL to compile each query to Java bytecode before running it. Codegen can make long queries or frequently repeated queries substantially faster, because it generates specialized code to run them. However, in a setting with very short (1–2 seconds) ad hoc queries, it may add overhead as it has to run a compiler for each query.[1] Codegen is also still experimental, but we recommend trying it for any workload with large queries, or with the same query repeated over and over.

The second option you may need to tune is `spark.sql.inMemoryColumnarStor age.batchSize`. When caching DataFrames, Spark SQL groups together the records in the RDD in batches of the size given by this option (default: `1000`), and compresses each batch. Very small batch sizes lead to low compression, but on the other hand, very large sizes can also be problematic, as each batch might be too large to build up in memory. If the rows in your tables are large (i.e., contain hundreds of fields or contain string fields that can be very long, such as web pages), you may need to lower the batch size to avoid out-of-memory errors. If not, the default batch size is likely fine, as there are diminishing returns for extra compression when you go beyond 1,000 records.

Conclusion

With Spark SQL, we have seen how to use Spark with structured and semistructured data. In addition to the queries explored here, it's important to remember that our previous tools from Chapter 3 through Chapter 6 can be used on the DataFrames Spark SQL provides. In many pipelines, it is convenient to combine SQL (for its conciseness) with code written in other programming languages (for their ability to express more complex logic). When you use Spark SQL to do this, you also gain some optimizations from the engine's ability to leverage schemas.

---

1 Note that the first few runs of codegen will be especially slow as it needs to initialize its compiler, so you should run four to five queries before measuring its overhead.

## CHAPTER 10

Spark Streaming

Many applications benefit from acting on data as soon as it arrives. For example, an application might track statistics about page views in real time, train a machine learning model, or automatically detect anomalies. Spark Streaming is Spark's module for such applications. It lets users write streaming applications using a very similar API to batch jobs, and thus reuse a lot of the skills and even code they built for those.

Much like Spark is built on the concept of RDDs, Spark Streaming provides an abstraction called *DStreams*, or *discretized streams*. A DStream is a sequence of data arriving over time. Internally, each DStream is represented as a sequence of RDDs arriving at each time step (hence the name "discretized"). DStreams can be created from various input sources, such as Flume, Kafka, or HDFS. Once built, they offer two types of operations: *transformations*, which yield a new DStream, and *output operations*, which write data to an external system. DStreams provide many of the same operations available on RDDs, plus new operations related to time, such as sliding windows.

Unlike batch programs, Spark Streaming applications need additional setup in order to operate 24/7. We will discuss *checkpointing*, the main mechanism Spark Streaming provides for this purpose, which lets it store data in a reliable file system such as HDFS. We will also discuss how to restart applications on failure or set them to be automatically restarted.

Finally, as of Spark 1.1, Spark Streaming is available only in Java and Scala. Experimental Python support was added in Spark 1.2, though it supports only text data. We will focus this chapter on Java and Scala to show the full API, but similar concepts apply in Python.

A Simple Example

Before we dive into the details of Spark Streaming, let's consider a simple example. We will receive a stream of newline-delimited lines of text from a server running at port 7777, filter only the lines that contain the word *error*, and print them.

Spark Streaming programs are best run as standalone applications built using Maven or sbt. Spark Streaming, while part of Spark, ships as a separate Maven artifact and has some additional imports you will want to add to your project. These are shown in Examples 10-1 through 10-3.

Example 10-1. Maven coordinates for Spark Streaming

```
groupId = org.apache.spark
artifactId = spark-streaming_2.10
version = 1.3.0
```

Example 10-2. Scala streaming imports

```
import org.apache.spark.streaming.StreamingContext
import org.apache.spark.streaming.StreamingContext._
import org.apache.spark.streaming.dstream.DStream
import org.apache.spark.streaming.Duration
import org.apache.spark.streaming.Seconds
```

Example 10-3. Java streaming imports

```
import org.apache.spark.streaming.api.java.JavaStreamingContext;
import org.apache.spark.streaming.api.java.JavaDStream;
import org.apache.spark.streaming.api.java.JavaPairDStream;
import org.apache.spark.streaming.Duration;
import org.apache.spark.streaming.Durations;
```

We will start by creating a StreamingContext, which is the main entry point for streaming functionality. This also sets up an underlying SparkContext that it will use to process the data. It takes as input a *batch interval* specifying how often to process new data, which we set to 1 second. Next, we use socketTextStream() to create a DStream based on text data received on port 7777 of the local machine. Then we transform the DStream with filter() to get only the lines that contain *error*. Finally, we apply the output operation print() to print some of the filtered lines. (See Examples 10-4 and 10-5.)

Example 10-4. Streaming filter for printing lines containing "error" in Scala

```
// Create a StreamingContext with a 1-second batch size from a SparkConf
val ssc = new StreamingContext(conf, Seconds(1))
// Create a DStream using data received after connecting to port 7777 on the
```

```
// local machine
val lines = ssc.socketTextStream("localhost", 7777)
// Filter our DStream for lines with "error"
val errorLines = lines.filter(_.contains("error"))
// Print out the lines with errors
errorLines.print()
```

Example 10-5. Streaming filter for printing lines containing "error" in Java

```
// Create a StreamingContext with a 1-second batch size from a SparkConf
JavaStreamingContext jssc = new JavaStreamingContext(conf, Durations.seconds(1));
// Create a DStream from all the input on port 7777
JavaDStream<String> lines = jssc.socketTextStream("localhost", 7777);
// Filter our DStream for lines with "error"
JavaDStream<String> errorLines = lines.filter(new Function<String, Boolean>() {
  @Override
  public Boolean call(String line) {
    return line.contains("error");
  }});
// Print out the lines with errors
errorLines.print();
```

This sets up only the computation that will be done when the system receives data. To start receiving data, we must explicitly call start() on the StreamingContext. Then, Spark Streaming will start to schedule Spark jobs on the underlying SparkContext. This will occur in a separate thread, so to keep our application from exiting, we also need to call awaitTermination to wait for the streaming computation to finish. (See Examples 10-6 and 10-7.)

Example 10-6. Streaming filter for printing lines containing "error" in Scala

```
// Start our streaming context and wait for it to "finish"
ssc.start()
// Wait for the job to finish
ssc.awaitTermination()
```

Example 10-7. Streaming filter for printing lines containing "error" in Java

```
// Start our streaming context and wait for it to "finish"
jssc.start();
// Wait for the job to finish
jssc.awaitTermination();
```

Note that a streaming context can be started only once, and must be started after we set up all the DStreams and output operations we want.

Now that we have our simple streaming application, we can go ahead and run it, as shown in Example 10-8.

Example 10-8. Running the streaming app and providing data on Linux/Mac

```
$ spark-submit --class com.oreilly.learningsparkexamples.scala.StreamingLogInput \
$ASSEMBLY_JAR local[4]

$ nc localhost 7777    # Lets you type input lines to send to the server
<your input here>
```

Windows users can use the ncat (*http://nmap.org/ncat/*) command in place of the nc command. ncat is available as part of nmap (*http://nmap.org/*).

In the rest of this chapter, we'll build on this example to process Apache logfiles. If you'd like to generate some fake logs, you can run the script ./bin/fakelogs.sh or ./bin/fakelogs.cmd in this book's Git repository to send logs to port 7777.

Architecture and Abstraction

Spark Streaming uses a "micro-batch" architecture, where the streaming computation is treated as a continuous series of batch computations on small batches of data. Spark Streaming receives data from various input sources and groups it into small batches. New batches are created at regular time intervals. At the beginning of each time interval a new batch is created, and any data that arrives during that interval gets added to that batch. At the end of the time interval the batch is done growing. The size of the time intervals is determined by a parameter called the *batch interval*. The batch interval is typically between 500 milliseconds and several seconds, as configured by the application developer. Each input batch forms an RDD, and is processed using Spark jobs to create other RDDs. The processed results can then be pushed out to external systems in batches. This high-level architecture is shown in Figure 10-1.

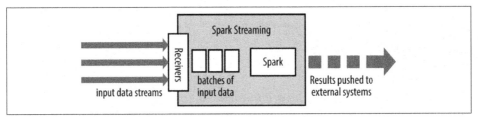

Figure 10-1. High-level architecture of Spark Streaming

As you've learned, the programming abstraction in Spark Streaming is a discretized stream or a DStream (shown in Figure 10-2), which is a sequence of RDDs, where each RDD has one time slice of the data in the stream.

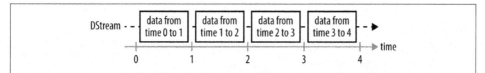

Figure 10-2. DStream as a continuous series of RDDs

You can create DStreams either from external input sources, or by applying *transformations* to other DStreams. DStreams support many of the transformations that you saw on RDDs in Chapter 3. Additionally, DStreams also have new "stateful" transformations that can aggregate data across time. We will discuss these in the next section.

In our simple example, we created a DStream from data received through a socket, and then applied a `filter()` transformation to it. This internally creates RDDs as shown in Figure 10-3.

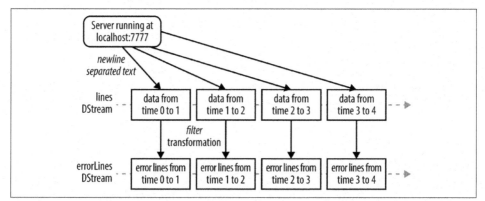

Figure 10-3. DStreams and transformation of Examples 10-4 through 10-8

If you run Example 10-8, you should see something similar to the output in Example 10-9.

Example 10-9. Log output from running Example 10-8

```
-------------------------------------------
Time: 1413833674000 ms
-------------------------------------------
71.19.157.174 - - [24/Sep/2014:22:26:12 +0000] "GET /error78978 HTTP/1.1" 404 505
...

-------------------------------------------
Time: 1413833675000 ms
-------------------------------------------
71.19.164.174 - - [24/Sep/2014:22:27:10 +0000] "GET /error78978 HTTP/1.1" 404 505
...
```

This output nicely illustrates the micro-batch architecture of Spark Streaming. We can see the filtered logs being printed every second, since we set the batch interval to 1 second when we created the StreamingContext. The Spark UI also shows that Spark Streaming is running many small jobs, as you can see in Figure 10-4.

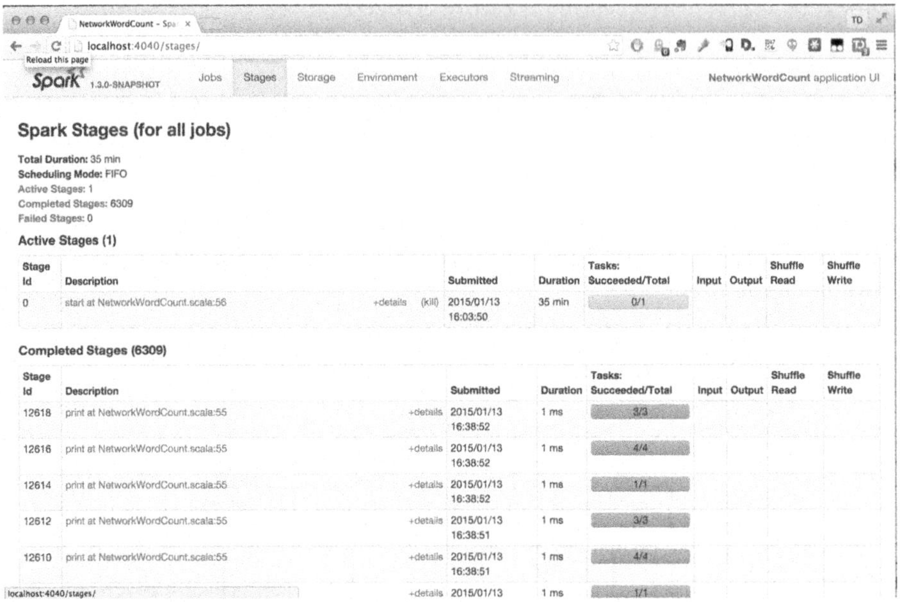

Figure 10-4. Spark application UI when running a streaming job

Apart from transformations, DStreams support *output operations*, such as the print() used in our example. Output operations are similar to RDD actions in that they write data to an external system, but in Spark Streaming they run periodically on each time step, producing output in batches.

The execution of Spark Streaming within Spark's driver-worker components is shown in Figure 10-5 (see Figure 2-3 earlier in the book for the components of Spark). For each input source, Spark Streaming launches *receivers*, which are tasks running within the application's executors that collect data from the input source and save it as RDDs. These receive the input data and replicate it (by default) to another executor for fault tolerance. This data is stored in the memory of the executors in the same way as cached RDDs.[1] The StreamingContext in the driver program then periodically runs Spark jobs to process this data and combine it with RDDs from previous time steps.

---

1 In Spark 1.2, receivers can also replicate data to HDFS. Also, some input sources, such as HDFS, are naturally replicated, so Spark Streaming does not replicate those again.

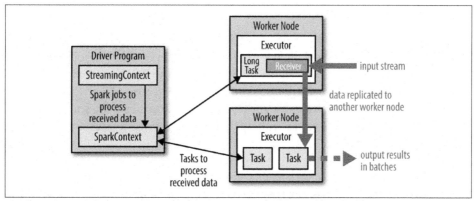

Figure 10-5. Execution of Spark Streaming within Spark's components

Spark Streaming offers the same fault-tolerance properties for DStreams as Spark has for RDDs: as long as a copy of the input data is still available, it can recompute any state derived from it using the lineage of the RDDs (i.e., by rerunning the operations used to process it). By default, received data is replicated across two nodes, as mentioned, so Spark Streaming can tolerate single worker failures. Using just lineage, however, recomputation could take a long time for data that has been built up since the beginning of the program. Thus, Spark Streaming also includes a mechanism called *checkpointing* that saves state periodically to a reliable filesystem (e.g., HDFS or S3). Typically, you might set up checkpointing every 5–10 batches of data. When recovering lost data, Spark Streaming needs only to go back to the last checkpoint.

In the rest of this chapter, we will explore the transformations, output operations, and input sources in Spark Streaming in detail. We will then return to fault tolerance and checkpointing to explain how to configure programs for 24/7 operation.

Transformations

Transformations on DStreams can be grouped into either *stateless* or *stateful*:

- In *stateless transformations* the processing of each batch does not depend on the data of its previous batches. They include the common RDD transformations we have seen in Chapters 3 and 4, like map(), filter(), and reduceByKey().
- *Stateful transformations*, in contrast, use data or intermediate results from previous batches to compute the results of the current batch. They include transformations based on sliding windows and on tracking state across time.

Stateless Transformations

Stateless transformations, some of which are listed in Table 10-1, are simple RDD transformations being applied on every batch—that is, every RDD in a DStream. We have already seen filter() in Figure 10-3. Many of the RDD transformations discussed in Chapters 3 and 4 are also available on DStreams. Note that key/value DStream transformations like reduceByKey() are made available in Scala by import StreamingContext._. In Java, as with RDDs, it is necessary to create a JavaPairD Stream using mapToPair().

Table 10-1. Examples of stateless DStream transformations (incomplete list)

Function name	Purpose	Scala example	Signature of user-supplied function on DStream[T]
map()	Apply a function to each element in the DStream and return a DStream of the result.	ds.map(x => x + 1)	f: (T) → U
flatMap()	Apply a function to each element in the DStream and return a DStream of the contents of the iterators returned.	ds.flatMap(x => x.split(" "))	f: T → Itera ble[U]
filter()	Return a DStream consisting of only elements that pass the condition passed to filter.	ds.filter(x => x != 1)	f: T → Boolean
reparti tion()	Change the number of partitions of the DStream.	ds.repartition(10)	N/A
reduceBy Key()	Combine values with the same key in each batch.	ds.reduceByKey((x, y) => x + y)	f: T, T → T
groupBy Key()	Group values with the same key in each batch.	ds.groupByKey()	N/A

Keep in mind that although these functions look like they're applying to the whole stream, internally each DStream is composed of multiple RDDs (batches), and each stateless transformation applies *separately* to each RDD. For example, reduceByKey() will reduce data within each time step, but not across time steps. The stateful transformations we cover later allow combining data across time.

As an example, in our log processing program from earlier, we could use map() and reduceByKey() to count log events by IP address in each time step, as shown in Examples 10-10 and 10-11.

Example 10-10. map() and reduceByKey() on DStream in Scala

```
// Assumes ApacheAccessLog is a utility class for parsing entries from Apache logs
val accessLogDStream = logData.map(line => ApacheAccessLog.parseFromLogLine(line))
val ipDStream = accessLogsDStream.map(entry => (entry.getIpAddress(), 1))
val ipCountsDStream = ipDStream.reduceByKey((x, y) => x + y)
```

Example 10-11. map() and reduceByKey() on DStream in Java

```
// Assumes ApacheAccessLog is a utility class for parsing entries from Apache logs
static final class IpTuple implements PairFunction<ApacheAccessLog, String, Long> {
  public Tuple2<String, Long> call(ApacheAccessLog log) {
    return new Tuple2<>(log.getIpAddress(), 1L);
  }
}

JavaDStream<ApacheAccessLog> accessLogsDStream =
  logData.map(new ParseFromLogLine());
JavaPairDStream<String, Long> ipDStream =
  accessLogsDStream.mapToPair(new IpTuple());
JavaPairDStream<String, Long> ipCountsDStream =
  ipDStream.reduceByKey(new LongSumReducer());
```

Stateless transformations can also combine data from multiple DStreams, again within each time step. For example, key/value DStreams have the same join-related transformations as RDDs—namely, cogroup(), join(), leftOuterJoin(), and so on (see "Joins" on page 58). We can use these operations on DStreams to perform the underlying RDD operations separately on each batch.

Let us consider a join between two DStreams. In Examples 10-12 and 10-13, we have data keyed by IP address, and we join the request count against the bytes transferred.

Example 10-12. Joining two DStreams in Scala

```
val ipBytesDStream =
  accessLogsDStream.map(entry => (entry.getIpAddress(), entry.getContentSize()))
val ipBytesSumDStream =
  ipBytesDStream.reduceByKey((x, y) => x + y)
val ipBytesRequestCountDStream =
  ipCountsDStream.join(ipBytesSumDStream)
```

Example 10-13. Joining two DStreams in Java

```java
JavaPairDStream<String, Long> ipBytesDStream =
  accessLogsDStream.mapToPair(new IpContentTuple());
JavaPairDStream<String, Long> ipBytesSumDStream =
  ipBytesDStream.reduceByKey(new LongSumReducer());
JavaPairDStream<String, Tuple2<Long, Long>> ipBytesRequestCountDStream =
  ipCountsDStream.join(ipBytesSumDStream);
```

We can also merge the contents of two different DStreams using the union() operator as in regular Spark, or using StreamingContext.union() for multiple streams.

Finally, if these stateless transformations are insufficient, DStreams provide an advanced operator called transform() that lets you operate directly on the RDDs inside them. The transform() operation lets you provide any arbitrary RDD-to-RDD function to act on the DStream. This function gets called on each batch of data in the stream to produce a new stream. A common application of transform() is to reuse batch processing code you had written on RDDs. For example, if you had a function, extractOutliers(), that acted on an RDD of log lines to produce an RDD of outliers (perhaps after running some statistics on the messages), you could reuse it within a transform(), as shown in Examples 10-14 and 10-15.

Example 10-14. transform() on a DStream in Scala

```scala
val outlierDStream = accessLogsDStream.transform { rdd =>
  extractOutliers(rdd)
}
```

Example 10-15. transform() on a DStream in Java

```java
JavaPairDStream<String, Long> ipRawDStream = accessLogsDStream.transform(
  new Function<JavaRDD<ApacheAccessLog>, JavaRDD<ApacheAccessLog>>() {
    public JavaPairRDD<ApacheAccessLog> call(JavaRDD<ApacheAccessLog> rdd) {
      return extractOutliers(rdd);
    }
});
```

You can also combine and transform data from multiple DStreams together using StreamingContext.transform or DStream.transformWith(otherStream, func).

Stateful Transformations

Stateful transformations are operations on DStreams that track data across time; that is, some data from previous batches is used to generate the results for a new batch. The two main types are windowed operations, which act over a sliding window of time periods, and updateStateByKey(), which is used to track state across events for each key (e.g., to build up an object representing each user session).

Stateful transformations require checkpointing to be enabled in your StreamingContext for fault tolerance. We will discuss checkpointing in more detail in "24/7 Operation" on page 208, but for now, you can enable it by passing a directory to `ssc.checkpoint()`, as shown in Example 10-16.

Example 10-16. Setting up checkpointing

```
ssc.checkpoint("hdfs://...")
```

For local development, you can also use a local path (e.g., */tmp*) instead of HDFS.

Windowed transformations

Windowed operations compute results across a longer time period than the StreamingContext's batch interval, by combining results from multiple batches. In this section, we'll show how to use them to keep track of the most common response codes, content sizes, and clients in a web server access log.

All windowed operations need two parameters, window duration and sliding duration, both of which must be a multiple of the StreamingContext's batch interval. The window duration controls how many previous batches of data are considered, namely the last `windowDuration/batchInterval`. If we had a source DStream with a batch interval of 10 seconds and wanted to create a sliding window of the last 30 seconds (or last 3 batches) we would set the `windowDuration` to 30 seconds. The sliding duration, which defaults to the batch interval, controls how frequently the new DStream computes results. If we had the source DStream with a batch interval of 10 seconds and wanted to compute our window only on every second batch, we would set our sliding interval to 20 seconds. Figure 10-6 shows an example.

The simplest window operation we can do on a DStream is `window()`, which returns a new DStream with the data for the requested window. In other words, each RDD in the DStream resulting from `window()` will contain data from multiple batches, which we can then process with `count()`, `transform()`, and so on. (See Examples 10-17 and 10-18.)

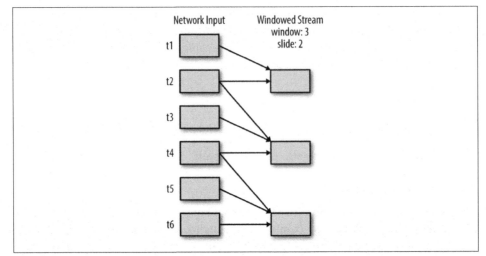

Figure 10-6. A windowed stream with a window duration of 3 batches and a slide duration of 2 batches; every two time steps, we compute a result over the previous 3 time steps

Example 10-17. How to use window() to count data over a window in Scala

```
val accessLogsWindow = accessLogsDStream.window(Seconds(30), Seconds(10))
val windowCounts = accessLogsWindow.count()
```

Example 10-18. How to use window() to count data over a window in Java

```
JavaDStream<ApacheAccessLog> accessLogsWindow = accessLogsDStream.window(
    Durations.seconds(30), Durations.seconds(10));
JavaDStream<Integer> windowCounts = accessLogsWindow.count();
```

While we can build all other windowed operations on top of window(), Spark Streaming provides a number of other windowed operations for efficiency and convenience. First, reduceByWindow() and reduceByKeyAndWindow() allow us to perform reductions on each window more efficiently. They take a single reduce function to run on the whole window, such as +. In addition, they have a special form that allows Spark to compute the reduction *incrementally*, by considering only which data is coming into the window and which data is going out. This special form requires an inverse of the reduce function, such as - for +. It is much more efficient for large windows if your function has an inverse (see Figure 10-7).

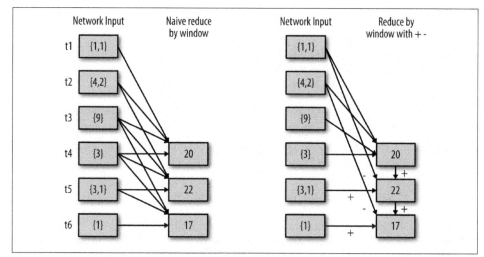

Figure 10-7. Difference between naive reduceByWindow() and incremental reduceBy-Window(), using an inverse function

In our log processing example, we can use these two functions to count visits by each IP address more efficiently, as you can see in Examples 10-19 and 10-20.

Example 10-19. Scala visit counts per IP address

```
val ipDStream = accessLogsDStream.map(logEntry => (logEntry.getIpAddress(), 1))
val ipCountDStream = ipDStream.reduceByKeyAndWindow(
  {(x, y) => x + y}, // Adding elements in the new batches entering the window
  {(x, y) => x - y}, // Removing elements from the oldest batches exiting the window
  Seconds(30),       // Window duration
  Seconds(10))       // Slide duration
```

Example 10-20. Java visit counts per IP address

```
class ExtractIp extends PairFunction<ApacheAccessLog, String, Long> {
  public Tuple2<String, Long> call(ApacheAccessLog entry) {
    return new Tuple2(entry.getIpAddress(), 1L);
  }
}
class AddLongs extends Function2<Long, Long, Long>() {
  public Long call(Long v1, Long v2) { return v1 + v2; }
}
class SubtractLongs extends Function2<Long, Long, Long>() {
  public Long call(Long v1, Long v2) { return v1 - v2; }
}

JavaPairDStream<String, Long> ipAddressPairDStream = accessLogsDStream.mapToPair(
  new ExtractIp());
JavaPairDStream<String, Long> ipCountDStream = ipAddressPairDStream.
```

```
reduceByKeyAndWindow(
new AddLongs(),       // Adding elements in the new batches entering the window
new SubtractLongs()
// Removing elements from the oldest batches exiting the window
Durations.seconds(30),  // Window duration
Durations.seconds(10)); // Slide duration
```

Finally, for counting data, DStreams offer countByWindow() and countByValueAnd
Window() as shorthands. countByWindow() gives us a DStream representing the number of elements in each window. countByValueAndWindow() gives us a DStream with
the counts for each value. See Examples 10-21 and 10-22.

Example 10-21. Windowed count operations in Scala

```
val ipDStream = accessLogsDStream.map{entry => entry.getIpAddress()}
val ipAddressRequestCount = ipDStream.countByValueAndWindow(Seconds(30), Seconds(10))
val requestCount = accessLogsDStream.countByWindow(Seconds(30), Seconds(10))
```

Example 10-22. Windowed count operations in Java

```
JavaDStream<String> ip = accessLogsDStream.map(
  new Function<ApacheAccessLog, String>() {
    public String call(ApacheAccessLog entry) {
      return entry.getIpAddress();
    }});
JavaDStream<Long> requestCount = accessLogsDStream.countByWindow(
  Dirations.seconds(30), Durations.seconds(10));
JavaPairDStream<String, Long> ipAddressRequestCount = ip.countByValueAndWindow(
  Dirations.seconds(30), Durations.seconds(10));
```

UpdateStateByKey transformation

Sometimes it's useful to maintain *state* across the batches in a DStream (e.g., to track
sessions as users visit a site). updateStateByKey() enables this by providing access to
a state variable for DStreams of key/value pairs. Given a DStream of (key, event)
pairs, it lets you construct a new DStream of (key, state) pairs by taking a function
that specifies how to update the state for each key given new events. For example, in a
web server log, our events might be visits to the site, where the key is the user ID.
Using updateStateByKey(), we could track the last 10 pages each user visited. This
list would be our "state" object, and we'd update it as each event arrives.

To use updateStateByKey(), we provide a function update(events, oldState) that
takes in the events that have arrived for a key and its previous state, and returns a
newState to store for it. This function's signature is as follows:

• events is a list of events that arrived in the current batch (may be empty).

- `oldState` is an optional state object, stored within an `Option`; it might be missing if there was no previous state for the key.

- `newState`, returned by the function, is also an `Option`; we can return an empty `Option` to specify that we want to delete the state.

The result of `updateStateByKey()` will be a new DStream that contains an RDD of (key, state) pairs on each time step.

As a simple example, we'll use `updateStateByKey()` to keep a running count of the number of log messages with each HTTP response code. Our keys here are the response codes, our state is an integer representing each count, and our events are page views. Note that unlike our window examples earlier, Examples 10-23 and 10-24 keep an "infinitely growing" count since the beginning of the program.

Example 10-23. Running count of response codes using updateStateByKey() in Scala

```scala
def updateRunningSum(values: Seq[Long], state: Option[Long]) = {
  Some(state.getOrElse(0L) + values.size)
}

val responseCodeDStream = accessLogsDStream.map(log => (log.getResponseCode(), 1L))
val responseCodeCountDStream = responseCodeDStream.updateStateByKey(updateRunningSum _)
```

Example 10-24. Running count of response codes using updateStateByKey() in Java

```java
class UpdateRunningSum implements Function2<List<Long>,
    Optional<Long>, Optional<Long>> {
  public Optional<Long> call(List<Long> nums, Optional<Long> current) {
    long sum = current.or(0L);
    return Optional.of(sum + nums.size());
  }
};

JavaPairDStream<Integer, Long> responseCodeCountDStream = accessLogsDStream.mapToPair(
    new PairFunction<ApacheAccessLog, Integer, Long>() {
      public Tuple2<Integer, Long> call(ApacheAccessLog log) {
        return new Tuple2(log.getResponseCode(), 1L);
      }})
    .updateStateByKey(new UpdateRunningSum());
```

Output Operations

Output operations specify what needs to be done with the final transformed data in a stream (e.g., pushing it to an external database or printing it to the screen).

Much like lazy evaluation in RDDs, if no output operation is applied on a DStream and any of its descendants, then those DStreams will not be evaluated. And if there are no output operations set in a StreamingContext, then the context will not start.

A common debugging output operation that we have used already is print(). This grabs the first 10 elements from each batch of the DStream and prints the results.

Once we've debugged our program, we can also use output operations to save results. Spark Streaming has similar save() operations for DStreams, each of which takes a directory to save files into and an optional suffix. The results of each batch are saved as subdirectories in the given directory, with the time and the suffix in the filename. For instance, we can save our IP address counts as shown in Example 10-25.

Example 10-25. Saving DStream to text files in Scala

```
ipAddressRequestCount.saveAsTextFiles("outputDir", "txt")
```

The more general saveAsHadoopFiles() takes a Hadoop OutputFormat. For instance, Spark Streaming doesn't have a built-in saveAsSequenceFile() function, but we can save SequenceFiles as shown in Examples 10-26 and 10-27.

Example 10-26. Saving SequenceFiles from a DStream in Scala

```
val writableIpAddressRequestCount = ipAddressRequestCount.map {
  (ip, count) => (new Text(ip), new LongWritable(count)) }
writableIpAddressRequestCount.saveAsHadoopFiles[
  SequenceFileOutputFormat[Text, LongWritable]]("outputDir", "txt")
```

Example 10-27. Saving SequenceFiles from a DStream in Java

```
JavaPairDStream<Text, LongWritable> writableDStream = ipDStream.mapToPair(
  new PairFunction<Tuple2<String, Long>, Text, LongWritable>() {
    public Tuple2<Text, LongWritable> call(Tuple2<String, Long> e) {
      return new Tuple2(new Text(e._1()), new LongWritable(e._2())));
  }});
class OutFormat extends SequenceFileOutputFormat<Text, LongWritable> {};
writableDStream.saveAsHadoopFiles(
  "outputDir", "txt", Text.class, LongWritable.class, OutFormat.class);
```

Finally, foreachRDD() is a generic output operation that lets us run arbitrary computations on the RDDs on the DStream. It is similar to transform() in that it gives you access to each RDD. Within foreachRDD(), we can reuse all the actions we have in Spark. For example, a common use case is to write data to an external database such as MySQL, where Spark may not have a saveAs() function, but we might use for eachPartition() on the RDD to write it out. For convenience, foreachRDD() can also give us the time of the current batch, allowing us to output each time period to a different location. See Example 10-28.

Example 10-28. Saving data to external systems with foreachRDD() in Scala

```
ipAddressRequestCount.foreachRDD { rdd =>
  rdd.foreachPartition { partition =>
    // Open connection to storage system (e.g. a database connection)
    partition.foreach { item =>
      // Use connection to push item to system
    }
    // Close connection
  }
}
```

Input Sources

Spark Streaming has built-in support for a number of different data sources. Some "core" sources are built into the Spark Streaming Maven artifact, while others are available through additional artifacts, such as `spark-streaming-kafka`.

This section walks through some of these sources. It assumes that you already have each input source set up, and is not intended to introduce the non-Spark-specific components of any of these systems. If you are designing a new application, we recommend trying HDFS or Kafka as simple input sources to get started with.

Core Sources

The methods to create DStream from the core sources are all available on the StreamingContext. We have already explored one of these sources in the example: sockets. Here we discuss two more, files and Akka actors.

Stream of files

Since Spark supports reading from any Hadoop-compatible filesystem, Spark Streaming naturally allows a stream to be created from files written in a directory of a Hadoop-compatible filesystem. This is a popular option due to its support of a wide variety of backends, especially for log data that we would copy to HDFS anyway. For Spark Streaming to work with the data, it needs to have a consistent date format for the directory names and the files have to be created *atomically* (e.g., by moving the file into the directory Spark is monitoring).[2] The data must also be in a consistent for-

---

2 *Atomically* means that the entire operation happens at once. This is important here since if Spark Streaming were to start processing the file and then more data were to appear, it wouldn't notice the additional data. In filesystems, the file rename operation is typically atomic.

mat. We can change Examples 10-4 and 10-5 to handle new logfiles as they show up in a directory instead, as shown in Examples 10-29 and 10-30.

Example 10-29. Streaming text files written to a directory in Scala

```
val logData = ssc.textFileStream(logDirectory)
```

Example 10-30. Streaming text files written to a directory in Java

```
JavaDStream<String> logData = jssc.textFileStream(logsDirectory);
```

We can use the provided *./bin/fakelogs_directory.sh* script to fake the logs, or if we have real log data we could replace the rotator with an `mv` command to rotate the logfiles into the directory we are monitoring.

In addition to text data, we can also read any Hadoop input format. As with "Hadoop Input and Output Formats" on page 83, we simply need to provide Spark Streaming with the Key, Value, and InputFormat classes. If, for example, we had a previous streaming job process the logs and save the bytes transferred at each time as a SequenceFile, we could read the data as shown in Example 10-31.

Example 10-31. Streaming SequenceFiles written to a directory in Scala

```
ssc.fileStream[LongWritable, IntWritable,
   SequenceFileInputFormat[LongWritable, IntWritable]](inputDirectory).map {
   case (x, y) => (x.get(), y.get())
}
```

Akka actor stream

The second core receiver is `actorStream`, which allows using Akka actors (*http:// akka.io*) as a source for streaming. To construct an actor stream we create an Akka actor and implement the `org.apache.spark.streaming.receiver.ActorHelper` interface. To copy the input from our actor into Spark Streaming, we need to call the `store()` function in our actor when we receive new data. Akka actor streams are less common so we won't go into detail, but you can look at the streaming documentation (*http://bit.ly/1BQzCdp*) and the ActorWordCount (*http://bit.ly/1BQzD0R*) example in Spark to see them in use.

Additional Sources

In addition to the core sources, additional receivers for well-known data ingestion systems are packaged as separate components of Spark Streaming. These receivers are still part of Spark, but require extra packages to be included in your build file. Some current receivers include Twitter, Apache Kafka, Amazon Kinesis, Apache Flume, and ZeroMQ. We can include these additional receivers by adding the Maven artifact spark-streaming-[projectname]_2.10 with the same version number as Spark.

Apache Kafka

Apache Kafka (*http://kafka.apache.org/*) is popular input source due to its speed and resilience. Using the native support for Kafka, we can easily process the messages for many topics. To use it, we have to include the Maven artifact spark-streaming-kafka_2.10 to our project. The provided KafkaUtils (*http://bit.ly/1BQzJFL*) object works on StreamingContext and JavaStreamingContext to create a DStream of your Kafka messages. Since it can subscribe to multiple topics, the DStream it creates consists of pairs of topic and message. To create a stream, we will call the create Stream() method with our streaming context, a string containing comma-separated ZooKeeper hosts, the name of our consumer group (a unique name), and a map of topics to number of receiver threads to use for that topic (see Examples 10-32 and 10-33).

Example 10-32. Apache Kafka subscribing to Panda's topic in Scala

```
import org.apache.spark.streaming.kafka._
...
// Create a map of topics to number of receiver threads to use
val topics = List(("pandas", 1), ("logs", 1)).toMap
val topicLines = KafkaUtils.createStream(ssc, zkQuorum, group, topics)
topicLines.print()
```

Example 10-33. Apache Kafka subscribing to Panda's topic in Java

```
import org.apache.spark.streaming.kafka.*;
...
// Create a map of topics to number of receiver threads to use
Map<String, Integer> topics = new HashMap<String, Integer>();
topics.put("pandas", 1);
topics.put("logs", 1);
JavaPairDStream<String, String> topicLines =
  KafkaUtils.createStream(jssc, zkQuorum, group, topics);
topicLines.print();
```

New in Spark 1.3, Spark can also receive from Kafka directly, removing the difficulty of dealing with receiver failure. Since the data is read directly, we don't need to replicate the data after read, since if we fail it can simply be re-read, similar to how we don't need to replicate data when reading from HDFS. This approach also allows us to have multiple readers without having to use Example 10-13 to combine streams.

Instead of using createStream() to read from Kafka directly, we will use the create DirectStream() method. Instead of providing the Zookeeper hosts, we will provide the list of Kafka brokers directly. As with `createStream()`, we can also subscribe to multiple topics, but we no longer need to specify a specific number of reader threads to use. Examples 10-34 and 10-35 illustrate the creation of a direct Kafka stream.

Example 10-34. Apache Kafka directly reading Panda's topic in Scala

```scala
import org.apache.spark.streaming.kafka._
import kafka.serializer.StringDecoder
...
// Specify the brokers in our kafkaParams
val kafkaParams = Map[String, String]("metadata.broker.list" -> brokers)
// Create a map of topics to number of receiver threads to use
val topicSet = List("pandas", "logs").toSet
val topicLines = KafkaUtils.createDirectStream[String, String,
  StringDecoder, StringDecoder](ssc, kafkaParams, topicSet)
StreamingLogInput.processLines(topicLines.map(_._2))
```

Example 10-35. Apache Kafka directly reading Panda's topic in Java

```java
import org.apache.spark.streaming.kafka.*;
import kafka.serializer.StringDecoder;
...
HashSet<String> topicsSet = new HashSet<String>();
topicsSet.put("pandas");
topicsSet.put("logs");
HashMap<String, String> kafkaParams = new HashMap<String, String>();
kafkaParams.put("metadata.broker.list", brokers);
JavaPairDStream<String, String> input =
  KafkaUtils.createDirectStream(jssc,
    String.class,
    String.class,
    StringDecoder.class,
    StringDecoder.class,
    kafkaParams,
    topics)
input.print();
```

Apache Flume

Spark has two different receivers for use with Apache Flume (*http://flume.apache.org/*) (see Figure 10-8). They are as follows:

Push-based receiver
> The receiver acts as an Avro sink that Flume pushes data to.

Pull-based receiver
> The receiver can pull data from an intermediate custom sink, to which other processes are pushing data with Flume.

Both approaches require reconfiguring Flume and running the receiver on a node on a configured port (not your existing Spark or Flume ports). To use either of them, we have to include the Maven artifact `spark-streaming-flume_2.10` in our project.

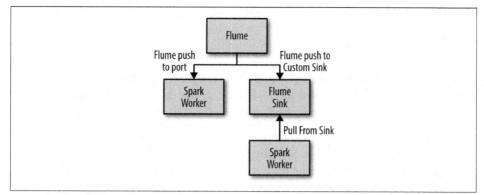

Figure 10-8. Flume receiver options

Push-based receiver

The push-based approach can be set up quickly but does not use transactions to receive data. In this approach, the receiver acts as an Avro sink, and we need to configure Flume to send the data to the Avro sink (Example 10-36). The provided `Flume Utils` object sets up the receiver to be started on a specific worker's hostname and port (Examples 10-37 and 10-38). These must match those in our Flume configuration.

Example 10-36. Flume configuration for Avro sink

```
a1.sinks = avroSink
a1.sinks.avroSink.type = avro
a1.sinks.avroSink.channel = memoryChannel
a1.sinks.avroSink.hostname = receiver-hostname
a1.sinks.avroSink.port = port-used-for-avro-sink-not-spark-port
```

Example 10-37. FlumeUtils agent in Scala

```
val events = FlumeUtils.createStream(ssc, receiverHostname, receiverPort)
```

Example 10-38. FlumeUtils agent in Java

```
JavaDStream<SparkFlumeEvent> events = FlumeUtils.createStream(ssc, receiverHostname,
                                    receiverPort)
```

Despite its simplicity, the disadvantage of this approach is its lack of transactions. This increases the chance of losing small amounts of data in case of the failure of the worker node running the receiver. Furthermore, if the worker running the receiver fails, the system will try to launch the receiver at a different location, and Flume will need to be reconfigured to send to the new worker. This is often challenging to set up.

Pull-based receiver

The newer pull-based approach (added in Spark 1.1) is to set up a specialized Flume sink Spark Streaming will read from, and have the receiver pull the data from the sink. This approach is preferred for resiliency, as the data remains in the sink until Spark Streaming reads and replicates it and tells the sink via a transaction.

To get started, we will need to set up the custom sink as a third-party plug-in for Flume. The latest directions on installing plug-ins are in the Flume documentation (*http://bit.ly/1BQASNt*). Since the plug-in is written in Scala we need to add both the plug-in and the Scala library to Flume's plug-ins. For Spark 1.3, the Maven coordinates are shown in Example 10-39.

Example 10-39. Maven coordinates for Flume sink

```
groupId = org.apache.spark
artifactId = spark-streaming-flume-sink_2.10
version = 1.3.0

groupId = org.scala-lang
artifactId = scala-library
version = 2.10.4
```

Once you have the custom flume sink added to a node, we need to configure Flume to push to the sink, as we do in Example 10-40.

Example 10-40. Flume configuration for custom sink

```
a1.sinks = spark
a1.sinks.spark.type = org.apache.spark.streaming.flume.sink.SparkSink
a1.sinks.spark.hostname = receiver-hostname
a1.sinks.spark.port = port-used-for-sync-not-spark-port
a1.sinks.spark.channel = memoryChannel
```

With the data being buffered in the sink we can now use FlumeUtils to read it, as shown in Examples 10-41 and 10-42.

Example 10-41. FlumeUtils custom sink in Scala

```
val events = FlumeUtils.createPollingStream(ssc, receiverHostname, receiverPort)
```

Example 10-42. FlumeUtils custom sink in Java

```java
JavaDStream<SparkFlumeEvent> events = FlumeUtils.createPollingStream(ssc,
  receiverHostname, receiverPort)
```

In either case, the DStream is composed of SparkFlumeEvents (*http://bit.ly/1BQBlzp*). We can access the underlying AvroFlumeEvent through event. If our event body was UTF-8 strings we could get the contents as shown in Example 10-43.

Example 10-43. SparkFlumeEvent in Scala

```scala
// Assuming that our flume events are UTF-8 log lines
 val lines = events.map{e => new String(e.event.getBody().array(), "UTF-8")}
```

Custom input sources

In addition to the provided sources, you can also implement your own receiver. This is described in Spark's documentation in the Streaming Custom Receivers guide (*http://bit.ly/1BQzCdp*).

Multiple Sources and Cluster Sizing

As covered earlier, we can combine multiple DStreams using operations like union(). Through these operators, we can combine data from multiple input DStreams. Sometimes multiple receivers are necessary to increase the aggregate throughput of the ingestion (if a single receiver becomes the bottleneck). Other times different receivers are created on different sources to receive different kinds of data, which are then combined using joins or cogroups.

It is important to understand how the receivers are executed in the Spark cluster to use multiple ones. Each receiver runs as a long-running task within Spark's executors, and hence occupies CPU cores allocated to the application. In addition, there need to be available cores for processing the data. This means that in order to run multiple receivers, you should have at least as many cores as the number of receivers, plus however many are needed to run your computation. For example, if we want to run 10 receivers in our streaming application, then we have to allocate at least 11 cores.

> Do not run Spark Streaming programs locally with master configured as "local" or "local[1]". This allocates only one CPU for tasks and if a receiver is running on it, there is no resource left to process the received data. Use at least "local[2]" to have more cores.

24/7 Operation

One of the main advantages of Spark Streaming is that it provides strong fault tolerance guarantees. As long as the input data is stored reliably, Spark Streaming will always compute the correct result from it, offering "exactly once" semantics (i.e., as if all of the data was processed without any nodes failing), even if workers or the driver fail.

To run Spark Streaming applications 24/7, you need some special setup. The first step is setting up *checkpointing* to a reliable storage system, such as HDFS or Amazon S3.[3] In addition, we need to worry about the fault tolerance of the driver program (which requires special setup code) and of unreliable input sources. This section covers how to perform this setup.

 An important part of deploying production Spark Streaming jobs is effective testing. The spark-testing-base package on *http:// www.spark-packages.org* provides utilities to test your Spark Streaming application.

Checkpointing

Checkpointing is the main mechanism that needs to be set up for fault tolerance in Spark Streaming. It allows Spark Streaming to periodically save data about the application to a reliable storage system, such as HDFS or Amazon S3, for use in recovering. Specifically, checkpointing serves two purposes:

- Limiting the state that must be recomputed on failure. As discussed in "Architecture and Abstraction" on page 188, Spark Streaming can recompute state using the lineage graph of transformations, but checkpointing controls how far back it must go.
- Providing fault tolerance for the driver. If the driver program in a streaming application crashes, you can launch it again and tell it to recover from a checkpoint, in which case Spark Streaming will read how far the previous run of the program got in processing the data and take over from there.

For these reasons, checkpointing is important to set up in any production streaming application. You can set it by passing a path (either HDFS, S3, or local filesystem) to the ssc.checkpoint() method, as shown in Example 10-44.

---

3 We do not cover how to set up one of these filesystems, but they come in many Hadoop or cloud environments. When deploying on your own cluster, it is probably easiest to set up HDFS.

Example 10-44. Setting up checkpointing

```
ssc.checkpoint("hdfs://...")
```

Note that even in local mode, Spark Streaming will complain if you try to run a stateful operation without checkpointing enabled. In that case, you can pass a local filesystem path for checkpointing. But in any production setting, you should use a replicated system such as HDFS, S3, or an NFS filer.

Driver Fault Tolerance

Tolerating failures of the driver node requires a special way of creating our StreamingContext, which takes in the checkpoint directory. Instead of simply calling new StreamingContext, we need to use the StreamingContext.getOrCreate() function. From our initial example we would change our code as shown in Examples 10-45 and 10-46.

Example 10-45. Setting up a driver that can recover from failure in Scala

```
def createStreamingContext() = {
  ...
  val sc = new SparkContext(conf)
  // Create a StreamingContext with a 1 second batch size
  val ssc = new StreamingContext(sc, Seconds(1))
  ssc.checkpoint(checkpointDir)
}
...
val ssc = StreamingContext.getOrCreate(checkpointDir, createStreamingContext _)
```

Example 10-46. Setting up a driver that can recover from failure in Java

```
JavaStreamingContextFactory fact = new JavaStreamingContextFactory() {
  public JavaStreamingContext call() {
    ...
    JavaSparkContext sc = new JavaSparkContext(conf);
    // Create a StreamingContext with a 1 second batch size
    JavaStreamingContext jssc = new JavaStreamingContext(sc, Durations.seconds(1));
    jssc.checkpoint(checkpointDir);
    return jssc;
  }};
JavaStreamingContext jssc = JavaStreamingContext.getOrCreate(checkpointDir, fact);
```

When this code is run the first time, assuming that the checkpoint directory does not yet exist, the StreamingContext will be created when you call the factory function (createStreamingContext() for Scala, and JavaStreamingContextFactory() for Java). In the factory, you should set the checkpoint directory. After the driver fails, if you restart it and run this code again, getOrCreate() will reinitialize a Streaming-Context from the checkpoint directory and resume processing.

In addition to writing your initialization code using getOrCreate(), you will need to actually restart your driver program when it crashes. On most cluster managers, Spark does not automatically relaunch the driver if it crashes, so you need to monitor it using a tool like monit and restart it. The best way to do this is probably specific to your environment. One place where Spark provides more support is the Standalone cluster manager, which supports a --supervise flag when submitting your driver that lets Spark restart it. You will also need to pass --deploy-mode cluster to make the driver run within the cluster and not on your local machine, as shown in Example 10-47.

Example 10-47. Launching a driver in supervise mode

```
./bin/spark-submit --deploy-mode cluster --supervise --master spark://... App.jar
```

When using this option, you will also want the Spark Standalone master to be fault-tolerant. You can configure this using ZooKeeper, as described in the Spark documentation (*http://bit.ly/1BQCEOO*). With this setup, your application will have no single point of failure.

Finally, note that when the driver crashes, executors in Spark will also restart. This may be changed in future Spark versions, but it is expected behavior in 1.2 and earlier versions, as the executors are not able to continue processing data without a driver. Your relaunched driver will start new executors to pick up where it left off.

Worker Fault Tolerance

For failure of a worker node, Spark Streaming uses the same techniques as Spark for its fault tolerance. All the data received from external sources is replicated among the Spark workers. All RDDs created through transformations of this replicated input data are tolerant to failure of a worker node, as the RDD lineage allows the system to recompute the lost data all the way from the surviving replica of the input data.

Receiver Fault Tolerance

The fault tolerance of the workers running the receivers is another important consideration. In such a failure, Spark Streaming restarts the failed receivers on other nodes in the cluster. However, whether it loses any of the received data depends on the nature of the source (whether the source can resend data or not) and the implementation of the receiver (whether it updates the source about received data or not). For example, with Flume, one of the main differences between the two receivers is the data loss guarantees. With the receiver-pull-from-sink model, Spark removes the elements only once they have been replicated inside Spark. For the push-to-receiver model, if the receiver fails before the data is replicated some data can be lost. In general, for any receiver, you must also consider the fault-tolerance properties of the upstream source (transactional, or not) for ensuring zero data loss.

In general, receivers provide the following guarantees:

- All data read from a reliable filesystem (e.g., with `StreamingContext.hadoop Files`) is reliable, because the underlying filesystem is replicated. Spark Streaming will remember which data it processed in its checkpoints and will pick up again where it left off if your application crashes.
- For unreliable sources such as receiver-based Kafka, push-based Flume, or Twitter, Spark replicates the input data to other nodes, but it can briefly lose data if a receiver task is down. In Spark 1.1 and earlier, received data was replicated in-memory only to executors, so it could also be lost if the driver crashed (in which case all executors disconnect). In Spark 1.2, received data can be logged to a reliable filesystem like HDFS so that it is not lost on driver restart.

To summarize, therefore, the best way to ensure all data is processed is to use a reliable input source (e.g., HDFS, directly consuming Kafka or pull-based Flume). If you have a non-reliable input source and wish to avoid any chance of data loss, post Spark 1.2, you should also enable write ahead logging by setting `spark.stream ing.receiver.writeAheadLog.enable` to `true`. This is generally also a best practice if you need to process the data later in batch jobs: it ensures that your batch jobs and streaming jobs will see the same data and produce the same results.

Processing Guarantees

Due to Spark Streaming's worker fault-tolerance guarantees, it can provide *exactly-once semantics* for all transformations—even if a worker fails and some data gets reprocessed, the final transformed result (that is, the transformed RDDs) will be the same as if the data were processed exactly once.

However, when the transformed result is to be pushed to external systems using output operations, the task pushing the result may get executed multiple times due to failures, and some data can get pushed multiple times. Since this involves external systems, it is up to the system-specific code to handle this case. We can either use transactions to push to external systems (that is, atomically push one RDD partition at a time), or design updates to be idempotent operations (such that multiple runs of an update still produce the same result). For example, Spark Streaming's `saveAs...File` operations automatically make sure only one copy of each output file exists, by atomically moving a file to its final destination when it is complete.

Streaming UI

Spark Streaming provides a special UI page that lets us look at what applications are doing. This is available in a Streaming tab on the normal Spark UI (typically *http://<driver>:4040*). A sample screenshot is shown in Figure 10-9.

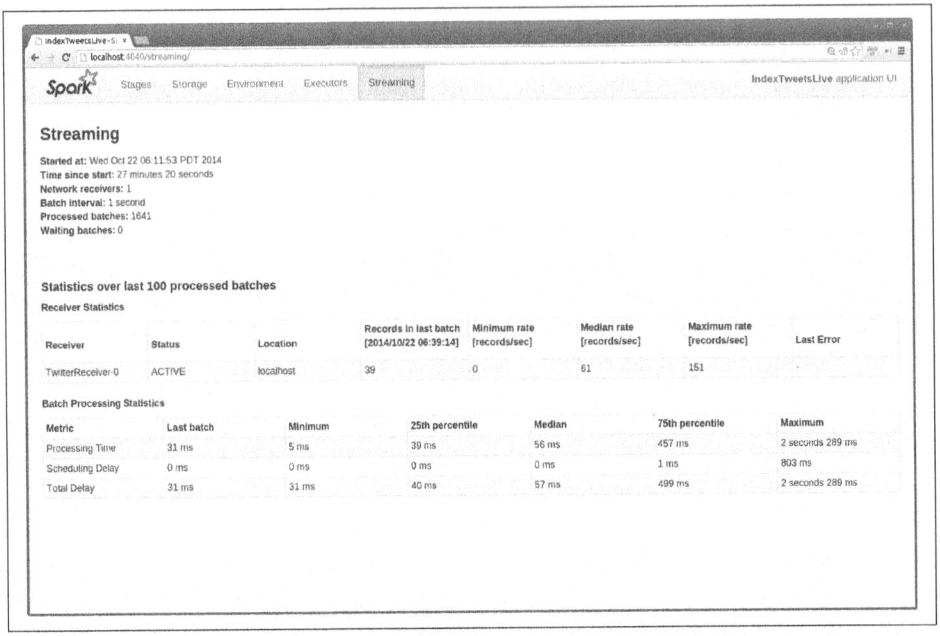

Figure 10-9. Streaming UI tab in the Spark UI

The Streaming UI exposes statistics for our batch processing and our receivers. In our example we have one network receiver, and we can see the message processing rates. If we were falling behind, we could see how many records each receiver is able to process. We can also see whether a receiver failed. The batch processing statistics show us how long our batches take and also break out the delay in scheduling the job. If a cluster experiences contention, then the scheduling delay may increase.

Performance Considerations

In addition to the existing performance considerations we have discussed in general Spark, Spark Streaming applications have a few specialized tuning options.

Batch and Window Sizes

The most common question is what minimum batch size Spark Streaming can use. In general, 500 milliseconds has proven to be a good minimum size for many applications. The best approach is to start with a larger batch size (around 10 seconds) and work your way down to a smaller batch size. If the processing times reported in the Streaming UI remain consistent, then you can continue to decrease the batch size, but if they are increasing you may have reached the limit for your application.

In a similar way, for windowed operations, the interval at which you compute a result (i.e., the slide interval) has a big impact on performance. Consider increasing this interval for expensive computations if it is a bottleneck.

Level of Parallelism

A common way to reduce the processing time of batches is to increase the parallelism. There are three ways to increase the parallelism:

Increasing the number of receivers
Receivers can sometimes act as a bottleneck if there are too many records for a single machine to read in and distribute. You can add more receivers by creating multiple input DStreams (which creates multiple receivers), and then applying union to merge them into a single stream.

Explicitly repartitioning received data
If receivers cannot be increased anymore, you can further redistribute the received data by explicitly repartitioning the input stream (or the union of multiple streams) using DStream.repartition.

Increasing parallelism in aggregation
For operations like reduceByKey(), you can specify the parallelism as a second parameter, as already discussed for RDDs.

Garbage Collection and Memory Usage

Another aspect that can cause problems is Java's garbage collection. You can minimize unpredictably large pauses due to GC by enabling Java's Concurrent Mark-Sweep garbage collector. The Concurrent Mark-Sweep garbage collector does consume more resources overall, but introduces fewer pauses.

We can control the GC by adding -XX:+UseConcMarkSweepGC to the spark.execu tor.extraJavaOptions configuration parameter. Example 10-48 shows this with spark-submit.

Example 10-48. Enable the Concurrent Mark-Sweep GC

```
spark-submit --conf spark.executor.extraJavaOptions=-XX:+UseConcMarkSweepGC App.jar
```

In addition to using a garbage collector less likely to introduce pauses, you can make a big difference by reducing GC pressure. Caching RDDs in serialized form (instead of as native objects) also reduces GC pressure, which is why, by default, RDDs generated by Spark Streaming are stored in serialized form. Using Kryo serialization further reduces the memory required for the in-memory representation of cached data.

Spark also allows us to control how cached/persisted RDDs are evicted from the cache. By default Spark uses an LRU cache. Spark will also explicitly evict RDDs older than a certain time period if you set `spark.cleaner.ttl`. By preemptively evicting RDDs that we are unlikely to need from the cache, we may be able to reduce the GC pressure.

Conclusion

In this chapter, we have seen how to work with streaming data using DStreams. Since DStreams are composed of RDDs, the techniques and knowledge you have gained from the earlier chapters remains applicable for streaming and real-time applications. In the next chapter, we will look at machine learning with Spark.

## CHAPTER 11

Machine Learning with MLlib

MLlib is Spark's library of machine learning functions. Designed to run in parallel on clusters, MLlib contains a variety of learning algorithms and is accessible from all of Spark's programming languages. This chapter will show you how to call it in your own programs, and offer common usage tips.

Machine learning itself is a topic large enough to fill many books,[1] so unfortunately, in this chapter, we will not have the space to explain machine learning in detail. If you are familiar with machine learning, however, this chapter will explain how to use it in Spark; and even if you are new to it, you should be able to combine the material here with other introductory material. This chapter is most relevant to data scientists with a machine learning background looking to use Spark, as well as engineers working with a machine learning expert.

Overview

MLlib's design and philosophy are simple: it lets you invoke various algorithms on distributed datasets, representing all data as RDDs. MLlib introduces a few data types (e.g., labeled points and vectors), but at the end of the day, it is simply a set of functions to call on RDDs. For example, to use MLlib for a text classification task (e.g., identifying spammy emails), you might do the following:

1. Start with an RDD of strings representing your messages.

2. Run one of MLlib's *feature extraction* algorithms to convert text into numerical features (suitable for learning algorithms); this will give back an RDD of vectors.

---

1 Some examples from O'Reilly include *Machine Learning with R* and *Machine Learning for Hackers*.

3. Call a classification algorithm (e.g., logistic regression) on the RDD of vectors; this will give back a model object that can be used to classify new points.

4. Evaluate the model on a test dataset using one of MLlib's evaluation functions.

One important thing to note about MLlib is that it contains only *parallel* algorithms that run well on clusters. Some classic ML algorithms are not included because they were not designed for parallel platforms, but in contrast MLlib contains several recent research algorithms for clusters, such as distributed random forests, K-means||, and alternating least squares. This choice means that MLlib is best suited for running each algorithm on a large dataset. If you instead have many small datasets on which you want to train different learning models, it would be better to use a single-node learning library (e.g., Weka (*http://www.cs.waikato.ac.nz/ml/weka/*) or SciKit-Learn (*http://scikit-learn.org/*)) on each node, perhaps calling it in parallel across nodes using a Spark `map()`. Likewise, it is common for machine learning pipelines to require training the *same* algorithm on a small dataset with many configurations of parameters, in order to choose the best one. You can achieve this in Spark by using `parallelize()` over your list of parameters to train different ones on different nodes, again using a single-node learning library on each node. But MLlib itself shines when you have a large, distributed dataset that you need to train a model on.

Finally, in Spark 1.0 and 1.1, MLlib's interface is relatively low-level, giving you the functions to call for different tasks but not the higher-level workflow typically required for a learning pipeline (e.g., splitting the input into training and test data, or trying many combinations of parameters). In Spark 1.2, MLlib gains an additional (and at the time of writing still experimental) *pipeline API* for building such pipelines. This API resembles higher-level libraries like SciKit-Learn, and will hopefully make it easy to write complete, self-tuning pipelines. We include a preview of this API at the end of this chapter, but focus primarily on the lower-level APIs.

System Requirements

MLlib requires some linear algebra libraries to be installed on your machines. First, you will need the `gfortran` runtime library for your operating system. If MLlib warns that `gfortran` is missing, follow the setup instructions on the MLlib website (*http://bit.ly/1yCoHox*). Second, to use MLlib in Python, you will need NumPy (*http://www.numpy.org/*). If your Python installation does not have it (i.e., you cannot `import numpy`), the easiest way to get it is by installing the `python-numpy` or `numpy` package through your package manager on Linux, or by using a third-party scientific Python installation like Anaconda (*http://bit.ly/1yCoMIC*).

MLlib's supported algorithms have also evolved over time. The ones we discuss here are all available as of Spark 1.2, but some of the algorithms may not be present in earlier versions.

Machine Learning Basics

To put the functions in MLlib in context, we'll start with a brief review of machine learning concepts.

Machine learning algorithms attempt to make predictions or decisions based on *training data*, often maximizing a mathematical objective about how the algorithm should behave. There are multiple types of learning problems, including classification, regression, or clustering, which have different objectives. As a simple example, we'll consider *classification*, which involves identifying which of several categories an item belongs to (e.g., whether an email is spam or non-spam), based on labeled examples of other items (e.g., emails known to be spam or not).

All learning algorithms require defining a set of *features* for each item, which will be fed into the learning function. For example, for an email, some features might include the server it comes from, or the number of mentions of the word *free*, or the color of the text. In many cases, defining the right features is the most challenging part of using machine learning. For example, in a product recommendation task, simply adding another feature (e.g., realizing that which book you should recommend to a user might also depend on which movies she's watched) could give a large improvement in results.

Most algorithms are defined only for numerical features (specifically, a vector of numbers representing the value for each feature), so often an important step is *feature extraction and transformation* to produce these feature vectors. For example, for text classification (e.g., our spam versus non-spam case), there are several methods to featurize text, such as counting the frequency of each word.

Once data is represented as feature vectors, most machine learning algorithms optimize a well-defined mathematical function based on these vectors. For example, one classification algorithm might be to define the plane (in the space of feature vectors) that "best" separates the spam versus non-spam examples, according to some definition of "best" (e.g., the most points classified correctly by the plane). At the end, the algorithm will return a *model* representing the learning decision (e.g., the plane chosen). This model can now be used to make predictions on new points (e.g., see which side of the plane the feature vector for a new email falls on, in order to decide whether it's spam). Figure 11-1 shows an example learning pipeline.

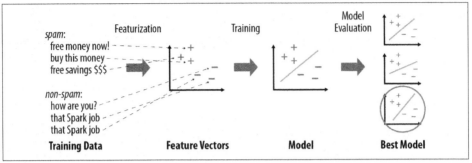

Figure 11-1. Typical steps in a machine learning pipeline

Finally, most learning algorithms have multiple parameters that can affect results, so real-world pipelines will train multiple versions of a model and *evaluate* each one. To do this, it is common to separate the input data into "training" and "test" sets, and train only on the former, so that the test set can be used to see whether the model *overfit* the training data. MLlib provides several algorithms for model evaluation.

Example: Spam Classification

As a quick example of MLlib, we show a very simple program for building a spam classifier (Examples 11-1 through 11-3). This program uses two MLlib algorithms: HashingTF, which builds *term frequency* feature vectors from text data, and Logistic RegressionWithSGD, which implements the logistic regression procedure using *stochastic gradient descent* (SGD). We assume that we start with two files, *spam.txt* and *normal.txt*, each of which contains examples of spam and non-spam emails, one per line. We then turn the text in each file into a feature vector with TF, and train a logistic regression model to separate the two types of messages. The code and data files are available in the book's Git repository.

Example 11-1. Spam classifier in Python

```
from pyspark.mllib.regression import LabeledPoint
from pyspark.mllib.feature import HashingTF
from pyspark.mllib.classification import LogisticRegressionWithSGD

spam = sc.textFile("spam.txt")
normal = sc.textFile("normal.txt")

# Create a HashingTF instance to map email text to vectors of 10,000 features.
tf = HashingTF(numFeatures = 10000)
# Each email is split into words, and each word is mapped to one feature.
spamFeatures = spam.map(lambda email: tf.transform(email.split(" ")))
normalFeatures = normal.map(lambda email: tf.transform(email.split(" ")))

# Create LabeledPoint datasets for positive (spam) and negative (normal) examples.
```

```
positiveExamples = spamFeatures.map(lambda features: LabeledPoint(1, features))
negativeExamples = normalFeatures.map(lambda features: LabeledPoint(0, features))
trainingData = positiveExamples.union(negativeExamples)
trainingData.cache() # Cache since Logistic Regression is an iterative algorithm.

# Run Logistic Regression using the SGD algorithm.
model = LogisticRegressionWithSGD.train(trainingData)

# Test on a positive example (spam) and a negative one (normal). We first apply
# the same HashingTF feature transformation to get vectors, then apply the model.
posTest = tf.transform("O M G GET cheap stuff by sending money to ...".split(" "))
negTest = tf.transform("Hi Dad, I started studying Spark the other ...".split(" "))
print "Prediction for positive test example: %g" % model.predict(posTest)
print "Prediction for negative test example: %g" % model.predict(negTest)
```

Example 11-2. Spam classifier in Scala

```
import org.apache.spark.mllib.regression.LabeledPoint
import org.apache.spark.mllib.feature.HashingTF
import org.apache.spark.mllib.classification.LogisticRegressionWithSGD

val spam = sc.textFile("spam.txt")
val normal = sc.textFile("normal.txt")

// Create a HashingTF instance to map email text to vectors of 10,000 features.
val tf = new HashingTF(numFeatures = 10000)
// Each email is split into words, and each word is mapped to one feature.
val spamFeatures = spam.map(email => tf.transform(email.split(" ")))
val normalFeatures = normal.map(email => tf.transform(email.split(" ")))

// Create LabeledPoint datasets for positive (spam) and negative (normal) examples.
val positiveExamples = spamFeatures.map(features => LabeledPoint(1, features))
val negativeExamples = normalFeatures.map(features => LabeledPoint(0, features))
val trainingData = positiveExamples.union(negativeExamples)
trainingData.cache() // Cache since Logistic Regression is an iterative algorithm.

// Run Logistic Regression using the SGD algorithm.
val model = new LogisticRegressionWithSGD().run(trainingData)

// Test on a positive example (spam) and a negative one (normal).
val posTest = tf.transform(
  "O M G GET cheap stuff by sending money to ...".split(" "))
val negTest = tf.transform(
  "Hi Dad, I started studying Spark the other ...".split(" "))
println("Prediction for positive test example: " + model.predict(posTest))
println("Prediction for negative test example: " + model.predict(negTest))
```

Example 11-3. Spam classifier in Java

```
import org.apache.spark.mllib.classification.LogisticRegressionModel;
import org.apache.spark.mllib.classification.LogisticRegressionWithSGD;
```

```java
import org.apache.spark.mllib.feature.HashingTF;
import org.apache.spark.mllib.linalg.Vector;
import org.apache.spark.mllib.regression.LabeledPoint;

JavaRDD<String> spam = sc.textFile("spam.txt");
JavaRDD<String> normal = sc.textFile("normal.txt");

// Create a HashingTF instance to map email text to vectors of 10,000 features.
final HashingTF tf = new HashingTF(10000);

// Create LabeledPoint datasets for positive (spam) and negative (normal) examples.
JavaRDD<LabeledPoint> posExamples = spam.map(new Function<String, LabeledPoint>() {
  public LabeledPoint call(String email) {
    return new LabeledPoint(1, tf.transform(Arrays.asList(email.split(" "))));
  }
});
JavaRDD<LabeledPoint> negExamples = normal.map(new Function<String, LabeledPoint>() {
  public LabeledPoint call(String email) {
    return new LabeledPoint(0, tf.transform(Arrays.asList(email.split(" "))));
  }
});
JavaRDD<LabeledPoint> trainData = positiveExamples.union(negativeExamples);
trainData.cache(); // Cache since Logistic Regression is an iterative algorithm.

// Run Logistic Regression using the SGD algorithm.
LogisticRegressionModel model = new LogisticRegressionWithSGD().run(trainData.rdd());

// Test on a positive example (spam) and a negative one (normal).
Vector posTest = tf.transform(
  Arrays.asList("O M G GET cheap stuff by sending money to ...".split(" ")));
Vector negTest = tf.transform(
  Arrays.asList("Hi Dad, I started studying Spark the other ...".split(" ")));
System.out.println("Prediction for positive example: " + model.predict(posTest));
System.out.println("Prediction for negative example: " + model.predict(negTest));
```

As you can see, the code is fairly similar in all the languages. It operates directly on
RDDs—in this case, of strings (the original text) and LabeledPoints (an MLlib data
type for a vector of features together with a label).

Data Types

MLlib contains a few specific data types, located in the org.apache.spark.mllib
package (Java/Scala) or pyspark.mllib (Python). The main ones are:

Vector
    A mathematical vector. MLlib supports both dense vectors, where every entry is
    stored, and sparse vectors, where only the nonzero entries are stored to save
    space. We will discuss the different types of vectors shortly. Vectors can be con‐
    structed with the mllib.linalg.Vectors class.

LabeledPoint

A labeled data point for supervised learning algorithms such as classification and regression. Includes a feature vector and a label (which is a floating-point value). Located in the mllib.regression package.

Rating

A rating of a product by a user, used in the mllib.recommendation package for product recommendation.

Various Model *classes*

Each Model is the result of a training algorithm, and typically has a predict() method for applying the model to a new data point or to an RDD of new data points.

Most algorithms work directly on RDDs of Vectors, LabeledPoints, or Ratings. You can construct these objects however you want, but typically you will build an RDD through transformations on external data—for example, by loading a text file or running a Spark SQL command—and then apply a map() to turn your data objects into MLlib types.

Working with Vectors

There are a few points to note for the Vector class in MLlib, which will be the most commonly used one.

First, vectors come in two flavors: dense and sparse. Dense vectors store all their entries in an array of floating-point numbers. For example, a vector of size 100 will contain 100 double values. In contrast, sparse vectors store only the nonzero values and their indices. Sparse vectors are usually preferable (both in terms of memory use and speed) if at most 10% of elements are nonzero. Many featurization techniques yield very sparse vectors, so using this representation is often a key optimization.

Second, the ways to construct vectors vary a bit by language. In Python, you can simply pass a NumPy array anywhere in MLlib to represent a dense vector, or use the mllib.linalg.Vectors class to build vectors of other types (see Example 11-4).[2] In Java and Scala, use the mllib.linalg.Vectors class (see Examples 11-5 and 11-6).

Example 11-4. Creating vectors in Python

```
from numpy import array
from pyspark.mllib.linalg import Vectors
```

---

2 If you use SciPy, Spark also recognizes scipy.sparse matrices of size $N \times 1$ as length-N vectors.

```
# Create the dense vector <1.0, 2.0, 3.0>
denseVec1 = array([1.0, 2.0, 3.0])  # NumPy arrays can be passed directly to MLlib
denseVec2 = Vectors.dense([1.0, 2.0, 3.0]) # .. or you can use the Vectors class

# Create the sparse vector <1.0, 0.0, 2.0, 0.0>; the methods for this take only
# the size of the vector (4) and the positions and values of nonzero entries.
# These can be passed as a dictionary or as two lists of indices and values.
sparseVec1 = Vectors.sparse(4, {0: 1.0, 2: 2.0})
sparseVec2 = Vectors.sparse(4, [0, 2], [1.0, 2.0])
```

Example 11-5. Creating vectors in Scala

```
import org.apache.spark.mllib.linalg.Vectors

// Create the dense vector <1.0, 2.0, 3.0>; Vectors.dense takes values or an array
val denseVec1 = Vectors.dense(1.0, 2.0, 3.0)
val denseVec2 = Vectors.dense(Array(1.0, 2.0, 3.0))

// Create the sparse vector <1.0, 0.0, 2.0, 0.0>; Vectors.sparse takes the size of
// the vector (here 4) and the positions and values of nonzero entries
val sparseVec1 = Vectors.sparse(4, Array(0, 2), Array(1.0, 2.0))
```

Example 11-6. Creating vectors in Java

```
import org.apache.spark.mllib.linalg.Vector;
import org.apache.spark.mllib.linalg.Vectors;

// Create the dense vector <1.0, 2.0, 3.0>; Vectors.dense takes values or an array
Vector denseVec1 = Vectors.dense(1.0, 2.0, 3.0);
Vector denseVec2 = Vectors.dense(new double[] {1.0, 2.0, 3.0});

// Create the sparse vector <1.0, 0.0, 2.0, 0.0>; Vectors.sparse takes the size of
// the vector (here 4) and the positions and values of nonzero entries
Vector sparseVec1 = Vectors.sparse(4, new int[] {0, 2}, new double[]{1.0, 2.0});
```

Finally, in Java and Scala, MLlib's Vector classes are primarily meant for data representation, but do not provide arithmetic operations such as addition and subtraction in the user API. (In Python, you can of course use NumPy to perform math on dense vectors and pass those to MLlib.) This was done mainly to keep MLlib small, because writing a complete linear algebra library is beyond the scope of the project. But if you want to do vector math in your programs, you can use a third-party library like Breeze (*https://github.com/scalanlp/breeze*) in Scala or MTJ (*https://github.com/fommil/matrix-toolkits-java*) in Java, and convert the data from it to MLlib vectors.

Algorithms

In this section, we'll cover the key algorithms available in MLlib, as well as their input and output types. We do not have space to explain each algorithm mathematically, but focus instead on how to call and configure these algorithms.

Feature Extraction

The `mllib.feature` package contains several classes for common feature transformations. These include algorithms to construct feature vectors from text (or from other tokens), and ways to normalize and scale features.

TF-IDF

Term Frequency–Inverse Document Frequency, or TF-IDF, is a simple way to generate feature vectors from text documents (e.g., web pages). It computes two statistics for each term in each document: the term frequency (TF), which is the number of times the term occurs in that document, and the inverse document frequency (IDF), which measures how (in)frequently a term occurs across the whole document corpus. The product of these values, TF × IDF, shows how relevant a term is to a specific document (i.e., if it is common in that document but rare in the whole corpus).

MLlib has two algorithms that compute TF-IDF: `HashingTF` and `IDF`, both in the `mllib.feature` package. `HashingTF` computes a term frequency vector of a given size from a document. In order to map terms to vector indices, it uses a technique known as the *hashing trick*. Within a language like English, there are hundreds of thousands of words, so tracking a distinct mapping from each word to an index in the vector would be expensive. Instead, `HashingTF` takes the hash code of each word modulo a desired vector size, S, and thus maps each word to a number between 0 and $S-1$. This always yields an S-dimensional vector, and in practice is quite robust even if multiple words map to the same hash code. The MLlib developers recommend setting S between 2^{18} and 2^{20}.

`HashingTF` can run either on one document at a time or on a whole RDD. It requires each "document" to be represented as an iterable sequence of objects—for instance, a list in Python or a `Collection` in Java. Example 11-7 uses `HashingTF` in Python.

Example 11-7. Using HashingTF in Python

```
>>> from pyspark.mllib.feature import HashingTF

>>> sentence = "hello hello world"
>>> words = sentence.split()  # Split sentence into a list of terms
>>> tf = HashingTF(10000)  # Create vectors of size S = 10,000
>>> tf.transform(words)
SparseVector(10000, {3065: 1.0, 6861: 2.0})
```

```
>>> rdd = sc.wholeTextFiles("data").map(lambda (name, text): text.split())
>>> tfVectors = tf.transform(rdd)    # Transforms an entire RDD
```

 In a real pipeline, you will likely need to preprocess and stem words in a document before passing them to TF. For example, you might convert all words to lowercase, drop punctuation characters, and drop suffixes like *ing*. For best results you can call a single-node natural language library like NLTK (*http://www.nltk.org*) in a map().

Once you have built term frequency vectors, you can use IDF to compute the inverse document frequencies, and multiply them with the term frequencies to compute the TF-IDF. You first call fit() on an IDF object to obtain an IDFModel representing the inverse document frequencies in the corpus, then call transform() on the model to transform TF vectors into IDF vectors. Example 11-8 shows how you would compute IDF starting with Example 11-7.

Example 11-8. Using TF-IDF in Python

```
from pyspark.mllib.feature import HashingTF, IDF

# Read a set of text files as TF vectors
rdd = sc.wholeTextFiles("data").map(lambda (name, text): text.split())
tf = HashingTF()
tfVectors = tf.transform(rdd).cache()

# Compute the IDF, then the TF-IDF vectors
idf = IDF()
idfModel = idf.fit(tfVectors)
tfIdfVectors = idfModel.transform(tfVectors)
```

Note that we called cache() on the tfVectors RDD because it is used twice (once to train the IDF model, and once to multiply the TF vectors by the IDF).

Scaling

Most machine learning algorithms consider the magnitude of each element in the feature vector, and thus work best when the features are scaled so they weigh equally (e.g., all features have a mean of 0 and standard deviation of 1). Once you have built feature vectors, you can use the StandardScaler class in MLlib to do this scaling, both for the mean and the standard deviation. You create a StandardScaler, call fit() on a dataset to obtain a StandardScalerModel (i.e., compute the mean and variance of each column), and then call transform() on the model to scale a dataset. Example 11-9 demonstrates.

Example 11-9. Scaling vectors in Python

```python
from pyspark.mllib.feature import StandardScaler

vectors = [Vectors.dense([-2.0, 5.0, 1.0]), Vectors.dense([2.0, 0.0, 1.0])]
dataset = sc.parallelize(vectors)
scaler = StandardScaler(withMean=True, withStd=True)
model = scaler.fit(dataset)
result = model.transform(dataset)

# Result: {[-0.7071, 0.7071, 0.0], [0.7071, -0.7071, 0.0]}
```

Normalization

In some situations, normalizing vectors to length 1 is also useful to prepare input data. The `Normalizer` class allows this. Simply use `Normalizer().transform(rdd)`. By default `Normalizer` uses the L^2 norm (i.e, Euclidean length), but you can also pass a power p to `Normalizer` to use the L^p norm.

Word2Vec

Word2Vec (*https://code.google.com/p/word2vec/*)[3] is a featurization algorithm for text based on neural networks that can be used to feed data into many downstream algorithms. Spark includes an implementation of it in the `mllib.feature.Word2Vec` class.

To train Word2Vec, you need to pass it a corpus of documents, represented as `Itera bles` of `Strings` (one per word). Much like in "TF-IDF" on page 223, it is recommended to normalize your words (e.g., mapping them to lowercase and removing punctuation and numbers). Once you have trained the model (with `Word2Vec.fit(rdd)`), you will receive a `Word2VecModel` that can be used to `trans form()` each word into a vector. Note that the size of the models in Word2Vec will be equal to the number of words in your vocabulary times the size of a vector (by default, 100). You may wish to filter out words that are not in a standard dictionary to limit the size. In general, a good size for the vocabulary is 100,000 words.

Statistics

Basic statistics are an important part of data analysis, both in ad hoc exploration and understanding data for machine learning. MLlib offers several widely used statistic functions that work directly on RDDs, through methods in the `mllib.stat.Statis tics` class. Some commonly used ones include:

---

3 Introduced in Mikolov et al., "Efficient Estimation of Word Representations in Vector Space," 2013.

`Statistics.colStats(`*`rdd`*`)`

Computes a statistical summary of an RDD of vectors, which stores the min, max, mean, and variance for each column in the set of vectors. This can be used to obtain a wide variety of statistics in one pass.

`Statistics.corr(`*`rdd, method`*`)`

Computes the correlation matrix between columns in an RDD of vectors, using either the Pearson or Spearman correlation (*method* must be one of `pearson` and `spearman`).

`Statistics.corr(`*`rdd1, rdd2, method`*`)`

Computes the correlation between two RDDs of floating-point values, using either the Pearson or Spearman correlation (*method* must be one of `pearson` and `spearman`).

`Statistics.chiSqTest(`*`rdd`*`)`

Computes Pearson's independence test for every feature with the label on an RDD of `LabeledPoint` objects. Returns an array of `ChiSqTestResult` objects that capture the p-value, test statistic, and degrees of freedom for each feature. Label and feature values must be categorical (i.e., discrete values).

Apart from these methods, RDDs containing numeric data offer several basic statistics such as `mean()`, `stdev()`, and `sum()`, as described in "Numeric RDD Operations" on page 113. In addition, RDDs support `sample()` and `sampleByKey()` to build simple and stratified samples of data.

Classification and Regression

Classification and regression are two common forms of *supervised learning*, where algorithms attempt to predict a variable from features of objects using labeled training data (i.e., examples where we know the answer). The difference between them is the type of variable predicted: in classification, the variable is *discrete* (i.e., it takes on a finite set of values called *classes*); for example, classes might be `spam` or `nonspam` for emails, or the language in which the text is written. In regression, the variable predicted is *continuous* (e.g., the height of a person given her age and weight).

Both classification and regression use the `LabeledPoint` class in MLlib, described in "Data Types" on page 220, which resides in the `mllib.regression` package. A `Label edPoint` consists simply of a `label` (which is always a `Double` value, but can be set to discrete integers for classification) and a `features` vector.

For binary classification, MLlib expects the labels 0 and 1. In some texts, –1 and 1 are used instead, but this will lead to incorrect results. For multiclass classification, MLlib expects labels from 0 to C–1, where C is the number of classes.

MLlib includes a variety of methods for classification and regression, including simple linear methods and decision trees and forests.

Linear regression

Linear regression is one of the most common methods for regression, predicting the output variable as a linear combination of the features. MLlib also supports L^1 and L^2 regularized regression, commonly known as *Lasso* and *ridge regression.*

The linear regression algorithms are available through the `mllib.regression.Line arRegressionWithSGD`, `LassoWithSGD`, and `RidgeRegressionWithSGD` classes. These follow a common naming pattern throughout MLlib, where problems involving multiple algorithms have a "With" part in the class name to specify the algorithm used. Here, SGD is Stochastic Gradient Descent.

These classes all have several parameters to tune the algorithm:

numIterations
Number of iterations to run (default: `100`).

stepSize
Step size for gradient descent (default: `1.0`).

intercept
Whether to add an intercept or bias feature to the data—that is, another feature whose value is always 1 (default: `false`).

regParam
Regularization parameter for Lasso and ridge (default: `1.0`).

The way to call the algorithms differs slightly by language. In Java and Scala, you create a `LinearRegressionWithSGD` object, call setter methods on it to set the parameters, and then call `run()` to train a model. In Python, you instead use the class method `LinearRegressionWithSGD.train()`, to which you pass key/value parameters. In both cases, you pass in an RDD of `LabeledPoints`, as shown in Examples 11-10 through 11-12.

Example 11-10. Linear regression in Python

```
from pyspark.mllib.regression import LabeledPoint
from pyspark.mllib.regression import LinearRegressionWithSGD
```

```
points = # (create RDD of LabeledPoint)
model = LinearRegressionWithSGD.train(points, iterations=200, intercept=True)
print "weights: %s, intercept: %s" % (model.weights, model.intercept)
```

Example 11-11. Linear regression in Scala

```
import org.apache.spark.mllib.regression.LabeledPoint
import org.apache.spark.mllib.regression.LinearRegressionWithSGD

val points: RDD[LabeledPoint] = // ...
val lr = new LinearRegressionWithSGD().setNumIterations(200).setIntercept(true)
val model = lr.run(points)
println("weights: %s, intercept: %s".format(model.weights, model.intercept))
```

Example 11-12. Linear regression in Java

```
import org.apache.spark.mllib.regression.LabeledPoint;
import org.apache.spark.mllib.regression.LinearRegressionWithSGD;
import org.apache.spark.mllib.regression.LinearRegressionModel;

JavaRDD<LabeledPoint> points = // ...
LinearRegressionWithSGD lr =
  new LinearRegressionWithSGD().setNumIterations(200).setIntercept(true);
LinearRegressionModel model = lr.run(points.rdd());
System.out.printf("weights: %s, intercept: %s\n",
  model.weights(), model.intercept());
```

Note that in Java, we need to convert our JavaRDD to the Scala RDD class by calling .rdd() on it. This is a common pattern throughout MLlib because the MLlib
methods are designed to be callable from both Java and Scala.

Once trained, the LinearRegressionModel returned in all languages includes a pre
dict() function that can be used to predict a value on a single vector. The RidgeRe
gressionWithSGD and LassoWithSGD classes behave similarly and return a similar
model class. Indeed, this pattern of an algorithm with parameters adjusted through
setters, which returns a Model object with a predict() method, is common in all of
MLlib.

Logistic regression

Logistic regression is a binary classification method that identifies a linear separating
plane between positive and negative examples. In MLlib, it takes LabeledPoints with
label 0 or 1 and returns a LogisticRegressionModel that can predict new points.

The logistic regression algorithm has a very similar API to linear regression, covered
in the previous section. One difference is that there are two algorithms available for

solving it: SGD and LBFGS.[4] LBFGS is generally the best choice, but is not available in some earlier versions of MLlib (before Spark 1.2). These algorithms are available in the `mllib.classification.LogisticRegressionWithLBFGS` and `WithSGD` classes, which have interfaces similar to `LinearRegressionWithSGD`. They take all the same parameters as linear regression (see the previous section).

The `LogisticRegressionModel` from these algorithms computes a score between 0 and 1 for each point, as returned by the logistic function. It then returns either 0 or 1 based on a *threshold* that can be set by the user: by default, if the score is at least 0.5, it will return 1. You can change this threshold via `setThreshold()`. You can also disable it altogether via `clearThreshold()`, in which case `predict()` will return the raw scores. For balanced datasets with about the same number of positive and negative examples, we recommend leaving the threshold at 0.5. For imbalanced datasets, you can increase the threshold to drive down the number of false positives (i.e., increase precision but decrease recall), or you can decrease the threshold to drive down the number of false negatives.

 When using logistic regression, it is usually important to scale the features in advance to be in the same range. You can use MLlib's StandardScaler to do this, as seen in "Scaling" on page 224.

Support Vector Machines

Support Vector Machines, or SVMs, are another binary classification method with linear separating planes, again expecting labels of 0 or 1. They are available through the `SVMWithSGD` class, with similar parameters to linear and logisitic regression. The returned `SVMModel` uses a threshold for prediction like `LogisticRegressionModel`.

Naive Bayes

Naive Bayes is a multiclass classification algorithm that scores how well each point belongs in each class based on a linear function of the features. It is commonly used in text classification with TF-IDF features, among other applications. MLlib implements Multinomial Naive Bayes, which expects nonnegative frequencies (e.g., word frequencies) as input features.

In MLlib, you can use Naive Bayes through the `mllib.classification.NaiveBayes` class. It supports one parameter, `lambda` (or `lambda_` in Python), used for smoothing.

---

4 LBFGS is an approximation to Newton's method that converges in fewer iterations than stochastic gradient descent. It is described at *http://en.wikipedia.org/wiki/Limited-memory_BFGS*.

You can call it on an RDD of LabeledPoints, where the labels are between 0 and $C{-}1$ for C classes.

The returned NaiveBayesModel lets you predict() the class in which a point best belongs, as well as access the two parameters of the trained model: theta, the matrix of class probabilities for each feature (of size $C \times D$ for C classes and D features), and pi, the C-dimensional vector of class priors.

Decision trees and random forests

Decision trees are a flexible model that can be used for both classification and regression. They represent a tree of *nodes*, each of which makes a binary decision based on a feature of the data (e.g., is a person's age greater than 20?), and where the leaf nodes in the tree contain a prediction (e.g., is the person likely to buy a product?). Decision trees are attractive because the models are easy to inspect and because they support both categorical and continuous features. Figure 11-2 shows an example tree.

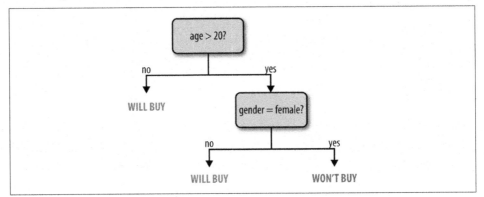

Figure 11-2. An example decision tree predicting whether a user might buy a product

In MLlib, you can train trees using the mllib.tree.DecisionTree class, through the static methods trainClassifier() and trainRegressor(). Unlike in some of the other algorithms, the Java and Scala APIs also use static methods instead of a DecisionTree object with setters. The training methods take the following parameters:

data
RDD of LabeledPoint.

numClasses *(classification only)*
Number of classes to use.

impurity
Node impurity measure; can be gini or entropy for classification, and must be variance for regression.

maxDepth

Maximum depth of tree (default: 5).

maxBins

Number of bins to split data into when building each node (suggested value: 32).

categoricalFeaturesInfo

A map specifying which features are categorical, and how many categories they each have. For example, if feature 1 is a binary feature with labels 0 and 1, and feature 2 is a three-valued feature with values 0, 1, and 2, you would pass {1: 2, 2: 3}. Use an empty map if no features are categorical.

The online MLlib documentation (*http://spark.apache.org/docs/latest/mllib-decision-tree.html*) contains a detailed explanation of the algorithm used. The cost of the algorithm scales linearly with the number of training examples, number of features, and maxBins. For large datasets, you may wish to lower maxBins to train a model faster, though this will also decrease quality.

The train() methods return a DecisionTreeModel. You can use it to predict values for a new feature vector or an RDD of vectors via predict(), or print the tree using toDebugString(). This object is serializable, so you can save it using Java Serialization and load it in another program.

Finally, in Spark 1.2, MLlib adds an experimental RandomForest class in Java and Scala to build ensembles of trees, also known as random forests. It is available through RandomForest.trainClassifier and trainRegressor. Apart from the per-tree parameters just listed, RandomForest takes the following parameters:

numTrees

How many trees to build. Increasing numTrees decreases the likelihood of overfitting on training data.

featureSubsetStrategy

Number of features to consider for splits at each node; can be auto (let the library select it), all, sqrt, log2, or onethird; larger values are more expensive.

seed

Random-number seed to use.

Random forests return a WeightedEnsembleModel that contains several trees (in the weakHypotheses field, weighted by weakHypothesisWeights) and can predict() an RDD or Vector. It also includes a toDebugString to print all the trees.

Clustering

Clustering is the unsupervised learning task that involves grouping objects into *clusters* of high similarity. Unlike the supervised tasks seen before, where data is labeled, clustering can be used to make sense of unlabeled data. It is commonly used in data exploration (to find what a new dataset looks like) and in anomaly detection (to identify points that are far from *any* cluster).

K-means

MLlib includes the popular K-means algorithm for clustering, as well as a variant called K-means|| that provides better initialization in parallel environments.[5] K-means|| is similar to the K-means++ initialization procedure often used in single-node settings.

The most important parameter in K-means is a target number of clusters to generate, K. In practice, you rarely know the "true" number of clusters in advance, so the best practice is to try several values of K, until the average intracluster distance stops decreasing dramatically. However, the algorithm takes only one K at a time. Apart from K, K-means in MLlib takes the following parameters:

initializationMode
> The method to initialize cluster centers, which can be either "k-means||" or "random"; k-means|| (the default) generally leads to better results but is slightly more expensive.

maxIterations
> Maximum number of iterations to run (default: 100).

runs
> Number of concurrent runs of the algorithm to execute. MLlib's K-means supports running from multiple starting positions concurrently and picking the best result, which is a good way to get a better overall model (as K-means runs can stop in local minima).

Like other algorithms, you invoke K-means by creating a mllib.clustering.KMeans object (in Java/Scala) or calling KMeans.train (in Python). It takes an RDD of Vectors. K-means returns a KMeansModel that lets you access the clusterCenters (as an array of vectors) or call predict() on a new vector to return its cluster. Note that predict() always returns the closest center to a point, even if the point is far from all clusters.

---

5 K-means|| was introduced in Bahmani et al., "Scalable K-Means++," VLDB 2008.

Collaborative Filtering and Recommendation

Collaborative filtering is a technique for recommender systems wherein users' ratings and interactions with various products are used to recommend new ones. Collaborative filtering is attractive because it only needs to take in a list of user/product interactions: either "explicit" interactions (i.e., ratings on a shopping site) or "implicit" ones (e.g., a user browsed a product page but did not rate the product). Based solely on these interactions, collaborative filtering algorithms learn which products are similar to each other (because the same users interact with them) and which users are similar to each other, and can make new recommendations.

While the MLlib API talks about "users" and "products," you can also use collaborative filtering for other applications, such as recommending users to follow on a social network, tags to add to an article, or songs to add to a radio station.

Alternating Least Squares

MLlib includes an implementation of Alternating Least Squares (ALS), a popular algorithm for collaborative filtering that scales well on clusters.[6] It is located in the `mllib.recommendation.ALS` class.

ALS works by determining a feature vector for each user and product, such that the dot product of a user's vector and a product's is close to their score. It takes the following parameters:

rank
> Size of feature vectors to use; larger ranks can lead to better models but are more expensive to compute (default: 10).

iterations
> Number of iterations to run (default: 10).

lambda
> Regularization parameter (default: 0.01).

alpha
> A constant used for computing confidence in implicit ALS (default: 1.0).

numUserBlocks, numProductBlocks
> Number of blocks to divide user and product data in, to control parallelism; you can pass –1 to let MLlib automatically determine this (the default behavior).

---

6 Two research papers on ALS for web-scale data are Zhou et al.'s "Large-Scale Parallel Collaborative Filtering for the Netflix Prize" and Hu et al.'s "Collaborative Filtering for Implicit Feedback Datasets," both from 2008.

To use ALS, you need to give it an RDD of `mllib.recommendation.Rating` objects, each of which contains a user ID, a product ID, and a rating (either an explicit rating or implicit feedback; see upcoming discussion). One challenge with the implementation is that each ID needs to be a 32-bit integer. If your IDs are strings or larger numbers, it is recommended to just use the hash code of each ID in ALS; even if two users or products map to the same ID, overall results can still be good. Alternatively, you can `broadcast()` a table of product-ID-to-integer mappings to give them unique IDs.

ALS returns a `MatrixFactorizationModel` representing its results, which can be used to `predict()` ratings for an RDD of (userID, productID) pairs.[7] Alternatively, you can use `model.recommendProducts(userId, numProducts)` to find the top `numProducts()` products recommended for a given user. Note that *unlike other models in MLlib, the `MatrixFactorizationModel` is large, holding one vector for each user and product.* This means that it cannot be saved to disk and then loaded back in another run of your program. Instead, you can save the RDDs of feature vectors produced in it, `model.userFeatures` and `model.productFeatures`, to a distributed filesystem.

Finally, there are two variants of ALS: for explicit ratings (the default) and for implicit ratings (which you enable by calling `ALS.trainImplicit()` instead of `ALS.train()`). With explicit ratings, each user's rating for a product needs to be a score (e.g., 1 to 5 stars), and the predicted ratings will be scores. With implicit feedback, each rating represents a confidence that users will interact with a given item (e.g., the rating might go up the more times a user visits a web page), and the predicted items will be confidence values. Further details about ALS with implicit ratings are described in Hu et al., "Collaborative Filtering for Implicit Feedback Datasets," ICDM 2008.

Dimensionality Reduction

Principal component analysis

Given a dataset of points in a high-dimensional space, we are often interested in reducing the dimensionality of the points so that they can be analyzed with simpler tools. For example, we might want to plot the points in two dimensions, or just reduce the number of features to train models more effectively.

The main technique for dimensionality reduction used by the machine learning community is principal component analysis (PCA) (*http://en.wikipedia.org/wiki/Principal_component_analysis*). In this technique, the mapping to the lower-dimensional space is done such that the variance of the data in the low-dimensional representation is maximized, thus ignoring noninformative dimensions. To compute the map-

---

7 In Java, start with a JavaRDD of `Tuple2<Integer, Integer>` and call `.rdd()` on it.

ping, the normalized correlation matrix of the data is constructed and the singular vectors and values of this matrix are used. The singular vectors that correspond to the largest singular values are used to reconstruct a large fraction of the variance of the original data.

PCA is currently available only in Java and Scala (as of MLlib 1.2). To invoke it, you must first represent your matrix using the `mllib.linalg.distributed.RowMatrix` class, which stores an RDD of Vectors, one per row.[8] You can then call PCA as shown in Example 11-13.

Example 11-13. PCA in Scala

```
import org.apache.spark.mllib.linalg.Matrix
import org.apache.spark.mllib.linalg.distributed.RowMatrix

val points: RDD[Vector] = // ...
val mat: RowMatrix = new RowMatrix(points)
val pc: Matrix = mat.computePrincipalComponents(2)

// Project points to low-dimensional space
val projected = mat.multiply(pc).rows

// Train a k-means model on the projected 2-dimensional data
val model = KMeans.train(projected, 10)
```

In this example, the projected RDD contains a two-dimensional version of the original points RDD, and can be used for plotting or performing other MLlib algorithms, such as clustering via K-means.

Note that `computePrincipalComponents()` returns a `mllib.linalg.Matrix` object, which is a utility class representing dense matrices, similar to Vector. You can get at the underlying data with `toArray`.

Singular value decomposition

MLlib also provides the lower-level singular value decomposition (SVD) primitive. The SVD factorizes an $m \times n$ matrix A into three matrices $A \approx U\Sigma V^T$, where:

- U is an orthonormal matrix, whose columns are called left singular vectors.
- Σ is a diagonal matrix with nonnegative diagonals in descending order, whose diagonals are called singular values.
- V is an orthonormal matrix, whose columns are called right singular vectors.

---

8 In Java, start with a JavaRDD of Vectors, and then call `.rdd()` on it to convert it to a Scala RDD.

For large matrices, usually we don't need the complete factorization but only the top singular values and its associated singular vectors. This can save storage, denoise, and recover the low-rank structure of the matrix. If we keep the top k singular values, then the dimensions of the resulting matrices will be $U : m \times k$, $\Sigma : k \times k$, and $V : n \times k$.

To achieve the decomposition, we call `computeSVD` on the `RowMatrix` class, as shown in Example 11-14.

Example 11-14. SVD in Scala

```scala
// Compute the top 20 singular values of a RowMatrix mat and their singular vectors.
val svd: SingularValueDecomposition[RowMatrix, Matrix] =
  mat.computeSVD(20, computeU=true)

val U: RowMatrix = svd.U  // U is a distributed RowMatrix.
val s: Vector = svd.s     // Singular values are a local dense vector.
val V: Matrix = svd.V     // V is a local dense matrix.
```

Model Evaluation

No matter what algorithm is used for a machine learning task, model evaluation is an important part of end-to-end machine learning pipelines. Many learning tasks can be tackled with different models, and even for the same algorithm, parameter settings can lead to different results. Moreover, there is always a risk of overfitting a model to the training data, which you can best evaluate by testing the model on a different dataset than the training data.

At the time of writing (for Spark 1.2), MLlib contains an experimental set of model evaluation functions, though only in Java and Scala. These are available in the `mllib.evaluation` package, in classes such as `BinaryClassificationMetrics` and `MulticlassMetrics`, depending on the problem. For these classes, you can create a `Metrics` object from an RDD of (prediction, ground truth) pairs, and then compute metrics such as precision, recall, and area under the receiver operating characteristic (ROC) curve. These methods should be run on a test dataset not used for training (e.g., by leaving out 20% of the data before training). You can apply your model to the test dataset in a `map()` function to build the RDD of (prediction, ground truth) pairs.

In future versions of Spark, the pipeline API at the end of this chapter is expected to include evaluation functions in all languages. With the pipeline API, you can define a pipeline of ML algorithms and an evaluation metric, and automatically have the system search for parameters and pick the best model using cross-validation.

Tips and Performance Considerations

Preparing Features

While machine learning presentations often put significant emphasis on the algorithms used, it is important to remember that in practice, each algorithm is only as good as the features you put into it! Many large-scale learning practitioners agree that feature preparation is the most important step to large-scale learning. Both adding more informative features (e.g., joining with other datasets to bring in more information) and converting the available features to suitable vector representations (e.g., scaling the vectors) can yield major improvements in results.

A full discussion of feature preparation is beyond the scope of this book, but we encourage you to refer to other texts on machine learning for more information. However, with MLlib in particular, some common tips to follow are:

- Scale your input features. Run features through `StandardScaler` as described in "Scaling" on page 224 to weigh features equally.

- Featurize text correctly. Use an external library like NLTK (*http://www.nltk.org*) to stem words, and use IDF across a representative corpus for TF-IDF.

- Label classes correctly. MLlib requires class labels to be 0 to $C-1$, where C is the total number of classes.

Configuring Algorithms

Most algorithms in MLlib perform better (in terms of prediction accuracy) with regularization when that option is available. Also, most of the SGD-based algorithms require around 100 iterations to get good results. MLlib attempts to provide useful default values, but you should try increasing the number of iterations past the default to see whether it improves accuracy. For example, with ALS, the default rank of 10 is fairly low, so you should try increasing this value. Make sure to evaluate these parameter changes on test data held out during training.

Caching RDDs to Reuse

Most algorithms in MLlib are iterative, going over the data multiple times. Thus, it is important to `cache()` your input datasets before passing them to MLlib. Even if your data does not fit in memory, try `persist(StorageLevel.DISK_ONLY)`.

In Python, MLlib automatically caches RDDs on the Java side when you pass them from Python, so there is no need to cache your Python RDDs unless you reuse them within your program. In Scala and Java, however, it is up to you to cache them.

Recognizing Sparsity

When your feature vectors contain mostly zeros, storing them in sparse format can result in huge time and space savings for big datasets. In terms of space, MLlib's sparse representation is smaller than its dense one if at most two-thirds of the entries are nonzero. In terms of processing cost, sparse vectors are generally cheaper to compute on if at most 10% of the entries are nonzero. (This is because their representation requires more instructions per vector element than dense vectors.) But if going to a sparse representation is the difference between being able to cache your vectors in memory and not, you should consider a sparse representation even for denser data.

Level of Parallelism

For most algorithms, you should have at least as many partitions in your input RDD as the number of cores on your cluster to achieve full parallelism. Recall that Spark creates a partition for each "block" of a file by default, where a block is typically 64 MB. You can pass a minimum number of partitions to methods like `SparkCon text.textFile()` to change this—for example, `sc.textFile("data.txt", 10)`. Alternatively, you can call `repartition(numPartitions)` on your RDD to partition it equally into `numPartitions` pieces. You can always see the number of partitions in each RDD on Spark's web UI. At the same time, be careful with adding too many partitions, because this will increase the communication cost.

Pipeline API

Starting in Spark 1.2, MLlib is adding a new, higher-level API for machine learning, based on the concept of *pipelines*. This API is similar to the pipeline API in SciKit-Learn (*http://scikit-learn.org*). In short, a pipeline is a series of algorithms (either feature transformation or model fitting) that transform a dataset. Each stage of the pipeline may have *parameters* (e.g., the number of iterations in `LogisticRegres sion`). The pipeline API can automatically search for the best set of parameters using a grid search, evaluating each set using an evaluation metric of choice.

The pipeline API uses a uniform representation of datasets throughout, which is SchemaRDDs from Spark SQL in Chapter 9. SchemaRDDs have multiple named columns, making it easy to refer to different fields in the data. Various pipeline stages may add columns (e.g., a featurized version of the data). The overall concept is also similar to data frames in R.

To give you a preview of this API, we include a version of the spam classification examples from earlier in the chapter. We also show how to augment the example to do a grid search over several values of the `HashingTF` and `LogisticRegression` parameters. (See Example 11-15.)

Example 11-15. Pipeline API version of spam classification in Scala

```scala
import org.apache.spark.sql.SQLContext
import org.apache.spark.ml.Pipeline
import org.apache.spark.ml.classification.LogisticRegression
import org.apache.spark.ml.feature.{HashingTF, Tokenizer}
import org.apache.spark.ml.tuning.{CrossValidator, ParamGridBuilder}
import org.apache.spark.ml.evaluation.BinaryClassificationEvaluator

// A class to represent documents -- will be turned into a SchemaRDD
case class LabeledDocument(id: Long, text: String, label: Double)
val documents = // (load RDD of LabeledDocument)

val sqlContext = new SQLContext(sc)
import sqlContext._

// Configure an ML pipeline with three stages: tokenizer, tf, and lr; each stage
// outputs a column in a SchemaRDD and feeds it to the next stage's input column
val tokenizer = new Tokenizer() // Splits each email into words
  .setInputCol("text")
  .setOutputCol("words")
val tf = new HashingTF() // Maps email words to vectors of 10000 features
  .setNumFeatures(10000)
  .setInputCol(tokenizer.getOutputCol)
  .setOutputCol("features")
val lr = new LogisticRegression() // Uses "features" as inputCol by default
val pipeline = new Pipeline().setStages(Array(tokenizer, tf, lr))

// Fit the pipeline to the training documents
val model = pipeline.fit(documents)

// Alternatively, instead of fitting once with the parameters above, we can do a
// grid search over some parameters and pick the best model via cross-validation
val paramMaps = new ParamGridBuilder()
  .addGrid(tf.numFeatures, Array(10000, 20000))
  .addGrid(lr.maxIter, Array(100, 200))
  .build()     // Builds all combinations of parameters
val eval = new BinaryClassificationEvaluator()
val cv = new CrossValidator()
  .setEstimator(lr)
  .setEstimatorParamMaps(paramMaps)
  .setEvaluator(eval)
val bestModel = cv.fit(documents)
```

The pipeline API is still experimental at the time of writing, but you can always find the most recent documentation for it in the MLlib documentation (*http://spark.apache.org/docs/latest/mllib-guide.html*).

Conclusion

This chapter has given an overview of Spark's machine learning library. As you can see, the library ties directly to Spark's other APIs, letting you work on RDDs and get back results you can use in other Spark functions. MLlib is one of the most actively developed parts of Spark, so it is still evolving. We recommend checking the official documentation (*http://spark.apache.org/documentation.html*) for your Spark version to see the latest functions available in it.

Index

Symbols

=> lambda syntax, 16

A

AccumulatorParam, 104
accumulators, 100
  and fault tolerance, 103
  custom, 103
  empty line count in Python and Scala
    (example), 100
  error count in Python (example), 102
  how they work, 102
aggregate(), 51
aggregations, 51
  conditional aggregate operations in Spark
    SQL, 181
  disabling map-side aggregation in combine-
    ByKey(), 54
  distributed word count, 53
  per-key average using combineByKey(), 54
  per-key average using reduceByKey() and
    mapValues(), 52
  per-key combiners, combineByKey() and,
    53
Akka actor stream, 202
Alternating Least Squares (ALS) algorithm, 233
Amazon EC2, 135-138
  launching clusters, 135
  logging into a cluster, 136
  pausing and restarting clusters, 137
  storage on the cluster, 138
Amazon S3, 89
Amazon Web Services (AWS) account, 135
Apache Flume, 204

pull-based receiver for, 206
  push-based receiver for, 205
Apache Hive, 91
  connecting Spark SQL to existing Hive
    installation, 91
  Hive JDBC/ODBC, 176
    (see also JDBC/ODBC server in Spark
    SQL))
  HiveServer2, 176
  loading and saving data from, in Spark SQL,
    171
  Spark SQL and, 162
  user defined functions (UDFs), 181
Apache Kafka, 203
Apache Mesos, 118, 134-135
  client and cluster mode, 135
  configuring resource usage, 135
  scheduling modes, 134
Apache Software Foundation
  Spark, 7
Apache ZooKeeper, 133
  using with Mesos, 134
applications, Spark, 117
  driver and executors, 118
  driver programs, 14
  runtime architecture, 117
    driver, 118
    executors, 119
    launching a program, 120
    summary of steps, 120
  standalone applications, 17
    building, 18
ascending parameter, sortByKey() function, 60
assembly JAR, 124

collectAsMap(), 60
combineByKey(), 52
    benefitting from partitioning, 65
    disabling map-side aggregation in, 54
    per-key average using, 54
    setting partitioner, 66
combiners, reduceByKey() and foldByKey()
    and, 52
comma-separated vaule file (see CSV files)
commutative operations, 104
compression
    choosing a compression codec, 88
    file compression options, 87
    ShemaRDD records, 183
computing cluster, 2
Concurrent Mark-Sweep garbage collector, 213
conf/spark-defaults.conf file, 143
configuration
    copying hive-site.xml file to Spark /conf/
      directory, 171
    information on, web UI environment page,
      153
configuring algorithms, 237
configuring Spark, 141
    common configuration values, 143
    configuration properties set in multiple
      places, 143
    local directories for shuffle data storage, 145
    setting configurations dynamically with
      spark-submit, 142
    with SparkConf, 141
connections, shared connection pool, 107
core input sources, Spark Streaming, 201
    Akka actor stream, 202
    stream of files, 201
cores, number for executors, 158
count(), 113
countByKey(), 60
countByValue(), 53
countByValueAndWindow(), 198
countByWindow(), 198
CSV files, 72, 77
    loading, 77
    saving, 79

D

data processing applications, 6
data science tasks, 5
data wrangling, 5

databases
    accessing from Spark, 92
    Cassandra, 94
    data sources from, 72
    Elasticsearch, 96
    external, writing data to, 200
    HBase, 96
    supporting JDBC, loading data from, 93
DataFrame, 161
DataFrames, 166
    caching of, 183
    converting regular RDDs to, 175
    in Spark SQL UI, 170
    registering as temporary table to query, 167
    saving to Parquet, 173
    types stored by, 168
    working with Row objects, 169
debugging Spark
    finding information, 150-154
      driver and executor logs, 154
      on executors, 153
      on Spark configuration, 153
    output operations, 200
decision trees, 230
    and random forests, 231
    DecisionTree class, training methods, 230
    DecisionTreeModel, 231
dependencies
    conflicts in, 128
    conflicts with Hive, 163
    for Spark SQL, 162
    information about, 153
    packaging your code with, 123
      in Python, 124
      in Scala and Java, 124
      Java Spark application built with Maven,
        124
      Scala Spark application built with sbt,
        126
    runtime dependencies of an application, 122
deployment modes
    and location of application logfiles, 154
    executor memory, cores, and number of
      executors, 158
    local disk configuration, 159
dimensionality reduction
    principal component analysis, 234
    singular value decomposition (SVD), 235
directed acyclic graph (DAG), 118, 146

About the Authors

Holden Karau is a software development engineer at Databricks and is active in open source. She is the author of an earlier Spark book. Prior to Databricks, she worked on a variety of search and classification problems at Google, Foursquare, and Amazon. She graduated from the University of Waterloo with a Bachelor of Mathematics in Computer Science. Outside of software she enjoys playing with fire, welding, and hula hooping.

Most recently, **Andy Konwinski** cofounded Databricks. Before that he was a PhD student and then postdoc in the AMPLab at UC Berkeley, focused on large-scale distributed computing and cluster scheduling. He cocreated and is a committer on the Apache Mesos project. He also worked with systems engineers and researchers at Google on the design of Omega, their next-generation cluster scheduling system. More recently, he developed and led the AMP Camp Big Data Bootcamps and Spark Summits, and contributes to the Spark project.

Patrick Wendell is a cofounder of Databricks as well as a Spark Committer and PMC member. In the Spark project, Patrick has acted as release manager for several Spark releases, including Spark 1.0. Patrick also maintains several subsystems of Spark's core engine. Before helping start Databricks, Patrick obtained an MS in Computer Science at UC Berkeley. His research focused on low-latency scheduling for large-scale analytics workloads. He holds a BSE in Computer Science from Princeton University.

Matei Zaharia is the creator of Apache Spark and CTO at Databricks. He holds a PhD from UC Berkeley, where he started Spark as a research project. He now serves as its Vice President at Apache. Apart from Spark, he has made research and open source contributions to other projects in the cluster computing area, including Apache Hadoop (where he is a committer) and Apache Mesos (which he also helped start at Berkeley).

Colophon

The animal on the cover of *Learning Spark* is a small-spotted catshark (*Scyliorhinus canicula*), one of the most abundant elasmobranchs in the Northeast Atlantic and Mediterranean Sea. It is a small, slender shark with a blunt head, elongated eyes, and a rounded snout. The dorsal surface is grayish-brown and patterned with many small dark and sometimes lighter spots. The texture of the skin is rough, similar to the coarseness of sandpaper.

This small shark feeds on marine invertebrates including mollusks, crustaceans, cephalopods, and polychaete worms. It also feeds on small bony fish, and occasionally larger fish. It is an oviparous species that deposits egg-cases in shallow coastal waters, protected by a horny capsule with long tendrils.

The small-spotted catshark is of only moderate commercial fisheries importance, however it is utilized in public aquarium display tanks. Though commercial landings are made and large individuals are retained for human consumption, the species is often discarded and studies show that post-discard survival rates are high.

Many of the animals on O'Reilly covers are endangered; all of them are important to the world. To learn more about how you can help, go to *animals.oreilly.com*.

The cover image is from Wood's Animate Creation. The cover fonts are URW Typewriter and Guardian Sans. The text font is Adobe Minion Pro; the heading font is Adobe Myriad Condensed; and the code font is Dalton Maag's Ubuntu Mono.

Get even more for your money.

Join the O'Reilly Community, and register the O'Reilly books you own. It's free, and you'll get:

- $4.99 ebook upgrade offer
- 40% upgrade offer on O'Reilly print books
- Membership discounts on books and events
- Free lifetime updates to ebooks and videos
- Multiple ebook formats, DRM FREE
- Participation in the O'Reilly community
- Newsletters
- Account management
- 100% Satisfaction Guarantee

Signing up is easy:

1. Go to: oreilly.com/go/register
2. Create an O'Reilly login.
3. Provide your address.
4. Register your books.

Note: English-language books only

To order books online:
oreilly.com/store

For questions about products or an order:
orders@oreilly.com

To sign up to get topic-specific email announcements and/or news about upcoming books, conferences, special offers, and new technologies:
elists@oreilly.com

For technical questions about book content:
booktech@oreilly.com

To submit new book proposals to our editors:
proposals@oreilly.com

O'Reilly books are available in multiple DRM-free ebook formats. For more information:
oreilly.com/ebooks

Lightning Source UK Ltd.
Milton Keynes UK
UKOW04f1546130417

299043UK00002B/3/P